CSR, Sustainability, Ethics & Governance

In recent years the discussion concerning the relation between business and society has made immense strides. This has in turn led to a broad academic and practical discussion on innovative management concepts, such as Corporate Social Responsibility, Corporate Governance and Sustainability Management. This series offers a comprehensive overview of the latest theoretical and empirical research and provides sound concepts for sustainable business strategies. In order to do so, it combines the insights of leading researchers and thinkers in the fields of management theory and the social sciences and from all over the world, thus contributing to the interdisciplinary and intercultural discussion on the role of business in society. The underlying intention of this series is to help solve the world's most challenging problems by developing new management concepts that create value for business and society alike. In order to support those managers, researchers and students who are pursuing sustainable business approaches for our common future, the series offers them access to cutting-edge management approaches. CSR, Sustainability, Ethics and Governance is accepted by the Norwegian Register for Scientific Journals, Series and Publishers, maintained and operated by the Norwegian Social Science Data Services (NSD).

Joy A. Debski

Corporate Social Responsibility in the Energy Sector

Governance for a Sustainable Host Environment

Springer

Joy A. Debski
Law and Social Science
Robert Gordon University
Scotland, UK

ISSN 2196-7075 ISSN 2196-7083 (electronic)
CSR, Sustainability, Ethics & Governance
ISBN 978-3-032-17747-6 ISBN 978-3-032-17748-3 (eBook)
https://doi.org/10.1007/978-3-032-17748-3

This Springer imprint is published by the registered company Springer Nature Switzerland AG
The registered company address is: Gewerbestrasse 11, 6330 Cham, Switzerland

To my daughter Ilona Debski, my reason and my strength.

Foreword

Putting a book together is not a joke! It is serious business, as the author puts themselves in the position of considering what readers would be interested in buying, reading, and finding helpful. The goal is to provide information that adds to their existing knowledge of life or the specific area the book addresses. In terms of this particular book, let me remind readers that we live in an era defined by Agenda 21, which was initiated at the Rio Conference of the Earth Summit in June 1992, orchestrated by the United Nations. This era has seen two 15-year development goals as a result of the Summit: the Millennium Development Goals (MDGs) in 2015 and the Sustainable Development Goals (SDGs) for 2030. It is likely that we will see at least five more 15-year development goals set for 2030, 2045, 2060, 2075, and 2090 before the end of this century.

Looking at the title of the great contribution to knowledge, it's an addition to many of the books we have seen in the literature on sustainability and governance, this one in particular focusing on the energy sector, which is an important sector in the world we live in. The sector, either rightly or wrongly, is often looked at in an unfavourable light when it comes to the environment and some of the challenges we talk about concerning planet Earth. In my view, it is a great addition to what we have and would shed more light on how our world can continue to be more sustainable for this generation and future generations of occupants of this our great planet.

To be asked to write the Foreword to the book is personally a great honour for me, and I hope that the trust the author, Dr. Debski, has placed in me with these few words has not been misplaced! I have browsed through the nine chapters that make up the book, and I am very impressed with what Dr. Debski is saying in them. It is a must-read book for anyone interested in sustainability, governance, and corporate social responsibility in general—undergraduate and graduate students, tutors in the field, researchers, international organisations, those who work and operate in the sector, NGOs, and both local and central governments. I recommend the book to everyone unreservedly.

Let me end this piece by congratulating Dr. Debski for her thoughtfulness in putting together a book that, in my view, would be impactful in academia and society in general. Well done, Joy.

December 2025

Samuel O. Idowu
Professor of Accounting & Sustainability
London Metropolitan University
UK

Preface

The genesis of this book lies at the intersection of academic inquiry and the pressing realities faced by resource-rich nations across the Global South. While my perspective is informed by the Nigerian context—and the specific challenges of the Niger Delta—the analysis within these pages extends to a global comparative framework. The central question driving this research is universal: how can we transform Corporate Social Responsibility from a peripheral activity into a core function of governance that ensures sustainable and equitable outcomes for host environments?

This work argues that effective CSR is not merely about corporate charity but about constructing robust, multi-stakeholder governance systems. The book moves beyond diagnosing failures to propose actionable models for institutional reform, including the strategic establishment of dedicated bodies like a CSR Commission, which can provide the necessary oversight and legitimacy.

I have written this with a diverse readership in mind: for policymakers seeking practical frameworks for regulation, for corporate leaders dedicated to integrating genuine sustainability into their operations, and for academics and community advocates who require a nuanced understanding of the dynamics between energy corporations, governments, and host communities.

It is my sincere hope that the comparative insights and strategic frameworks presented here will contribute to meaningful dialogue and inspire the tangible policy reforms needed to build a more just and sustainable energy future, both in Nigeria and in other resource-rich developing economies.

December 2025

Dr. Joy A. Debski
Robert Gordon University
Aberdeen, UK

Acknowledgements This book is the culmination of a journey supported by many individuals and institutions. I gratefully acknowledge the Petroleum Technology Development Fund (PTDF) for sponsoring the initial research that laid the foundation for this work.

My profound gratitude goes to Professor Samuel O. Idowu, a true luminary in the field of Corporate Social Responsibility. His pioneering work has been a beacon throughout my academic journey, and his generous mentorship and insightful engagement with the manuscript were a constant source of inspiration and clarity. This book owes its existence to his guidance.

I am deeply indebted to a trio of remarkable mentors: Dr. Elimma Ezeani, whose steadfast belief and leadership shaped this work from an idea into its best form; Dr. Leon, whose wise counsel and perceptive insights were a constant source of inspiration; and Professor John Karlberg, whose support and perspective were invaluable.

From the depths of my heart, I thank my mother, Chief Mrs Ada Okolocha, for her boundless love and foundational support. My sincere thanks also extend to my brother and dear sister, Constantine and Nikky Micheals, for their unwavering prayers; to my senior mum, Professor Charity Emaviewe, for her constant support; and to my uncle, Associate Professor Emeka Ochem, for his gracious encouragement.

My exceptional thanks go to my daughter, Ilona, the sunshine of my life. Your "quiet" presence beside me, painting and practising your writing, made everything worthwhile.

I also thank Robert Gordon University for providing an excellent academic environment and the research support that enabled the completion of this work.

I extend my sincere appreciation to Dr. Prashanth Mahagaonkar, Executive Editor at Springer Nature, and the entire publishing team for their expertise and support in bringing this book to fruition.

Competing Interests The author has no competing interests to declare that are relevant to the content of this manuscript.

About the Book

Navigating the complex intersection of energy development, corporate responsibility, and environmental justice requires a robust and integrated framework. *Corporate Social Responsibility in the Energy Sector: Governance for a Sustainable Host Environment* provides precisely that. This comprehensive textbook moves beyond theoretical discussions to offer a critical, practical examination of how CSR must evolve from a peripheral public relations tool into a core strategic governance mechanism.

The book systematically analyses the persistent governance deficits that fail to translate global sustainability principles into equitable outcomes for communities hosting energy projects. It begins by establishing the conceptual and theoretical foundations of environmental sustainability and CSR before conducting in-depth, sector-specific reviews. These span the oil and gas industry, renewables, electricity, and the critical minerals supply chain, revealing that significant social and environmental externalities are challenges common to all energy forms.

A central pillar of the work is its focus on multi-stakeholder strategies and the indispensable role of host communities. It argues that proactive, rights-based community partnerships are fundamental to securing a social licence to operate and achieving genuine sustainability. Through comparative case studies from Nigeria, Canada, Brazil, the European Union, and others, the book dissects diverse regulatory models, corporate approaches, and community engagement practices.

Ultimately, this volume serves as an essential resource for students, researchers, policymakers, and industry leaders. It provides the conceptual clarity and actionable frameworks needed to build accountable, participatory, and resilient governance systems, ensuring the global energy transition is both environmentally sound and socially just. This is an indispensable guide for anyone committed to forging a sustainable path forward for the energy sector and the communities it impacts.

Contents

Abbreviations

ADB	Asian Development Bank
AfCFTA	African Continental Free Trade Area
AfDB	African Development Bank
AREI	Africa Renewable Energy Initiative
AU	African Union
BOEMRE	Bureau of Ocean Energy Management, Regulation and Enforcement
BSEE	Bureau of Safety and Environmental Enforcement
CAFE	Corporate Average Fuel Efficiency
CBDR	Common But Differentiated Responsibilities
CCS	Carbon Capture and Storage
CDAs	Community Development Agreements
CDP	Carbon Disclosure Project
CED	Committee for Economic Development
CETs	Community Energy Trusts
CISAP	Comisso Interministerial De Sustentabilidade Na Administraço Publica
CO_2	Carbon Dioxide
COP26	2021 United Nations Climate Change Conference
COP27	2022 United Nations Climate Change Conference
COP28	2023 United Nations Climate Change Conference
CSDDD	Corporate Sustainability Due Diligence Directive
CSOs	Chief Sustainability Officers
CSR	Corporate Social Responsibility
CSRD	Corporate Sustainability Reporting Directive
DMCs	Developing Member Countries
DRC	Democratic Republic of Congo
EAPs	Environment Action Programmes
EEA	European Environment Agency
EIA	Environmental Impact Assessment
EIR	Environmental Implementation Review

EITI	Extractive Industries Transparency Initiative
EMT	Ecological Modernisation Theory
EPA	Environmental Protection Agency
ESF	Environmental and Social Framework
ESG	Environmental, Social, And Governance
ESIAs	Environmental and Social Impact Assessments
ESS	Environmental Stewardship Strategy
ETP	Energy Transition Plan
FPIC	Free, Prior and Informed Consent
GDC	Geothermal Development Company
GHGs	Green-House Gases
GMoUs	Global Memoranda of Understanding
GRI	Global Reporting Initiative
HCDF	Host Communities Development Fund
HCRTs	Host Community Development Trusts
IAAPCCSDA	Integrated Assessment of Air Pollution and Climate Change for Sustainable Development in Africa
IBAs	Impact and Benefit Agreements
IEA	International Energy Agency
IFC	International Finance Corporation
ILO	International Labour Organisation
IMPEL	European Union Network for The Implementation and Enforcement of Environmental Law
IOGP	International Oil and Gas Producers
IPCC	Intergovernmental Panel on Climate Change
IRENA	International Renewable Energy Agency
ISO	International Organisation for Standardisation
ISSB	International Sustainability Standards Board
JET-IP	Just Energy Transition Investment Plan
LTWP	Lake Turkana Wind Power
MDGs	Millennium Development Goals
MMS	Minerals Management Service
MMS	Mineral And Mining Service
MNCs	Multinational Corporations
NCSC	National CSR and Sustainability Commission
NDC	Nationally Determined Contribution
NDCs	Nationally Determined Contributions
NEITI	Nigeria Extractive Industries Transparency Initiative
NEPA	National Environmental Policy Act
NESF	National Energy Sustainability Forum
NESREA	National Environmental Standards and Regulations Enforcement Agency
NGX	Nigerian Exchange
NHTSA	National Highway Traffic Safety Administration
NO_2	Nitrogen Oxides

NUPRC	Nigerian Upstream Petroleum Regulatory Commission
OCS	Outer Continental Shelf
OECD	Organisation For Economic Co-Operation and Development
PM	Particulate Matter
PPP	Public-Private Partnerships
PRC	People's Republic of China
REACT	Renewable Energy and Climate Technologies Programme
REIPPP	Renewable Energy Independent Power Producer Programme
SASB	Sustainability Accounting Standards Board
SDGs	Sustainable Development Goals
SEC	Securities and Exchange Commission
SFDR	Sustainable Finance Disclosure Regulation
SIF	Social Investment Forum
SLO	Social Licence to Operate
SO_2	Sulfur Dioxide
SPDC	Shell Petroleum Development Company
TBL	Triple Bottom Line
TCFD	Task Force on Climate-Related Financial Disclosures
UCLA	University of California
UN	United Nations
UNDRIP	United Nations Right of Indigenous Peoples Declaration
UNEP	United Nations Environment Programme
UNFCCC	United Nations Framework Convention on Climate Change
UNGC	United Nations Global Compact
UNGP	United Nations Guiding Principles
UNIDO	United Nations Industrial Development Organisation
UNPRI	United Nations Principles for Responsible Investment
US	United States
WEEE	Waste Electrical and Electronic Equipment
WHO	World Health Organisation
WSSD	World Summit on Sustainable Development

List of All Cases

List of All Legislations

Brazil

Canada

European Union

Ghana

India

International

Kenya

Netherlands

Nigeria

Phillipines

United Kingdom

United States

Tanzania

Chapter 1
Introduction

1.1 Background to the Book

The global energy system is experiencing a major shift in the twenty-first century, shaped by the growing urgency of climate change, rapid technological progress, and increasing public concern about environmental and social impacts. For many decades, fossil fuels especially oil and gas, have powered economic growth around the world. However, their environmental costs have become too heavy to ignore. Rising greenhouse gas emissions, deforestation, pollution, and biodiversity loss from extractive industries have all fuelled global pressure for a cleaner and more sustainable energy future [International Energy Agency (IEA), 2023; United Nations Environment Programme (UNEP), 2022].

Today, sustainability in the energy sector goes far beyond meeting environmental regulations. It is increasingly tied to Corporate Social Responsibility (CSR), as companies are now expected to manage environmental impacts as part of their broader responsibilities to society. The idea focuses not only on reducing environmental harm but also on actively adopting renewable technologies, promoting circular economy practices, and involving different stakeholders in decision-making (World Bank, 2023). As renewables such as solar, wind, hydro, and biomass expand, and electricity becomes central to global decarbonisation, CSR-driven sustainability has become essential for the reputation and long-term survival of energy companies (IEA, 2021).

In developing countries like Nigeria, these global changes interact with local challenges such as weak regulation, overdependence on oil, widespread energy poverty, and community conflicts in resource-rich areas. Yet, these same challenges also open new opportunities for innovation, green growth, and inclusive development if guided by CSR-oriented sustainability strategies [African Development Bank (AfDB), 2023]. This book therefore examines how environmental sustainability, as a core component of CSR, can be integrated across the energy sector including oil

J. A. Debski, *Corporate Social Responsibility in the Energy Sector*, CSR, Sustainability, Ethics & Governance, https://doi.org/10.1007/978-3-032-17748-3_1

and gas, renewables, electricity, and mining through institutional design, responsible corporate practices, and collaboration among key stakeholders.

1.2 Purpose and Objectives of the Book

The main aim of this book is to offer a broad and practical understanding of environmental sustainability across the entire energy industry, with CSR serving as the major framework through which sustainability responsibilities are interpreted and implemented. It goes beyond the usual focus on oil and gas to include renewable energy, power generation, and related extractive sectors. The book seeks to show how sustainability can move from being a mere policy statement to a practical and measurable CSR obligation within corporate and national frameworks.

More specifically, the objectives of this work are to:

1. Examine the theoretical foundations of environmental sustainability as they apply to different parts of the energy sector and how these foundations interact with CSR principles.
2. Identify policy, institutional, and legal gaps that prevent the effective implementation of sustainability goals in developing contexts.
3. Assess how corporate social responsibility (CSR) practices across energy subsectors align with global sustainability targets.
4. Explore the roles and interactions of governments, corporations, and host communities in promoting or obstructing sustainable practices.
5. Develop a framework for advancing environmental sustainability in developing economies, using Nigeria as a reference case.

By addressing these objectives, the book provides both analysis and guidance linking academic theory with real-world policy and business action, while keeping CSR as the operational base for sustainability performance.

1.3 Scope and Thematic Orientation

Unlike earlier studies that focused on a single branch of the energy industry, this work takes a sector-wide view. It acknowledges that energy systems are deeply connected, and that environmental challenges in one part often affect the others. The discussion therefore covers:

(a) The environmental impacts of different energy sources fossil, renewable, and mineral-based and how they influence sustainable development and CSR obligations.
(b) The policies and regulations that guide environmental protection, climate action, and the energy transition.

(c) Corporate strategies and community engagement efforts that determine environmental outcomes within CSR frameworks.
(d) Global frameworks such as the Paris Agreement (2015), the UN Sustainable Development Goals (SDGs), and the Corporate Sustainability Reporting Directive (European Commission, 2023), which increasingly shape how energy businesses operate and report CSR performance.

Through this broad approach, the book presents environmental sustainability as the common thread linking diverse energy systems, governance models, and CSR-related policy frameworks.

1.4 Relevance and Rationale

Environmental sustainability has become one of the most pressing issues in today's energy sector, and it sits at the centre of modern CSR obligations. As the world gets closer to the 1.5 °C global warming threshold, dependence on carbon-heavy fuels is proving unsustainable. The Intergovernmental Panel on Climate Change (IPCC, 2023) estimates that the energy industry contributes about 75% of total global greenhouse gas emissions. This makes it not only a major driver of the climate crisis but also a key part of the solution. For that reason, sustainability is no longer optional it is a matter of corporate and societal responsibility.

In recent years, the global shift towards cleaner energy has accelerated. Advances in technology, supportive policies, and investor pressure are pushing countries and companies to embrace low-carbon solutions. Governments are now embedding sustainability targets into economic strategies for instance, through the European Union's Green Deal, the United States' Inflation Reduction Act, and China's 2060 carbon-neutrality commitment (Stern & Xie, 2022). At the same time, private investors and financial institutions are increasingly using environmental, social, and governance (ESG) criteria to guide funding decisions, which shapes how capital is allocated within the global energy system (World Bank, 2023). These ESG principles strengthen the CSR expectations placed on companies, especially regarding environmental protection.

However, many developing countries face a difficult balance between growth and sustainability. In sub-Saharan Africa, energy demand is expected to more than double by 2040, yet over 600 million people still live without electricity (IEA, 2023). Nations such as Nigeria rich in oil, gas, and renewable potential face the challenge of using these resources to support development while keeping pace with global decarbonisation goals (African Union, 2023).

This book is therefore valuable for policymakers, researchers, and industry actors who must navigate this complex landscape. It argues that achieving sustainability in the energy sector requires more than adopting clean technologies. It also requires stronger CSR systems that promote institutional reforms, multi-stakeholder cooperation, and accountability systems that integrate social fairness with environmental responsibility. By combining global and local perspectives, this work provides a realistic and contextual guide for embedding CSR-driven sustainability principles into energy governance and practice.

1.5 Conceptual and Methodological Approach

This book is guided by three main theoretical perspectives Sustainable Development Theory, Stakeholder Theory, and Shared Value Theory. These ideas together shape how environmental sustainability is examined as both a guiding principle and a practical approach across the energy sector, especially as they connect directly to Corporate Social Responsibility (CSR) obligations.

Sustainable Development Theory, first presented by the World Commission on Environment and Development (1987), provides the foundation for balancing environmental protection, economic progress, and social welfare. In the energy context, this theory stresses the need to separate economic growth from environmental damage by using cleaner technologies and responsible resource management (United Nations, 2022). Within CSR, this theory supports the expectation that companies should integrate environmental responsibility into their business conduct.

Stakeholder Theory (Freeman, 1984; Harrison & Wicks, 2021) adds another important dimension. It argues that companies have obligations not just to their shareholders but also to employees, local communities, governments, and the natural environment. This is particularly relevant to the energy sector, where extraction, production, and infrastructure projects have direct effects on people's livelihoods and ecosystems. The theory strengthens the CSR position that environmental sustainability is part of the broader responsibility companies owe to their stakeholders.

Shared Value Theory, introduced by Porter and Kramer (2011), provides a practical way of connecting business goals with social progress. It suggests that companies can create economic value while also addressing social and environmental needs for example, through investment in clean technologies, expanding community access to energy, or supporting carbon reduction projects. Applied to the energy sector, this theory shows how profit-making and sustainability can reinforce each other rather than conflict, which aligns with the CSR idea that corporate success should advance environmental and social well-being.

Methodologically, this book takes a comparative and qualitative approach. It draws from a wide range of secondary sources, including academic research, international policy reports, sustainability disclosures by corporations, and documents from development organisations. The study combines sectoral analysis covering oil, gas, renewables, and electricity with regional insights that reflect both global trends and specific national contexts, especially Nigeria's changing energy governance landscape.

By using this interdisciplinary method, the analysis remains grounded in real-world conditions while still engaging with theory and policy. The aim is not only to critique existing practices but also to suggest practical frameworks that can guide future improvements in environmental governance, corporate accountability, and CSR-driven sustainable energy transitions.

1.6 Structure of the Book

The book is made up of nine connected chapters, each one building on the previous to form a complete story about environmental sustainability in the energy sector. The organisation moves from broad ideas to applied strategies and from global issues to local contexts.

1.6.1 Chapter One: Introduction

Chapter 1 sets the stage by outlining the background, purpose, scope, rationale, theoretical foundations, and methodology of the book. It introduces environmental sustainability as a central pillar of Corporate Social Responsibility (CSR) across the global energy sector and outlines how the remaining chapters are organised.

1.6.2 Chapter Two: The Concept of Environmental Sustainability in the Energy Sector

Chapter 2 serves as the intellectual foundation of the book, offering a detailed explanation of what environmental sustainability means within the modern energy landscape. It begins by tracing the roots of the concept, showing how early ideas about conservation and resource management gradually evolved into today's global sustainability agenda. Key historical milestones such as the *Brundtland Commission Report* (1987), the *Rio Declaration* (1992), and the *United Nations Sustainable Development Goals* (2015) help readers see how the idea of sustainability has developed over time (World Commission on Environment and Development, 1987; United Nations, 1992, 2015).

Rather than treating sustainability as a fixed or universal concept, this chapter presents it as an evolving response to shifting political, technological, and moral realities. It emphasises that within the energy sector, sustainability must be understood both as an aspiration and as a practical discipline. The discussion connects sustainability with three essential environmental dimensions land, air, and water highlighting how extraction, pollution, and emissions intersect across different energy systems. Using examples from fossil fuels, renewable energy, and emerging clean technologies, the chapter exposes a key paradox: while renewable energy plays a crucial role in sustainable development, it is not automatically sustainable unless its production and supply chains are equitable, ethical, and environmentally sound.

Drawing from research on planetary boundaries and the notion of *dynamic resilience* (Rockström et al., 2009), the chapter challenges static definitions of sustainability. It encourages readers to see sustainability not as a final state, but as a continuous balancing act between ecological preservation and human progress. This rethinking invites readers to move past simplistic judgments such as assuming that renewables are always "good" and fossil fuels are always "bad" and instead to view sustainability as something that must be constantly negotiated. Ultimately, Chapter 2 invites readers to ask deeper questions: not just *what* is sustainable, but *how* and *for whom* sustainability is achieved.

1.6.3 Chapter Three: Theoretical and Conceptual Framework for Environmental Sustainability in the Energy Sector

While Chapter 2 defines and contextualises sustainability, Chapter 3 builds the theoretical framework that supports the rest of the book. It brings together several influential perspectives *Systems Theory*, *Ecological Modernisation Theory*, *Institutional Theory*, and the *Triple Bottom Line framework* to explain how energy systems function within interlinked ecological, economic, and social structures (Bertalanffy, 1968; Jeurissen & Elkington, 2000). These theories are presented not as abstract academic ideas, but as practical tools for understanding the complex realities of sustainability governance.

The chapter argues that sustainability cannot be achieved through one-off technical fixes or isolated projects. Rather, it requires a systemic transformation that aligns industry practices, institutional behavior, and societal expectations through adaptive and inclusive governance mechanisms. By comparing theories of modernisation and institutional learning, the chapter reveals that achieving sustainability involves transforming not only technologies but also the social norms, institutions, and governance systems that shape them.

A unique contribution of this chapter is its insistence that sustainability has a moral and ethical dimension. Energy governance is portrayed as a deeply human enterprise one that must balance economic ambition with social justice and environmental responsibility. Using conceptual diagrams, the chapter illustrates how governments, corporations, and communities form an interconnected ecosystem where actions in one sphere influence outcomes in others. This approach helps readers visualise sustainability as a dynamic equilibrium rather than a static goal.

In essence, Chapter 3 provides the intellectual compass for the empirical and policy-oriented discussions that follow. By linking theory to practice, it helps readers appreciate sustainability not as a slogan, but as a living framework that demands cooperation, accountability, and continuous learning.

1.6.4 Chapter Four: Empirical Review of Environmental Sustainability in the Energy Sector

Building on the conceptual insights of the earlier chapters, Chapter 4 turns to the real world. It examines how environmental sustainability principles are applied or ignored in practice across various national and corporate energy systems. Through a broad comparative review, the chapter draws on evidence from both developed and developing economies to reveal how institutional strength, political will, and social inclusion determine real-world sustainability outcomes.

The chapter presents contrasting examples: Scandinavian countries, for instance, have successfully integrated renewable energy through coherent policies and public trust, while resource-dependent nations continue to struggle with environmental degradation, inequality, and weak governance. This comparison shows that progress towards sustainability depends not only on technology or wealth but also on effective institutions and genuine stakeholder engagement.

Additionally, the chapter explores the enabling role of data, innovation, and green finance. It analyses how instruments such as green bonds, carbon pricing, and sustainability reporting influence both corporate decisions and government policies (World Bank, 2022). However, it also identifies critical barriers such as uneven access to finance, policy inconsistency, and weak enforcement that continue to undermine progress, particularly in developing regions.

Chapter 4 closes with an important reminder: empirical evidence gains meaning only when interpreted through a solid theoretical lens. Without that bridge, sustainability risks becoming a collection of disconnected projects rather than a unified system of transformation. By linking evidence to theory, this chapter marks the completion of the book's first major section moving from defining and theorising sustainability to observing how it unfolds in practice.

1.6.5 Chapter Five: Corporate Social Responsibility (CSR) and Environmental Sustainability in the Energy Sector

Chapter 5 marks a turning point in the book's focus from general discussions of theory and evidence to the specific domain of corporate responsibility and governance. It highlights how Corporate Social Responsibility (CSR) has evolved from being a voluntary gesture to becoming a key pillar of sustainable corporate practice. In the energy sector, CSR now functions as both a governance tool and a moral framework for managing environmental and social obligations (Carroll, 1999; Freeman, 1984).

Using foundational models such as Carroll's *Pyramid of CSR*, Elkington's *Triple Bottom Line*, and Freeman's *Stakeholder Theory*, the chapter explains how environmental stewardship, social inclusion, and profitability are intertwined in modern business operations. It underscores that in today's energy industry, CSR is no longer an optional add-on it is the ethical backbone of sustainability.

The chapter also examines how modern CSR aligns with *Environmental, Social, and Governance (ESG)* principles and international sustainability frameworks such as the *UN Global Compact* and the *Global Reporting Initiative*. A particularly thought-provoking section discusses the concept of the Social Licence to Operate (SLO) the informal but powerful approval granted by local communities that determines whether a company can function without resistance (Gunningham et al., 2004). Examples from the oil, gas, and renewable sectors show that even legally compliant projects can fail if they lose community trust.

In the Nigerian context, the chapter demonstrates how CSR can act as a bridge between corporate interests and community welfare, especially when implemented through partnerships, institutional reforms, and renewable-energy initiatives. However, it also acknowledges the continuing challenges posed by weak institutions, corruption, and limited technical capacity.

Ultimately, Chapter 5 reinforces the idea that CSR connects the moral imperatives of sustainability with the operational realities of business. It sets the stage for the more specialised analyses in subsequent chapters, where issues of corporate accountability, governance, and policy reform are explored in-depth.

1.6.6 Chapter Six: CSR in the Oil and Gas Sector Environmental Sustainability, Governance, and Community Impacts

Chapter 6 brings the discussion squarely into the oil and gas sector an industry where environmental sustainability issues are both the most visible and the most contested. This chapter offers a candid examination of how Corporate Social Responsibility (CSR) has developed in one of the world's most influential yet environmentally challenging industries. It evaluates the extent to which oil and gas corporations whether multinational or state-owned have evolved from practising reactive philanthropy to adopting proactive environmental and social governance (ESG) strategies (Frynas, 2010).

Using ESG principles and the concept of the *Social Licence to Operate (SLO)* as analytical lenses, the chapter explores how these companies address critical issues such as pollution control, land remediation, community development, and climate commitments (Gunningham et al., 2004). However, it uncovers a sharp contrast between corporate sustainability rhetoric and actual on-the-ground practices, particularly in contexts where weak regulation and political interference prevail.

The Nigerian *Niger Delta* is presented as a central case study. Decades of oil extraction in the region have left behind a complex legacy of environmental degradation, economic dislocation, and social unrest (Watts, 2008). Although many oil companies have formal CSR policies, their impact remains limited due to poor implementation, lack of transparency, and uneven power relations between corporations, state authorities, and host communities. This case is not treated merely as a local tragedy but as a mirror reflecting global patterns of environmental and governance failures across the extractive sector.

To balance the analysis, the chapter draws comparisons with oil-producing countries such as Norway, Canada, and Brazil contexts where effective governance, strong institutions, and cultural commitments to transparency have produced more accountable CSR practices. These comparative insights highlight how good governance, community participation, and institutional trust can transform CSR from a public relations exercise into a framework for genuine environmental responsibility.

Chapter 6 presents the oil and gas industry as both a warning and an opportunity. It warns that unless CSR efforts become more transparent, measurable, and transformative, the sector will remain caught in the cycle of unsustainable development. At the same time, it shows that with stronger institutions and community trust, CSR can become a meaningful tool for ecological and social reform. This discussion sets the stage for Chapter 7, which extends the analysis to the newer and supposedly "greener" frontiers of energy production.

1.6.7 Chapter Seven: CSR in Renewable Energy, Electricity, and Mining Sectors

Chapter 7 shifts the focus from the extractive industries to the emerging arenas of renewable energy, electricity, and critical-mineral mining. It challenges the popular assumption that renewable energy is automatically sustainable, arguing instead that even clean energy systems can generate serious environmental and social risks if not properly managed (Sovacool et al., 2020).

Through a blend of legal, policy, and empirical analysis, the chapter exposes the hidden costs of the global transition to clean energy. It examines cases of land conflicts, biodiversity loss, and technological waste linked to large-scale solar, wind, and hydroelectric projects. The discussion also turns to the mining of critical minerals such as lithium, cobalt, and rare earth elements essential for renewable technologies but often extracted under conditions that replicate the same injustices associated with fossil fuels (Ali et al., 2017).

The chapter further explores CSR practices within the electricity sector, focusing on issues of governance, affordability, and *energy justice* the idea that energy transitions should distribute both benefits and burdens fairly (Jenkins et al., 2016). It critiques the policy inconsistencies and regulatory gaps that undermine accountability in many developing countries, where public–private utilities often operate without strong oversight.

Comparative analysis is once again used to great effect. Renewable-energy companies tend to focus on climate alignment and technological advancement, electricity utilities emphasise service reliability and access, and mining firms prioritise supply-chain transparency. Yet all face similar challenges: fragmented regulation, weak community engagement, and the growing threat of "greenwashing".

Ultimately, Chapter 7 argues that CSR must evolve into a governance instrument integrated within national sustainability strategies. This requires robust legal frameworks, standardised data reporting, and genuine stakeholder participation. By exposing the moral and environmental dilemmas of the so-called green transition, the chapter broadens the reader's understanding of sustainability as a shared governance problem, not one confined to fossil fuels. It also prepares the ground for Chapter 8, which centers on the experiences and perspectives of host communities.

1.6.8 Chapter Eight: Host Communities and Environmental Sustainability Impacts in the Energy Sector

Chapter 8 shifts attention from institutions and corporations to the people living in the shadow of energy projects host communities. By doing so, it reintroduces the human dimension into discussions of sustainability, emphasising that environmental governance is ultimately about people, justice, and dignity.

The chapter examines communities affected by a range of energy activities, from oil extraction to renewable projects, in countries such as Nigeria, Kenya, and Canada. It shows that, regardless of geography, these communities face recurring problems: environmental damage, economic displacement, poor compensation, and lack of meaningful participation in decision-making (Hilson, 2012).

Central to the discussion is the idea of co-producing sustainability the notion that host communities should not merely receive corporate goodwill but should be partners in shaping and monitoring environmental outcomes. Genuine sustainability, the chapter argues, must be participatory. It should combine ecological repair with social empowerment and recognition of historical inequalities.

The chapter critiques token CSR programmes that deliver temporary relief but fail to address structural causes of underdevelopment. It highlights alternative approaches such as community-led monitoring in Canada's energy corridors, Kenya's renewable mini-grid partnerships, and Nigeria's evolving *Host Community Development Trusts (HCDTs)* as practical models where shared ownership and accountability foster better outcomes (Lawal, 2021).

In essence, Chapter 8 restores the human face of sustainability. It redefines host communities as active co-architects of energy governance, rather than as passive recipients of corporate interventions. By reframing sustainability around inclusion and justice, the chapter naturally transitions to Chapter 9, which presents a broader multi-stakeholder governance framework.

1.6.9 Chapter Nine: Effective Multi-Stakeholder Strategies Roles of Government, Corporations, and Host Communities Across the Energy Sector

Chapter 9 brings together the book's central arguments into a unified model for sustainable energy governance. It asserts that environmental sustainability can only be achieved when governments, corporations, and host communities work collaboratively within a system of shared responsibility (Freeman, 1984).

Building on *Stakeholder Theory*, the chapter explains that these three groups each have distinct but interdependent roles. Governments must function as regulators and facilitators setting clear policies, enforcing environmental standards, and providing incentives for innovation. Corporations should act as innovators and implementers, integrating sustainability principles into their strategies and operations. Host communities, meanwhile, must be recognised as legitimate partners whose participation and consent determine the social legitimacy of energy projects.

The chapter advocates for hybrid governance a blend of mandatory regulations and voluntary initiatives such as CSR and ESG programs. It argues that this balance creates both accountability and flexibility, fostering innovation while ensuring compliance.

One of the chapter's most forward-looking proposals is the creation of a *National CSR and Sustainability Commission (NCSC)*, envisioned as an institutional hub to harmonise sustainability standards, coordinate stakeholder efforts, and institutionalise community participation across sectors. The chapter also calls for internal reforms within corporations, such as establishing *Chief Sustainability Officers (CSOs)* and Sustainability Departments to embed environmental and social metrics into business performance.

At the community level, it proposes the formation of *Community Energy Trusts (CETs)* grassroots platforms that enable host communities to manage development funds, monitor compliance, and plan for sustainable livelihoods.

Beyond institutional design, Chapter 9 stresses the softer but equally essential foundations of sustainability trust, transparency, and accountability. It concludes that without these, even the most sophisticated governance frameworks will falter. Ultimately, it presents a vision of an integrated sustainability ecosystem where governments provide direction, corporations drive innovation, and communities ensure legitimacy. This, it argues, is the only pathway through which the energy sector can achieve the delicate balance among economic growth, social inclusion, and environmental protection.

Together, these chapters form a connected discussion that moves from theory to application, from international frameworks to local realities, and from identifying challenges to offering realistic and actionable solutions for environmental sustainability and the CSR responsibilities that support it across the global energy sector.

1.7 Gap/Contribution to Knowledge

In recent years, discussions about environmental sustainability in the energy sector have grown rapidly, reflecting both the urgency of climate change and the global shift in how energy systems are organised. Yet, much of the existing scholarship remains fragmented divided by industries, disciplines, or regional focus. Many studies concentrate on the oil and gas sector, which has a long history of environmental and social impact, but this focus often overlooks valuable insights from other areas such as renewables, electricity, and mining (Ritchie & Roser, 2023). In addition, the CSR dimensions of environmental responsibility are not always applied across these subsectors in a consistent way, leaving gaps in how companies understand and manage their obligations.

This book aims to fill that gap by providing an integrated framework that treats environmental sustainability not only as a governance issue but also as a core CSR responsibility that shapes corporate behaviour across the energy sector. It contributes to both academic and policy discussions in several key ways.

1.7.1 Integrating Sustainability Across Energy Subsectors

One major contribution of this work is the effort to harmonise sustainability concepts across different energy industries. While traditional research tends to view sustainability in oil and gas through a compliance or corporate social responsibility (CSR) lens, and in renewables as automatically positive, this monograph challenges such distinctions. It argues that every energy source whether fossil-based or renewable comes with its own environmental trade-offs, governance structures, and social dynamics (UNEP, 2023; World Bank, 2023). These differences shape the specific CSR obligations that companies must address.

By comparing environmental challenges, regulatory responses, and stakeholder relationships across subsectors, the book promotes a "sector-neutral" understanding of sustainability that captures the interconnections within the wider energy system and the CSR responsibilities embedded within them.

1.7.2 Advancing Theory

This work also strengthens theory by combining elements of Sustainable Development Theory, Stakeholder Theory, and Shared Value Theory into a single, integrated perspective. Although these frameworks have been widely studied separately, their joint application to the energy sector is still uncommon. This combined lens allows for a richer understanding of sustainability as not only an environmental or ethical ideal but also a corporate strategy and a principle of governance within CSR practice (Harrison & Wicks, 2021; Porter & Kramer, 2011).

The approach aligns with recent scholarship that views sustainability as a process of continuous interaction among institutions, markets, and communities rather than a fixed end goal (Scoones et al., 2015). This fresh theoretical blend contributes to both academic thinking and practical approaches to energy governance, while clarifying the CSR expectations that follow from these theories.

1.7.3 Connecting Global and Developing Countries

A further contribution of this book lies in its strong focus on the developing world, particularly Africa. While much of the global literature examines sustainability transitions in advanced economies, there is still limited research on how institutional weaknesses, energy poverty, and political realities shape sustainability in developing contexts (AfDB, 2023). These conditions also influence how CSR duties are interpreted, enforced, and implemented across different energy subsectors.

Using Nigeria as a focal case, the book situates sustainability debates within real-world challenges faced by resource-dependent countries. It shows how developing nations must balance the dual demands of environmental protection and urgent development needs. In doing so, it offers an alternative to the largely Eurocentric narratives that dominate sustainability research, emphasising context-specific innovation, CSR accountability, and resilience.

1.7.4 Methodological Innovation

Methodologically, this book adopts a comparative and interdisciplinary approach that captures the complexity of sustainability in the energy sector. By blending legal, economic, and social perspectives, it avoids the oversimplifications common in single-discipline studies. This design makes the analysis both theoretically rich and policy-relevant, highlighting practical lessons that can be applied across different energy subsectors and governance systems, especially regarding CSR responsibilities and corporate conduct.

The book's main contribution lies in reframing sustainability as an integrative, cross-sectoral process one that unites theory, practice, and policy within the realities of both the Global North and the Global South, while positioning CSR as the key operational mechanism for delivering environmental responsibility.

1.8 Policy and Practical Implications

The pursuit of environmental sustainability in the energy sector is not just an academic discussion; it carries deep practical implications for governments, corporations, communities, and development partners. Because sustainability in the energy sector is closely tied to Corporate Social Responsibility (CSR), the lessons drawn from this monograph are meant to inform real-world decision-making and guide how both sustainability and CSR strategies are designed and implemented.

1.8.1 Implications for Governments and Regulators

Governments are central to steering the direction of sustainable energy transitions. Yet, in many developing countries, fragmented policies, weak institutions, and inconsistent enforcement continue to hinder progress (Okhirebhu et al., 2025). These governance challenges also affect how CSR responsibilities are interpreted and enforced across the energy sector.

This book emphasises the need for:

(a) Coherent governance frameworks that align environmental, economic, and energy policies and provide clarity for CSR expectations
(b) Strong and independent regulatory bodies capable of enforcing environmental standards and monitoring compliance.
(c) Policy and fiscal incentives such as carbon pricing, feed-in tariffs, and green subsidies to encourage investment in renewable energy.
(d) Transparent data systems and participatory processes that build accountability and public confidence.

These recommendations align with international frameworks like the UN High-Level Dialogue on Energy (2021) and the African Union's Climate Change and Resilient Development Strategy (2022–2032), both of which stress institutional reform and policy coherence as key pillars of sustainability (African Union, 2023). In this context, CSR becomes a tool through which companies meet these environmental and governance expectations.

1.8.2 Implications for Energy Corporations

For energy companies, sustainability has evolved into a strategic necessity rather than a voluntary gesture. Stakeholders, investors, regulators, and consumers now expect companies to demonstrate environmental responsibility and social integrity in their operations, which forms the core of CSR practice.

Firms must integrate sustainability into their governance systems and long-term strategies, moving beyond mere compliance or reporting. This includes setting measurable Environmental, Social, and Governance (ESG) targets, conducting life cycle assessments, and aligning supply chains with global sustainability standards (Porter & Kramer, 2011).

Doing so not only enhances corporate reputation but also reduces operational risk and strengthens investor confidence (IEA, 2021). The comparative insights presented in this book offer practical guidance for business leaders on emerging trends, from decarbonisation pathways to inclusive community engagement models that enhance both profitability and legitimacy within CSR frameworks.

1.8.3 Implications for Host Communities

Host communities remain vital stakeholders in the sustainability landscape, yet they are often excluded from meaningful participation. Since CSR requires companies to respond to the needs and concerns of affected communities, sustainable energy development demands rebuilding the social contract between corporations and communities based on fairness, inclusion, and shared benefits (Moffat & Zhang, 2014; Prno & Slocombe, 2012).

This monograph supports models that:

(a) Incorporate local knowledge and participation in environmental planning;
(b) Guarantee fair compensation and livelihood restoration where land or resources are affected; and
(c) Establish joint monitoring systems to hold both companies and governments accountable.

These approaches create what is known as a social license to operate a form of legitimacy grounded in mutual trust and respect. Without it, no energy project can truly achieve long-term sustainability or fulfil its CSR obligations.

1.8.4 Implications for International Development Partners

For international organisations and development financiers, this book provides guidance on how to design sustainability initiatives that reflect local realities rather than impose external models. It stresses the importance of empowering domestic institutions, supporting policy integration, and investing in capacity-building rather than short-term financial aid. These measures also strengthen national systems for monitoring CSR and environmental performance.

True partnership means enabling countries to take ownership of their sustainability agendas, tailoring global frameworks to national needs, and promoting mutual learning through knowledge exchange. In doing so, development partners can help create energy transitions that are not only environmentally sound but also socially just, economically viable, and consistent with CSR commitments across the energy sector.

1.9 Conclusion: Building a Common Path for Sustainability

Environmental sustainability in the energy sector is one of the most important issues of our time. As this opening chapter has shown, achieving real sustainability goes beyond changing technology or following regulations, it requires a deep shift in how energy is produced, managed, and used, and how these responsibilities are integrated into Corporate Social Responsibility (CSR) practices.

This chapter places the idea of sustainability within the broader story of global energy transitions. It explains how theories, institutions, and stakeholder relationships shape what sustainability looks like in practice. More importantly, it emphasises sustainability as a complete system that connects environmental care with social fairness and economic strength, and how these dimensions inform the CSR duties of energy companies.

The next chapters continue to build on these ideas in a step-by-step way. Together, these chapters form a unified picture of how sustainability can move from being an abstract principle to a real and inclusive practice across the global energy landscape, with CSR as a central mechanism for implementation.

In summary, this chapter sets the stage for the whole book: sustainability is not a final goal but an ongoing process that balances technology, policy, and society, and requires corporate responsibility as a driving force.

This introductory chapter has provided a broad foundation for understanding the complex and interlinked nature of environmental sustainability within the global energy sector. It has shown that sustainability is no longer an optional consideration but a guiding principle shaping how energy is produced, distributed, and governed, and how CSR commitments are defined.

The discussion traced the global momentum towards cleaner energy systems, the theoretical roots of sustainability, and the institutional and social constraints that continue to influence implementation. Yet, as the world moves from policy rhetoric to practical action, it becomes increasingly important to clarify what environmental sustainability truly means. The concept is widely invoked in government policy and corporate strategy, but its interpretations and applications vary greatly across contexts. A renewable-energy project in sub-Saharan Africa, for instance, may prioritise access and community inclusion, whereas sustainability in offshore drilling might emphasise emissions control and biodiversity protection differences that translate into distinct CSR expectations.

Chapter 2, *The Concept of Environmental Sustainability in the Energy Sector*, builds directly on these reflections. It explores how sustainability thinking has evolved, from early conservationist ideals to the more integrative approaches of ecological economics. The chapter also examines how international legal frameworks, corporate standards, and ethical principles have collectively shaped today's understanding of sustainable energy systems and the CSR obligations associated with them.

By clarifying these conceptual foundations, Chapter 2 bridges theory and practice. It establishes a common vocabulary through which subsequent chapters can analyse how policies, institutions, and corporations operationalise environmental sustainability within CSR frameworks and where gaps still remain between ambition and reality.

References

African Development Bank Group. (2023). *African economic outlook 2023*. https://www.afdb.org/en/documents/african-economic-outlook-2023

African Union (AU). (2023). *Environmental, social, and governance: The African private sector study*. African Union Commission. https://au.int/en/announcements/20230329/environmental-social-and-governance-african-private-sector-study

Ali, S. H., Giurco, D., Arndt, N., Nickless, E., Brown, G., Demetriades, A., Durrheim, R., Enríquez, M. A., Kinnaird, J., Littleboy, A., Meinert, L. D., Oberhänsli, R., Salem, J., Schodde, R., Schneider, G., Vidal, O., & Yakovleva, N. (2017). Mineral supply for sustainable development requires resource governance. *Nature, 543*(7645), 367–372. https://doi.org/10.1038/nature21359

von Bertalanffy, L. (1968). *General system theory: Foundations, development*. George Braziller.

Carroll, A. B. (1999). Corporate social responsibility: Evolution of a definitional construct. *Business & Society, 38*(3), 268–295. https://doi.org/10.1177/000765039903800303

European Commission. (2023). *The European green deal: Delivering the European Union's climate ambitions*. European Commission. https://commission.europa.eu/strategy-and-policy/priorities-2019-2024/european-green-deal_en

Freeman, R. E. (1984). *Strategic management: A stakeholder approach*. Pitman. https://doi.org/10.1017/CBO9781139192675

Frynas, J. G. (2010). Corporate social responsibility and societal governance: Lessons from transparency in the oil and gas sector. *Journal of Business Ethics, 93*(Suppl 2), 163–179. https://doi.org/10.1007/s10551-010-0559-1

Gunningham, N., Kagan, R. A., & Thornton, D. (2004). Social license and environmental protection: Why businesses go beyond compliance. *Law & Social Inquiry, 29*(2), 307–341. https://doi.org/10.1111/j.1747-4469.2004.tb00338.x

Harrison, J. S., & Wicks, A. C. (2021). Harmful stakeholder strategies. *Journal of Business Ethics, 169*(3), 405–419. https://doi.org/10.1007/s10551-019-04310-9

Hilson, G. (2012). Corporate social responsibility in the extractive industries: Experiences from developing countries. *Resources Policy, 37*(2), 131–137. https://doi.org/10.1016/j.resourpol.2012.01.002

Intergovernmental Panel on Climate Change (IPCC). (2023). *Climate change 2023: Synthesis report of the IPCC sixth assessment cycle*. IPCC. https://www.ipcc.ch/report/sixth-assessment-report-cycle

International Energy Agency. (2021). *Financing clean energy transitions in emerging and developing economies*. IEA. https://www.iea.org/reports/financing-clean-energy-transitions-in-emerging-and-developing-economies

International Energy Agency (IEA). (2023). *World energy outlook 2023*. IEA. https://www.iea.org/reports/world-energy-outlook-2023

Jenkins, K., McCauley, D., Heffron, R., Stephan, H., & Rehner, R. (2016). Energy justice: A conceptual review. *Energy Research & Social Science, 11*, 174–182. https://doi.org/10.1016/j.erss.2015.10.004
Jeurissen, R., & Elkington, J. (2000). Cannibals with forks: The triple bottom line of 21st century business. *Journal of Business Ethics, 23*, 229–231. https://doi.org/10.1023/A:1006129603978
Lawal, K. T. (2021). Law, policy, and the development of renewable energy for electricity: A case for a Renewable Energy Law in Nigeria. *International Journal of Legal Information, 49*(1), 3–15. https://doi.org/10.1017/jli.2021.7
Moffat, K., & Zhang, A. (2014). The paths to social licence to operate: An integrative model explaining community acceptance of mining. *Resources Policy, 39*(1), 61–70. https://doi.org/10.1016/j.resourpol.2013.11.003
Okhirebhu, D., Johnson, O., Oluwasola, M., & Agboola, P. (2025). Overcoming policy and regulatory barriers: Accelerating Nigeria's transition to renewable energy. *IIARD International Journal of Geography and Environmental Management, 11*(2), 88–108.
Porter, M. E., & Kramer, M. R. (2011). Creating shared value: How to reinvent capitalism—and unleash a wave of innovation and growth. *Harvard Business Review, 89*(1–2), 62–77.
Prno, J., & Slocombe, D. S. (2012). Exploring the origins of 'social licence to operate' in the mining sector: Perspectives from governance and sustainability theories. *Resources Policy, 37*(3), 346–357. https://doi.org/10.1016/j.resourpol.2012.04.002
Ritchie, H., & Roser, M. (2023). *Energy mix and transition*. Our World in Data. https://ourworldindata.org/energy-mix
Rockström, J., et al. (2009). A safe operating space for humanity. *Nature, 461*(7263), 472–475. https://doi.org/10.1038/461472a
Scoones, I., Leach, M., & Newell, P. (Eds.). (2015). *The politics of green transformations*. Routledge. https://doi.org/10.4324/9781315747378
Sovacool, B. K., Burke, M., Baker, L., Kotikalapudi, C. K., & Wlokas, H. (2020). New frontiers and conceptual frameworks for energy justice. *Energy Policy, 105*, 677–691. https://doi.org/10.1016/j.enpol.2017.03.005
Stern, N., & Xie, C. (2022). China's new growth story: Linking the 14th Five-Year Plan with the 2060 carbon neutrality pledge. *Journal of Chinese Economic and Business Studies, 21*(1), 5–25. https://doi.org/10.1080/14765284.2022.2073172
United Nations. (1992). *Rio declaration on environment and development*. UN.
United Nations. (2015). *Transforming our world: The 2030 agenda for sustainable development*. United Nations: https://sdgs.un.org/2030agenda
United Nations. (2022). *Transforming our world: The 2030 agenda for sustainable development*. United Nations. https://sdgs.un.org/2030agenda
United Nations Environment Programme (UNEP). (2023). *Global environment outlook 7: Steering transformations to sustainability*. UNEP. Global Environment Outlook (GEO-7) | Global Environment Outlook (GEO)
Watts, M. (2008). *Curse of the black gold: 50 years of oil in the Niger Delta*. PowerHouse Books.
World Bank. (2022). *Good practice note for energy and extractive sectors*. World Bank. http://documents.worldbank.org/curated/en/589081642702749624
World Bank. (2023, April 20). *Scaling up to phase down: Financing energy transition in developing countries* [Press release]. World Bank. https://www.worldbank.org/en/news/press-release/2023/04/20/scaling-up-to-phase-down-financing-energy-transition-in-developing-countries
World Commission on Environment and Development (WCED). (1987). *Our common future*. Oxford University Press.

Chapter 2
The Concept of Environmental Sustainability in the Energy Sector

2.1 Introduction

Environmental sustainability in the energy sector serves as a foundational pillar for addressing the pressing global challenges of climate change, resource depletion, and social justice and equity. While fossil fuels remain the largest contributor to global greenhouse gas emissions, accounting for 37.4 billion tonnes of CO_2 emitted in 2024 (Global Carbon Project, 2024; Hassan et al., 2024), the entire energy sector; including renewables and emerging technologies—is not immune to environmental degradation capabilities which pose risks to future generations' well-being. This chapter begins by situating environmental sustainability within the broader energy context, emphasising the critical need to transition from traditional, carbon-intensive energy sources to more sustainable ones, without compromising economic development and societal needs (World Commission on Environment and Development, 1987); and beyond transitioning to renewables, to sustainable energy sources.

Scope-wise, the chapter covers the evolutionary definitions of environment, sustainability, and environmental sustainability vis-à-vis energy production and consumption. It integrates the expanded energy sector including renewables, electricity, and mining, and contrasts these with legacy oil and gas practices. It also examines environmental impacts such as emissions, resource use, and ecosystem effects, alongside socio-economic considerations like energy access, equity, and justice.

This chapter is vital to the overall book theme as it lays the conceptual groundwork for subsequent discussions on corporate social responsibility, multi-stakeholder governance, and sustainability frameworks in various energy subsectors. Also, the analytical framework guiding this chapter, leverages global definitions such as those from the Brundtland Commission "meeting the needs of the present without compromising future generations' ability to meet theirs" (World Commission on Environment and Development, 1987).

The chapter is organised into key sections: first, justifying the need to discuss sustainability within the energy sector and then defining and contextualising key

J. A. Debski, *Corporate Social Responsibility in the Energy Sector*, CSR, Sustainability, Ethics & Governance, https://doi.org/10.1007/978-3-032-17748-3_2

terms like; environment, sustainability, and environmental sustainability in energy sectoral sense.

2.2 Why Discuss Sustainability in the Energy Sector?

The importance of discussing the concept of sustainability within the energy sector is both theoretically justified and empirically underpinned by scholarly analysis, reality, and data flowing from many global conversations about the future. Energy is the fundamental currency of all complex systems, and human civilisation is no exception. Energy has come to underpin every shade of modern life to such extents that a systemic reliance has been formed across the globe. This deep systemic reliance makes any discussion of "doing without" energy a philosophical abstraction. The critical question, therefore, is not if we need energy, but how to provide it sustainably to secure our future.

The global nudge towards answering this question has led to policies and targets to transition to renewable-energy sources. Even at this, renewable energy is not an unequivocal good—since an energy source may be renewable yet, not sustainable. While such source may be clean at the point of use, the manufacturing of green technologies demands vast quantities of critical minerals; including lithium, cobalt, rare earth elements. The extraction of these materials frequently replicates destructive patterns of the fossil era: causing large-scale land degradation, contaminating freshwater sources, and generating toxic waste. Furthermore, these "green" mines can displace indigenous and local communities, creating environmental injustice and undermining the social pillars of sustainability (Adator & Li, 2021; Onifade et al., 2024). This demonstrates that an energy source is not truly sustainable if its supply chain inflicts irreparable ecological damage and social displacement. A significant socio-ecological paradox is hence formed, making sustainability considerations in the energy sector more critical than it used to be when the danger was with fossil fuel alone.

The concept of sustainability encompasses the responsible management of natural resources and conservation of the ecosystems and minimisation of waste and pollution of the environment in order to preserve health and resilience of the planet (Hajian & Kashani, 2021). As the world grapples with the challenges of climate change, biodiversity loss, and ecosystem degradation; environmental sustainability has emerged as a critical concept in humanity's modern era. The concept includes the responsible management of natural resources, minimisation of waste and pollution and conservation of the ecosystem to ensure the long-term health of the inhabitants of the environment.

The necessity to discuss sustainability in the energy sector is also vindicated by its central position in important global discussions about safety of the future. According to the Brundtland Commission in its 1987 report "Our Common Future" (World Commission on Environment and Development, 1987), sustainable development was the key to overcoming environmental concerns. The Report identified a range of serious problems associated with environmental degradation: explicitly, that human activity had led to profoundly adverse effects on the earth, and that development and growth would be unsustainable if this process of environmental exploitation continued. Foundational scholarship of Carson (1962a, 1962b), Hardin's (1968), Goldsmith and Allen (1973), and Meadows et al (1972); all attested to the growing extent of environmental degradation and the desirability of the creation of a new ideology to guarantee a common future for mankind—and sustainability is that ideology.

The importance of the concept of sustainable development has notably inspired the formulation of the United Nations (UN) Environment and Development Conference held in Rio de Janeiro in 1992. This meeting represented the first global effort to develop strategies and action plans for environmental sustainability and more sustainable development. Almost every country in the world sent delegates the Rio Conference, including more than 100 leaders. In addition to national delegates, some international groups representing civil society also sent representatives to the Conference.

2.3 Defining Sustainability

Achieving a definition for sustainability is crucial as it forms the bedrock which informs policymaking and engagements for sustainable future in every sector—including the energy sector. Sustainability, in essence, is about the future and its needs. By definition, the Brundtland Commission established that sustainability means "meeting the needs of the present without compromising future generations' ability to meet theirs" (World Commission on Environment and Development, 1987). This postulation goes to the essence of the concept of sustainability in intergenerational reasonable resource management to meet needs, while understanding resource limitations. Sustainability has also been defined by UCLA Sustainability Charter (2016) as the "the integration of environmental health, social equity and economic vitality in order to create thriving, healthy, diverse and resilient communities for this generation and generations to come" (see Section 2). This precise definition by the UCLA Sustainability via this Charter, succinctly captures the widely accepted three-pillar framework (environment, equity, and economy) essential for achieving holistic and enduring sustainable development.

While some definitions are general others are framed in manners that refer to what they envisage to sustain—ecology, economy, finance, or institutions. Therefore, Scholars have established that "term 'sustainability' refers to the way of defending, applying, or arguing in favor of sustainable development" (Damico et al., 2022). Generality and specificity of definitions being real issues some scholars have proposed that a more inclusive definition, rationalisation, and contextualisation be given to sustainability which covers the situations of indigenous people—"context-based relationality, community-based governance, education, language, quality of life and health, and communal recognition of certain nonhumans as life-givers" (Virtanen et al., 2020).

Instructively, some Scholars argue that sustainability stands for a "continual process and not an end product", hence, must include a dynamic process requiring the adaptive capacity of social and ecological systems in maintaining and supporting the quality of social systems (Sakalasooriya, 2021). Agreeably, sustainability as a continual process rather than an end product emphasises the necessity of ongoing adaptation, learning, and iterative improvement to effectively address the dynamic and complex challenges of balancing environmental protection, economic viability, and social equity over time. For instance, in the energy sector where sustainability focuses on both decarbonisation and energy utility, the systems and strategies ensuring these must be continuous in process. The common denominator in the several definitions of sustainability draws attention to the need for humanity to conserve resources at its disposal. However, transforming current global cultural norms relating to the environment has been identified as the most pressing challenge confronting humanity, since it has to consider the capability of the earth to sustain human life (Hák et al., 2016).

Much recent research draws attention to cross-generational needs. Still, since the future's needs are not easy to ascertain, contemporary research focuses on prioritising environmental, economic, and social challenges in a manner deemed beneficial (Basiago, 2020). The economic model attempts to do this by sustainably accumulating and using natural and financial capital. The social model aims to enhance political, cultural, religious, educational, and healthcare frameworks. This ensures fundamental human rights and well-being to achieve sustainable development (Evers, 2020). The environmental model is based on biodiversity and ecological integrity. All these must be integrative and remain continuous to really ground sustainability. In the energy sector, sustainability refers to the changes and risks in energy utility.

Sustainability in the energy sector necessitates an integrative and continuous approach, recognising that it is an ongoing process of managing changes and risks in energy utility. Simply framing sustainability as discrete outcomes, such as the transition to renewables, is insufficient because it overlooks the imperative of sustained adaptation and utility optimisation over time to achieve genuinely sustainable energy systems (Bakhsh et al., 2024; Halawa, 2024). Effective sustainability must encompass technical, economic, social, and institutional dimensions in a dynamic manner, ensuring resiliency and long-term balance rather than episodic achievements.

2.4 Environmental Impacts and Sustainability in the Energy Sector

The activities of the energy sector as identified above, poses serious environmental problem especially at the point of extraction of raw materials (Adator & Li, 2021; Onifade et al., 2024). Both the environment being impacted by these activities and the environmental problems, are often multifaceted. For example, a global issue such as climate change does not arise spontaneously; it is a build-up of carbon dioxide in the atmosphere caused by the combustion of fossil fuels, related in turn to air pollution in a more local context (Dryzek, 2005; Kabir et al., 2023; Nunes, 2023). Also, the intricacies are also shown in natural realities, polluted land can contaminate water and air through several processes, such as runoff, leaching, and gas emissions. It is therefore essential in this discourse on environmental sustainability to first clarify the meaning of 'environment' to provide a clear foundation for subsequent analysis.

The noun "environment" has its etymological roots in the old French words "environ" and "environer", meaning "circuit", "surround", "enclose", and "circumstances" (Jessop, 2012, 708). When the term environment is used, they mean the natural environment, which includes living and non-living things. The Cambridge Dictionary defines the environment as the air, water, and land in or on which people, animals, and plants live. The OECD Glossary of Statistical Terms defines the environment as "the totality of all the external conditions affecting the life, development and survival of an organism" (OECD, 2008).

The environment sustains all types of life. Rocks, soils, minerals, air, water, bacteria, fungi, plants, and animals all work together to maintain life and its potential to provide and sustainably regulate cultural advantages. The environment's ability to support all of this depends on billions of physical, chemical, and biological interactions. Exploration of the environment to accommodate the needs of society is causing a range of severe environmental impacts (Ripple et al., 2019), including global warming, environmental degradation (Wuebbles, 2017), such as ocean acidification, mass extinction, and biodiversity loss (Leakey & Lewin, 1996) and ecological crises and collapse. Other human activities causing damage, either directly or indirectly to the environment on a global scale, including population growth, (Crist et al., 2022), overconsumption, overexploitation, pollution, and deforestation. Some of the problems, including global warming and biodiversity loss, have been suggested as representing catastrophic risks to the survival of the human species (Torres, 2016).

Drawing from prevailing definitions and as is relevant to the energy sector, this research classifies the environment to encompass land, air, and water as the primary natural components impacted by energy production and consumption (Allaby, 1994; Ikpeze et al., 2015). And the heavy greenhouse gases (GHGs) emissions from energy production—particularly CO2 (CHAS, 2024) impact life and survival in these environmental components (Pan et al., 2024). These different components of the environment are contextually espoused below.

2.4.1 *Land*

Land is typically described as the earth's solid, dry surface. Land cover, rivers, shallow lakes, natural resources, non-marine fauna, and vegetation (the biosphere), lower regions of the atmosphere (the troposphere), groundwater reserves, and the physical products of human activities on land, such as construction and agriculture, are all examples of land (UN, 2017). The UN 2017 Outlook Report confirms that land is finite in quantity. It suggests that with planning, changes in consumer and corporate behaviour, and adaptation to sustainable practices, there is enough available land in the long run to meet both the demand for basic essentials and the need for a broader range of goods and services. Some natural resources, such as wood, are considered renewable because they revert to their original levels when managed sustainably. Coal and other fossil fuels are not regarded as renewable, since they take millions of years to develop. The current coal supply is predicted to peak around the middle of the twenty-first century.

Predicated on these concepts, the United Nations has suggested that to deal with land problems, integrative systems, and participatory stakeholder methods such as the "circular economy", rather than linear, sectoral plans, are necessary to effectively negotiate the sustainable use, management, and planning of land resources.

2.4.2 Air

The Earth is surrounded by a mixture of gases which we call "air". Most living things rely on the air around them for vital nutrients and gases like oxygen and nitrogen. Sometimes "atmosphere" is used instead of "air" (Webster 2025). Air is a fundamental component of the environment, playing a critical role in sustaining life and maintaining ecological balance. In the context of the energy sector, air quality is profoundly impacted by energy production and consumption, particularly through the emission of pollutants such as carbon dioxide (CO_2), nitrogen oxides (NO_X), sulfur dioxide (SO_2), and particulate matter (PM) (Pan et al., 2024). Fossil fuel combustion remains the dominant source of these emissions, contributing significantly to ambient air pollution and climate change (World Health Organisation, 2024). Such pollutants adversely affect human health by exacerbating respiratory and cardiovascular diseases, while also damaging ecosystems through acid rain and ozone depletion (IEA, 2025a).

Recent research indicates that although renewable-energy sources generate substantially lower air pollutants, associated activities such as manufacturing and installation can produce localised emissions, which should not be overlooked in comprehensive environmental assessments (Liu et al., 2021). Technological advances in energy efficiency and air pollution controls within the sector are critical pathways to mitigating these impacts (IEA, 2025a). Moreover, policies aimed at reducing air pollution, such as stringent emissions standards and transitioning to cleaner energy technologies, are essential to improving air quality and protecting public health (United Nations Environment Programme, 2025). In sum, understanding and managing air pollution remains a pivotal concern for achieving environmental sustainability in the energy sector.

2.4.3 *Water*

Water (H_2O) is a vital, inorganic solvent that sustains all known life and dominates Earth's hydrosphere, covering 71% of the planet—96.5% of which resides in oceans and seas (IERE Team, 2025). This abundance notwithstanding, there are underlying deception as only 2.5% of it is freshwater, and much of that is inaccessible (Isukuru et al., 2024). This illusion of plenty masks the harsh reality of water scarcity and pollution, especially in regions like Nigeria. Water is a crucial component of the environment and plays a vital role in sustaining ecological balance and human well-being.

Disrupting the natural properties of water through harmful activities threatens environmental stability and global ecosystems. For instance, when industries and human activities pollute water sources, they disrupt its natural balance and pose dangers for ecosystems and communities. Alarmingly, nearly 80% of global wastewater flows back untreated into rivers, lakes, and seas, poisoning life-sustaining waters and deepening environmental degradation (Peacock, 2019). In a world that is currently energy-dependent, this silent crisis demands urgent, compassionate action by all stakeholders.

In the context of the energy sector (especially amidst energy transition to renewables), water usage is intertwined with energy production processes, and this often leads to substantial environmental impacts. Recent studies have highlighted that transitioning to renewable-energy sources can drastically reduce water consumption (up to 95% in some cases); by eliminating the need for water-intensive processes like cooling in fossil fuel plants (Earth Day, 2025). Fossil fuel extraction and conventional power generation, particularly through cooling systems, deplete freshwater resources and cause thermal pollution, disrupting aquatic ecosystems and biodiversity.

Innovative approaches, such as recycling produced water and using advanced treatment techniques, have proven worthy tools to caution waste and enforce sustainability. These methods are adopted by energy companies to minimise water impacts and promote sustainability (ERM, 2025). Recognising water as a strategic asset, contemporary energy policies emphasise integrated water stewardship to ensure resilient and sustainable energy systems, especially amid climate change-induced water scarcity. Thus, judicious management of water is integral to achieving environmental sustainability and addressing global water-energy challenges (WeForum, 2025).

While water pollution is usually linked to fossil fuel production (Sophie, 2022), hydropower's impact on water pollution and sustainability is also a complex terrain. In the legitimate course of producing clean electricity, dams, and reservoirs alter water quality by changing temperature, flow, and sediment transport, which harms aquatic ecosystems (U.S.A. Energy Information Administration, 2022). Also, reservoirs can emit methane, a potent greenhouse gas, due to decomposition of submerged biomass, and this affects climate sustainability (BKV Energy, 2025). Again, sediment trapping by dams degrades downstream habitats and agricultural productivity (Abbasi,

2018). Although hydropower supports renewable-energy goals, effective environmental management practices; like minimum flow regulations and dam removal are essential for mitigating negative water impacts and achieving sustainable energy systems (Abbasi, 2018; U.S.A. EIA, 2022).

Studies assessing water contamination consistently reveal a direct link between polluted water sources and serious health risks. The research by Ngoa Manga et al. (2024) underscores this connection, showing how contaminated surface water endangers the health of nearby populations. We must therefore highlight that such findings are not merely academic because they reflect lived realities where environmental degradation breeds distrust, resentment, and unrest among host communities where energy explorative activities happen.

The energy sector poses serious threats to land, air, and water; which are core elements of life and ecological balance. Mining and drilling done to achieve energy production (traditional or renewables) degrade environments and destroy natural habitats (TotalEnergies, 2025). Fossil fuel combustion releases billions of tonnes of CO_2 annually—which worsens air condition and climate change and harms public health (IEA, 2025b). Earth's water systems suffer from excessive withdrawals and contamination, and these endanger aquatic life and clean water access (Earth Day, 2025). These impacts demand urgent, sustainability-centered strategies, such that restores land, reduce emissions, and protect water to safeguard both the planet and the people who depend on it.

2.5 Achieving Sustainability in the Energy Sector

To embed sustainability effectively within the energy sector, we must engage with its foundations. This requires three steps: (a) tracing its historical origins, (b) redefining it for contemporary realities, and (c) confronting the systemic challenges that impede progress. First, understanding its origins reveals how ecological thought emerged in response to industrial impacts. This will provide crucial context for modern policies. Second, redefinition moves the concept from a vague ideal to an actionable framework, in order to balance ecological, social, and technological needs with measurable goals. Finally, a clear-eyed examination of persistent economic, political, and ethical challenges is essential to develop strategies that are both resilient and equitable.

Together, these dimensions transform sustainability from a principle into a practical guide for energy development. The following sections will explore each in detail.

2.5.1 The Origins of Environmental Sustainability

The modern concept of sustainability could be traced to the pollution awareness of the 1960s and 1970s which was catalysed by seminal works like Rachel Carson's *Silent*

Spring and the rise of advocacy groups like Greenpeace (Carson, 1962a, 1962b). This era shifted concern from isolated pollution to the systemic protection of ecosystems and the human environment and as such, laying the direct groundwork for sustainable development. These were subsequently expanded to include all of the systems that support life on earth, including human society (Raskin, 2002). It was perceived that reducing such negative environmental consequences would enhance environmental sustainability.

While pollution is an ancient challenge, it was historically a local issue. This changed with the public consciousness raised by Carson's *Silent Spring*, which inspired the U.S. National Environmental Policy Act (NEPA) of 1969. Effective 1 January 1970, NEPA revolutionised global environmental governance by mandating public-participatory Environmental Impact Assessments (EIA) for major projects. This approach was later adopted in Germany and elsewhere in Europe (Spindler, 2013). Article 2 of NEPA states (U.S. NEPA, 1969) that an EIA must identify, anticipate, and assess the consequences of a project with public engagement on:

(a) Humans, including human health, animals, plants, and biological variety.
(b) The earth, its resources, atmosphere, weather, and topography
(c) Cultural assets and other material assets; and
(d) The interplay of the foregoing assets.

This diverse method treats environmental preservation as an ecosystemic problem, laying the groundwork for both environmental management and sustainability administration (Spindler, 2013). A series of UN Environmental Conferences significantly impacted the development of the new global environmental policy (Stockholm, 1972, Stockholm 1982, Rio de Janeiro 1992, Rio de Janeiro 2012). This is also another historical foundation of the concept of environmental sustainability and it achieved widespread attention. The most notable conference, known as the Earth Summit, was highly productive, resulting in the adoption of six agendas that were recognised as the most critical areas of action in global environmental sustainability concerns:

1. Rio Declaration on the Status of the Environment and Development (known as the Rio Declaration)
2. Forest Principles
3. Framework Convention on Climate Change
4. Convention on Biological Diversity
5. Convention to Combat Desertification (United Nations Convention to Combat Desertification, 2017)
6. Agenda 21

A subsequent and major initiative, known as the Sustainable Development Conference of 2015, (UN, 2015) reaffirms all of Agenda 21's goals as the foundation for sustainable development, identifying a total of 17 goals, all of which revolve around the same themes as Agenda 21: people, planet, prosperity, peace, and collaboration. Environmental sustainability is intimately connected to Goals 6, 7, 12, 13, 14, and

15. The aims underpinning these goals are primarily related to the natural environment. These goals focus on preventing biodiversity loss, battling land degradation and desertification, providing access to inexpensive, clean energy, using natural resources sustainably, and protecting life in aquatic and terrestrial ecosystems from climate change.

Climate change has been described as an existential threat to humanity.Global warming gases (GHGs) are projected to grow by 50% by 2050 due to rising population and energy consumption (OECD, 2012). According to the International Energy Agency's global assessment report, carbon emissions increased in 2018 by 1.7% due to a 2.3% increase in energy consumption, which is ten times faster than the previous decade (*SDG Knowledge Hub,* 2025). About 90% of the world's population breathes dirty air, and the World Health Organisation estimates that 7 million lives are lost annually due to exposure to particulate matter (WHO, 2025).

This historical context of rising awareness stands in stark contrast to a worsening planetary reality. Despite decades of environmental policy, critical data indicate a state of climate emergency. Atmospheric CO_2 has surged to 421 ppm (NOAA, 2024), driving global temperatures to unprecedented levels; 2023 was the warmest year on record at 1.48 °C above pre-industrial levels (Copernicus, 2024). With global wildlife populations declining by an average of 69% since 1970, this warming intensifies extreme weather and accelerates a devastating biodiversity crisis (WWF, 2022). Humanity's demand for resources now exceeds Earth's regenerative capacity by a factor of 1.7 (Global Footprint Network, 2023).

Therefore, while twentieth-century efforts established sustainability as a concept, twenty-first-century evidence reveals an escalating crisis. The foundational work traced from *Silent Spring* to NEPA was necessary but has proven insufficient. This data underscores an urgent imperative: the energy sector's transition must be radically accelerated, moving beyond incremental policy to transformative action that match the scale of the emergency.

2.5.2 Redefining Environmental Sustainability

This section begins with dictionary definitions of sustainability as a foundation, progressing to internationally recognised institutional explanations. The Cambridge English Dictionary defines sustainability as *"the quality of being able to continue over a period of time"* (Cambridge University Press, 2025), while the Oxford English Dictionary emphasises avoiding long-term depletion of natural resources (Oxford University Press, 2025). The U.S. Environmental Policy Act (EPA) frames environmental sustainability as maintaining conditions for productive harmony between humans and nature across generations (The National Academies Press, 2011; U.S. Environmental Protection Agency, 2025). Scholars view it as a balance of resilience and interconnectedness that preserves ecosystems while meeting human needs (Goodland, 1995; Morelli, 2011). Holdren et al. (1995) stress the need to conserve air, water, land, and biodiversity for social and economic progress. The OECD (2001) further refines sustainability with criteria such as regeneration, substitutability, assimilation, and irreversibility avoidance, proposing goals for governance and ecosystem integrity.

A critical analysis of environmental sustainability must move beyond dictionary-derived and institutionally static definitions. While foundational, classic formulations like Goodland's (1995) and the OECD's (2001) criteria, which focus on resource regeneration and waste assimilation, present a model of ecological stability to be maintained in a steady state. Their framework is ill-suited for a human era defined by extraordinary, human-driven planetary changes where a return to an original natural baseline is no longer feasible (Steffen et al., 2015). The Cambridge and Oxford definitions, with their emphasis on mere "continuation", are particularly inadequate, as they lack any normative dimension for justice or ecological health.

The U.S. EPA's definition of "productive harmony" is a diplomatic ideal, but it fails to address the inherent power imbalances and trade-offs in resource allocation. It obscures the critical question: harmonious for whom? The costs of environmental degradation are invariably borne disproportionately by the poor, Indigenous communities, and the Global South (environment of the poor), while the benefits of resource exploitation are often concentrated elsewhere (Martinez-Alier, 2002). Therefore, any contemporary definition must centrally incorporate distributive and procedural justice, moving beyond a generic concern for "future generations" to explicitly safeguard the most vulnerable in the *present.*

In this book therefore, we put forward a more exquisite and operational definition thus: "environmental sustainability is the dynamic, equitable, and resilient integration of human societies within ecological systems; to be achieved through socio-economic structures that operate within planetary boundaries, actively enhance biological and cultural diversity, and ensure a just distribution of environmental benefits and burdens across and within generations".

This definition expands the concept in four important ways:

1. It moves from "Stability to Dynamic Resilience": by rejecting the idea of a static balance and embraces the need for systems that can adapt to inevitable change and shocks.
2. It emphasises "Explicit Equity": since it moves beyond vague "human welfare" to mandate a *just distribution.* Thus, making environmental justice a core tenet, not an ancillary consideration.
3. It projects "Active Regeneration": as it calls not merely for avoiding harm but for actions that *actively enhance* natural and cultural capital. Hence, acknowledging humanity's new role as a planetary steward.
4. It recognises a "Structural Foundation": by locating the responsibility not in individual choice alone, but in the redesign of underlying *socio-economic structures; to wit,* laws, economies, and energy systems—which currently drive unsustainability.

Our effort makes an agreeable sense in terms of bringing the past to present. And to say the least, it seeks to transform sustainability from a passive goal of conservation into an active, ethical, and political project of co-creating a viable and just future.

2.5.3 Challenges of Sustainability in the Energy Sector

The discussion of sustainability in the energy sector, while critically important, is constrained by several notable limitations that deserve scholarly attention. First, the multidimensional nature of sustainability in energy generation is underexplored in research, with a predominant focus on environmental indicators such as greenhouse gas (GHG) emissions, often overshadowing equally pertinent dimensions like water use intensity, land footprint, and socio-economic factors (Georgakellos & Didaskalou, 2014). This narrow focus limits a comprehensive understanding of sustainability challenges and solutions applicable across diverse energy technologies (Turney & Fthenakis, 2011). Second, despite the global recognition of Sustainable Development Goals (SDGs), there remains a significant research gap in empirically linking sustainable energy generation technologies with broader socio-environmental impacts, especially in underdeveloped countries where data paucity and infrastructural deficits hinder detailed analysis (Emerging Issues in Energy Sustainability, 2023).

Economically, the transition to sustainable energy systems encounters cost-related challenges. Many renewable-energy technologies entail higher upfront capital investments and operational costs compared to established fossil fuel systems, impacting the economic feasibility for utilities and governments, particularly in developing contexts (Polzin et al., 2021; Adebayo et al., 2024). Furthermore, the sustainable energy sector faces persistent challenges such as skill shortages, technological immaturity, and uncertain policy environments, which complicate scaling efforts and delay impact realisation (Polzin et al., 2021; Adebayo et al., 2024). There is also resistance from entrenched fossil fuel industries and communities wary of change due to perceived socio-economic risks or environmental concerns associated with renewable infrastructure development, which creates social and political barriers to sustainability transitions (Polzin et al., 2021; Adebayo et al., 2024).

Such constraints emphasise that while the concept of sustainability in energy is essential and widely advocated, its practical implementation and scholarly treatment must advance beyond theoretical postulations. Addressing these limitations demands interdisciplinary research approaches that integrate technological innovation, socio-economic evaluation, and policy analysis, with a particular focus on localised contexts. It also calls for enhanced empirical studies on resource use efficiency and socio-environmental impacts, supported by robust data collection and reporting mechanisms worldwide. By confronting these limitations transparently, the academic and policy discourse on energy sustainability can evolve to propose more nuanced, feasible, and contextually sensitive solutions that bridge theory and practice effectively.

2.6 Conclusion

This chapter has provided a comprehensive exploration of environmental sustainability within the energy sector and highlighted its critical importance and complexity. The chapter began by contextualising why sustainability must be prioritised in an industry that remains a major contributor to environmental degradation. Definitions from authoritative sources clarified the multifarious nature of sustainability, surrounding ecological balance, resource regeneration, and intergenerational equity. The chapter examined the varied environmental impacts of energy production; particularly on land, air, and water resources, highlighting both the challenges and opportunities they pose. In order to achieve sustainability in the energy sector requires integrating principles of resource efficiency, pollution control, and socio-economic inclusion. While the chapter redefined environmental sustainability in contemporary terms and emphasised the need for adaptive and continuous approaches; historical perspectives helped trace the evolution of sustainability concepts. The energy sector faces significant challenges including technological, economic, and policy barriers, but also presents vast potential for transformative shifts towards renewable energy and cleaner technologies. Also crucial in the contribution of this chapter, is its conclusion that sustainability in the energy sector is not a fixed destination but an ongoing process of negotiation and balance among environmental preservation, economic development, and social well-being. Finally, the discussions of this chapter lay a strong foundation for the subsequent chapters, which will explore key theories that explain the principles and complexities behind sustainable energy practices. It will also address frameworks that seek to balance economic growth, environmental protection, and social equity across energy industries. Additionally, it will further analyse contemporary challenges.

References

Abbasi, T. (2018). Environmental impacts of hydropower and alternative mitigation measures. *Lupine Publishers*. https://lupinepublishers.com/agriculture-journal/fulltext/environmental-impacts-of-hydropower-and-alternative-mitigation-measures.ID.000133.php

Adator, S. W., & Li, J. (2021). Evaluating the environmental and economic impact of mining for post-mined land restoration and land-use: A review. *Journal of Environmental Management, 279*, Article 111623. https://doi.org/10.1016/j.jenvman.2020.111623

Adebayo, Y. A., Ikevuje, A. H., Kwakye, J. M., & Esiri, A. E. (2024). A model for assessing the economic impact of renewable energy adoption in traditional oil and gas companies. *GSC Advanced Research and Reviews, 20*(3), 298–315. https://doi.org/10.30574/gscarr.2024.20.3.0355

Allaby, M. (1994). *Macmillan dictionary of the environment*. Macmillan Press.

Bakhsh, S., Zhang, W., Ali, K., & Oláh, J. (2024). Strategy towards sustainable energy transition: The effect of environmental governance, economic complexity and geopolitics. *Energy Strategy Reviews, 52*, Article 101330. https://doi.org/10.1016/j.esr.2024.101330

Basiago, A. D. (2020). Economic, social, and environmental sustainability in development theory and urban planning practice. *Environmentalist, 19*. https://link.springer.com/article/ https://doi.org/10.1023/A:1006697118620

BKV Energy. (2025). Environmental impact of hydropower. https://bkvenergy.com/learning-center/environmental-impact-of-hydropower/

Cambridge University Press. (2025). Sustainability. In *Cambridge Dictionary*. Retrieved October 17, 2025, from https://dictionary.cambridge.org/dictionary/english/sustainability

Carson, R. (1962a). *Silent spring*. Penguin Books.

Carson, R. (1962b, June 9). Silent Spring—I: If we are living so intimately with chemicals, we had better know something about their power. *The New Yorker*. https://www.newyorker.com/magazine/1962/06/16/silent-spring-part-1

CHAS. (2024, May 27). Impact of the energy sector on the environment. *CHAS*. https://www.chas.co.uk/blog/energy-sector-impact-on-environment/

Copernicus Climate Change Service. (2024). *2023 is the hottest year on record, with global temperatures close to the 1.5°C limit*. European Centre for Medium-Range Weather Forecasts. https://climate.copernicus.eu/copernicus-2023-hottest-year-record

Crist, E., Bradshaw, C. J. A., & Ehrlich, P. R. (2022). Scientists' warning on population. *Science of the Total Environment, 845*, Article 157166. https://doi.org/10.1016/j.scitotenv.2022.157166

Damico, A. B., Aulicino, J. M., & Di Pasquale, J. (2022). What does sustainability mean? Perceptions of future professionals across disciplines. *Sustainability, 14*(15), 9650. https://doi.org/10.3390/su14159650

Dryzek, J. S. (2005). *The politics of the earth: Environmental discourses* (2nd ed.). Oxford University Press.

EarthDay. (2025, March 22). Powering the future without draining the planet. https://www.earthday.org/powering-the-future-without-draining-the-planet/

ERM. (2025, March 20). Powering the future: Water as a strategic asset for the energy sector. https://www.erm.com/insights/powering-the-future-water-as-a-strategic-asset-for-the-energy-sector/

Evers, B. (2020). *Why adopt the Sustainable Development Goals? The case of multinationals in the Colombian coffee and extractive sector* (Master's thesis, Erasmus University Rotterdam). https://thesis.eur.nl/pub/41819/Evers-Bas.pdf

Georgakellos, D. A., & Didaskalou, E. A. (2014). Air pollutants externalities associated with the life cycle of renewable energy sources power plants: A comparative appraisal. *International Journal of Energy and Environment, 8*, 154–161.

Global Carbon Project. (2024, November 13). Fossil fuel CO_2 emissions increase again in 2024. Retrieved from https://globalcarbonbudget.org/fossil-fuel-co2-emissions-increase-again-in-2024/

Global Footprint Network. (2023). *Open Data Platform*. https://data.footprintnetwork.org

Goldsmith, E., & Allen, R. (1973). *A blueprint for survival* (2nd ed., Revised ed.). Penguin.

Goodland, R. (1995). The concept of environmental sustainability. *Annual Review of Ecology and Systematics, 26*, 1–24.

Hajian, M. H., & Kashani, S. J. (2021). Sustainable resource management: Modern approaches and contexts. In C. M. Hussain & J. F. Velasco-Munoz (Eds.), *Evolution of the concept of sustainability: From Brundtland Report to Sustainable Development Goals*. Elsevier.

Hák, T., Janoušková, S., & Moldan, B. (2016). Sustainable Development Goals: A need for relevant indicators. *Ecological Indicators, 60*, 565–573. https://doi.org/10.1016/j.ecolind.2015.08.003

Halawa, E. (2024). Sustainable energy: Concept and definition in the context of the energy transition—A critical review. *Sustainability (Switzerland), 16*(4), Article 1523. https://doi.org/10.3390/su16041523

Hardin, G. (1968). The tragedy of the commons. *Science, 162*(3859), 1243–1248.

Hassan, Q., Algburi, S., Sameen, A. Z., Al-Musawi, T. J., Al-Jiboory, A. K., Salman, H. M., Ali, B. M., & Jaszczur, M. (2024). A comprehensive review of international renewable energy growth. *Energy and Built Environment*. Advance online publication. https://doi.org/10.1016/j.enbenv.2024.01.004

Holdren, J. P., Daily, G. C., & Ehrlich, P. R. (1995). The meaning of sustainability: Biogeophysical aspects. In M. Munasinghe & W. Shearer (Eds.), *Defining and measuring sustainability* (pp. 3–17). Distributed for the United Nations University by the World Bank.

IERE Team. (2025, March 3). How much water is there on and in the Earth? *Institute for Environmental Research and Education.* https://iere.org/how-much-water-is-there-on-and-in-the-earth/

Ikpeze, O. V. C., Osaro, E., & Ikpeze, N. G. (2015). Analysis of energy sources, impact on environment and sustainable development referencing landmark cases in the USA, South Africa and Nigeria. *Journal of Environment and Earth Science, 5*(18), 146–155.

International Energy Agency. (2025a). *Air pollution and energy.* https://www.iea.org/reports/air-pollution-and-energy

International Energy Agency. (2025b). *Global energy review 2025.* https://iea.blob.core.windows.net/assets/5b169aa1-bc88-4c96-b828-aaa50406ba80/GlobalEnergyReview2025.pdf

Isukuru, E. J., Opha, J. O., Isaiah, O. W., Orovwighose, B., & Emmanuel, S. S. (2024). Nigeria's water crisis: Abundant water, polluted reality. *Cleaner Water, 2*, Article 100026. https://doi.org/10.1016/j.clwat.2024.100026

ITOPF. (2022). *International tanker owners pollution federation.* https://www.itopf.org/

Jessop, R. (2012). Coinage of the term environment: A word without authority and Carlyle's displacement of the mechanical metaphor. *Literature Compass, 9*(10), 708–717.

Kabir, M., Habiba, U. E., Khan, W., Shah, A., Rahim, S., De los Rios-Escalante, P. R., Farooqi, Z.-U.-R., Ali, L., & Shafiq, M. (2023). Climate change due to increasing concentration of carbon dioxide and its impacts on environment in 21st century: A mini review. *Journal of King Saud University—Science, 35*(5), 102693. https://doi.org/10.1016/j.jksus.2023.102693

Leakey, R. E., & Lewin, R. (1996). *The sixth extinction: Patterns of life and the future of humankind.* Anchor Books.

Liu, X., Wang, D., & Li, A. (2021). Biodiesel production of *Rhodosporidium toruloides* using different carbon sources of sugar-containing wastewater: Experimental analysis and model verification. *Journal of Cleaner Production, 323*, Article 129112. https://doi.org/10.1016/j.jclepro.2021.129112

Martínez-Alier, J. (2002). *The environmentalism of the poor: A study of ecological conflicts and valuation.* Edward Elgar Publishing.

Meadows, D., Randers, J., Behrens, W., & Club of Rome. (1972). *The limits to growth: A report for the Club of Rome's project on the predicament of mankind.* Potomac Associates Books.

Merriam-Webster. (n.d.). Air definition & meaning. *Merriam-Webster Dictionary.* Retrieved November 13, 2024, from https://www.merriam-webster.com/dictionary/air

Morelli, J. (2011). Environmental sustainability: A definition for environmental professionals. *Journal of Environmental Sustainability, 1*(1), 1–9.

National Geographic Society. (n.d.). Air. *National Geographic Education.* Retrieved November 13, 2022, from https://education.nationalgeographic.org/resource/air

National Oceanic and Atmospheric Administration. (2024, June). *Carbon dioxide now more than 50% higher than pre-industrial levels.* https://www.noaa.gov/news-release/carbon-dioxide-now-more-than-50-higher-than-pre-industrial-levels

Ngoa Manga, E. S., Ekoa Bessa, A. Z., Ayissi Mbomo, R.-E., Akono, J. V., Dairou, B., & Kamtchouing, P. (2024). Evaluation of surface water contamination and its impacts on health in the mining districts of Kambélé and Bétaré-Oya (Eastern-Cameroon). *Heliyon, 10*(7), Article e29189. https://doi.org/10.1016/j.heliyon.2024.e29189

Nunes, L. J. R. (2023). The rising threat of atmospheric CO_2: A review on the causes, impacts, and mitigation strategies. *Environments, 10*(4), 66. https://doi.org/10.3390/environments10040066

Onifade, M., Zvarivadza, T., Adebisi, J. A., Said, K. O., Dayo-Olupona, O., Lawal, A. I., & Khandelwal, M. (2024). Advancing toward sustainability: The emergence of green mining technologies and practices. *Green and Smart Mining Engineering, 1*(2), 157–174.

Oxford University Press. (2025). Sustainability. In *Oxford Learner's Dictionaries*. Retrieved October 17, 2025, from https://www.oxfordlearnersdictionaries.com/definition/english/sustainability

OECD. (2001). *OECD environmental strategy for the first decade of the 21st century*. Organisation for Economic Co-operation and Development.

OECD. (2008). OECD glossary of statistical terms—Environment definition. *Organisation for Economic Co-operation and Development*. Retrieved November 13, 2024, from https://doi.org/10.1787/9789264055087-en

OECD. (2012). *Environmental outlook to 2050*. Organisation for Economic Co-operation and Development.

Pan, A., Xu, S., & Zaidi, S. A. H. (2024). Environmental impact of energy imports: Natural resources income and natural gas production profitability in the Asia-Pacific Economic Cooperation countries. *Geoscience Frontiers, 15*(2), Article 101756. https://doi.org/10.1016/j.gsf.2023.101756

Peacock, C. (2019, August 27). What are the biggest sources of water pollution? *Aquaread*. https://www.aquaread.com/blog/what-are-the-biggest-sources-of-water-pollution/

Polzin, F., Sanders, M., Steffen, B., & et al. (2021). The effect of differentiating costs of capital by country and technology on the European energy transition. *Climatic Change, 167*(26). https://doi.org/10.1007/s10584-021-03163-4

Raskin, P. (2002). *Great transition: The promise and lure of the times ahead* (p. 31). Stockholm Environment Institute.

Rentizelas, A., & Georgakellos, D. (2014). Incorporating life cycle external cost in optimization of the electricity generation mix. *Energy Policy, 65*, 134–149.

Ripple, W. J., Wolf, C., Newsome, T. M., Barnard, P., & Moomaw, W. R. (2019). World scientists' warning of a climate emergency. *BioScience, 70*(1), 8–12. https://doi.org/10.1093/biosci/biz088

Sakalasooriya, N. (2021). Conceptual analysis of sustainability and sustainable development. *Open Journal of Social Sciences, 9*(3), 396–414. https://doi.org/10.4236/jss.2021.93026

Sophie, I. (2022, September 6). The top most water polluting sectors. *Tariff*. https://www.tariff.com/news-and-insights/top-water-polluting-sectors/

Spindler, E. (2013). The history of sustainability: The origins and effects of a popular concept. In I. Jenkins & R. Schröder (Eds.), *Sustainability in tourism* (pp. 9–31). Springer Gabler. https://doi.org/10.1007/978-3-8349-7043-5_1

Steffen, W., Richardson, K., Rockström, J., Cornell, S. E., Fetzer, I., Bennett, E. M., & Sörlin, S. (2015). Planetary boundaries: Guiding human development on a changing planet. *Science, 347*(6223), 1259855. https://doi.org/10.1126/science.1259855

The World Bank. (2017). *Atlas of sustainable development goals: From world development indicators: World Bank Atlas*. Elibrary.worldbank.org. https://elibrary.worldbank.org/ https://doi.org/10.1596/978-1-4648-1080-0

Torres, P. (2016, April 11). Biodiversity loss: An existential risk comparable to climate change. *Bulletin of the Atomic Scientists*. https://thebulletin.org/2016/04/biodiversity-loss-an-existential-risk-comparable-to-climate-change/

TotalEnergies. (2025). *Sustainability & climate 2025 progress report*. https://totalenergies.com/system/files/documents/totalenergies_sustainability-climate-2025-progress-report_2025_en.pdf

UCLA Sustainability Committee. (2016). *UCLA Sustainability Charter*. University of California, Los Angeles. https://sustain.ucla.edu/wp-content/uploads/UCLA-Sustainability-Charter.pdf

United Nations Convention to Combat Desertification. (2017). *Global Land Outlook (GLO)*. UNCCD.

United Nations Environment Programme. (2025). *Global status of clean energy transition 2025*. https://www.unep.org/resources/report/global-status-clean-energy-transition-2025

United Nations General Assembly. (2015). *Transforming our world: The 2030 Agenda for Sustainable Development*. United Nations.

U.S. Energy Information Administration. (2022, November 6). Hydropower and the environment. https://www.eia.gov/energyexplained/hydropower/hydropower-and-the-environment.php

U.S. Environmental Protection Agency. (2025, August 21). Climate change impacts on energy. https://www.epa.gov/climateimpacts/climate-change-impacts-energy

Virtanen, P. K., Siragusa, L., & Guttorm, H. (2020). Introduction: Toward more inclusive definitions of sustainability. *Current Opinion in Environmental Sustainability, 43*, 77–82. https://doi.org/10.1016/j.cosust.2020.03.002

World Commission on Environment and Development. (1987). *Our common future*. Brundtland Commission.

World Economic Forum. (2025, July). How we tackle the energy, food and water nexus. https://www.weforum.org/stories/2025/07/energy-food-and-water-nexus/

World Health Organisation. (2024). *Ambient (outdoor) air quality and health*. https://www.who.int/news-room/fact-sheets/detail/ambient-(outdoor)-air-quality-and-health

World Health Organization. (2025). *Air pollution*. https://www.who.int/health-topics/air-pollution#tab=tab_1

World Wildlife Fund. (2022). *Living Planet Report 2022—Building a nature-positive society* (R. E. A. Almond, M. Grooten, D. Juffe Bignoli, & T. Petersen, Eds.). WWF. https://www.worldwildlife.org/publications/living-planet-report-2022

Wuebbles, D. J. (2017). Executive summary. In D. J. Wuebbles (Ed.), *Climate science special report: Fourth National Climate Assessment*. U.S. Global Change Research Program.

Chapter 3
Theories and Challenges of Environmental Sustainability

3.1 Introduction

Environmental sustainability is no longer a side topic; it now sits at the very heart of the global energy conversation. The way we produce, distribute, and consume energy today will determine the kind of planet future generations inherit. The same systems that have powered economic growth for over a century are also the ones driving climate change, biodiversity loss, and the steady depletion of natural resources. As the United Nations Environment Programme (2024) cautions, the energy sector must undergo a deep transformation if the world is to make genuine progress towards a sustainable future.

This chapter explores the main ideas and theories that shape how we understand environmental sustainability ideas drawn from sustainability science, systems theory, resilience thinking, stakeholder theory, ecological modernisation, and environmental justice. Each of these frameworks adds a different layer of meaning to sustainability. Sustainability science connects research to real-world action, emphasising the interdependence of environmental, economic, and social systems. Systems theory helps explain how energy, water, and climate are interconnected, reminding us that true sustainability requires coordination across sectors rather than isolated reforms. Resilience thinking focuses on how societies and institutions adapt to shocks such as climate crises or market disruptions, with stakeholder theory (Freeman, 1994) underlining that decisions about the environment must include the voices of all affected governments, corporations, and communities alike. The notion of ecological modernisation introduces a more practical dimension, showing how innovation and policy reform can make growth compatible with environmental care, and environmental justice completes the picture by insisting that sustainability must be fair, inclusive, and grounded in dignity for all.

While early debates about sustainability often centered on oil and gas, this discussion takes a much wider view. It includes the full range of energy systems from electricity and renewables like solar, wind, hydro, and bioenergy to transitional options

J. A. Debski, *Corporate Social Responsibility in the Energy Sector*, CSR, Sustainability, Ethics & Governance, https://doi.org/10.1007/978-3-032-17748-3_3

such as hydrogen, energy storage, and carbon capture, utilisation and storage (CCUS). By drawing examples from both developed and developing contexts, the chapter highlights how countries and corporations are interpreting and acting on sustainability goals in their own ways. The outcomes of COP28, for instance, renewed the global call to move away from fossil fuels while also raising tough questions about how governments and investors will turn those promises into reality (UNFCCC, 2023).

Energy trends today tell a mixed story. On one hand, renewable energy is growing faster than any other source of electricity, showing that the transition is underway. On the other, many nations still struggle to balance sustainability with affordability, reliability, and universal access (IEA, 2024). National examples such as Nigeria's Energy Transition Plan (Federal Government of Nigeria, 2022) illustrate the difficult balancing act between meeting development needs and cutting emissions.

The discussion that follows weaves together theory, policy, and on-the-ground experience from across the energy sector. It begins by outlining the main conceptual foundations of sustainability before moving through its economic, social, and environmental dimensions. It then examines the governance and financial factors that shape how quickly the energy transition can happen. The chapter closes by identifying the major gaps that still exist questions that naturally lead into the next chapter, which focuses on concrete sustainability initiatives and how they are being put into practice.

3.2 The Evolution of the Concept of Environmental Sustainability

The idea of environmental sustainability has evolved alongside the broader concept of sustainable development itself. From the outset, rests on the understanding that economic progress, social well-being, and environmental protection are deeply interconnected. Early concerns arose as people began to see how unrestrained industrial growth and the careless use of natural resources were threatening both ecological balance and human welfare (Meadows et al., 1972). Over time, this awareness matured through a series of global efforts and agreements that gradually transformed sustainability thinking from a narrow focus on protecting the environment to a more comprehensive view of how entire energy and development systems function.

The 1972 United Nations Conference on the Human Environment, often referred to as the Stockholm Conference, marked the first major global attempt to confront environmental challenges collectively. One of its most enduring legacies was the creation of the United Nations Environment Programme (UNEP), which became the institutional foundation for coordinated environmental action worldwide. Two decades later, the Brundtland Report (1987) put up a definition that remains central to sustainability discourse: *development that meets the needs of the present without compromising the ability of future generations to meet their own* (World Commission on Environment and Development, 1987). This idea of intergenerational equity and ecological responsibility provided both the moral and policy compass for global sustainability thinking in the decades that followed.

Momentum grew further at the 1992 Rio Earth Summit, which produced the Rio Declaration and Agenda 21. These introduced what would become the "three pillars" of sustainability economic, social, and environmental and established the principle of "common but differentiated responsibilities". Together, these concepts shaped how governments and corporations would frame their environmental and energy policies. The early 2000s brought a new wave of attention through the Millennium Development Goals (MDGs), which explicitly linked environmental protection to human well-being. The 2002 Johannesburg Summit built on this momentum by stressing the need for cross-sectoral collaboration and practical implementation.

A major shift occurred with the Copenhagen Accord in 2009 and, more decisively, the 2015 Paris Agreement. These milestones moved climate action from voluntary pledges to binding international commitments. The Paris Agreement, in particular, placed the energy transition at the centre of efforts to achieve net-zero emissions, compelling carbon-intensive industries from oil and gas to electricity and renewables to align with global decarbonisation pathways (UNFCCC, 2015). That same year, the 2030 Agenda for Sustainable Development was adopted, with its 17 Sustainable Development Goals (SDGs) firmly positioning energy at the heart of global development through Goal 7: *Affordable and Clean Energy*.

In recent years, sustainability thinking has broadened further to include fairness, inclusion, and justice. The notion of a *just transition* ensuring that the shift to low-carbon economies does not leave workers or communities behind has gained traction across policy debates. Similarly, circular economy principles have become more prominent, promoting efficiency and reuse across industries. The 2019 European Green Deal laid out a pathway towards climate neutrality by 2050, while the United States' Inflation Reduction Act (2022) introduced large-scale incentives for renewable energy and low-carbon technologies. In the Global South, initiatives such as Nigeria's Energy Transition Plan (2022) and similar frameworks in South Africa and India demonstrate growing efforts to pursue sustainable industrialisation that aligns with national contexts and development priorities.

The more recent climate summits COP26 in Glasgow (2021), COP27 in Sharm el-Sheikh (2022), and COP28 in Dubai (2023) have maintained international momentum. COP28, in particular, marked a defining moment by calling for a "transition away from fossil fuels in energy systems" and setting a collective goal to triple renewable-energy capacity by 2030 (UNFCCC, 2023).

Retrospectively, the story of environmental sustainability reveals a clear and steady transformation from isolated environmental protection efforts to an integrated framework that connects climate action, energy reform, and sustainable development. It reflects a growing understanding that sustainability is not just about conserving nature; it is about reshaping how societies produce energy, manage resources, and define progress itself (Table 3.1).

Table 3.1 Timeline of global sustainable development and environmental sustainability milestones (1972–2024)

Year/initiative	Sustainable development milestone	Key environmental or energy principle	Implications for the energy sector and this research
1972—Stockholm Conference (UN Conference on the Human Environment)	First global recognition of environmental issues and need for international cooperation	Environmental protection becomes a shared human concern	Laid foundation for global environmental governance; created UNEP
1987—Brundtland Report ("Our Common Future")	Introduced the modern definition of sustainable development	Intergenerational equity and ecological prudence	Framed sustainability as a development issue, influencing national and corporate energy policies
1992—Rio Earth Summit (Rio Declaration, Agenda 21)	Established three pillars of sustainability: economic, social, and environmental	Common but differentiated responsibilities (CBDR)	Introduced principles later used in corporate sustainability frameworks and climate agreements
2000—Millennium Development Goals (MDGs)	Linked poverty eradication with environmental protection	Human development and environmental stewardship	Highlighted energy access as essential to social progress
2002—Johannesburg World Summit on Sustainable Development (WSSD)	Focused on implementation of SD principles	Multi-stakeholder participation and corporate accountability	Broadened private sector responsibility for sustainable operations
2009—Copenhagen Accord	Introduced voluntary emission reduction pledges	Recognition of national commitments and climate finance	Opened the path for energy transition finance and technology transfer
2012—Rio + 20 Summit	Introduced the "Green Economy" and the institutional framework for sustainable development	Integration of economic growth with environmental resilience	Encouraged renewable energy and clean technology investments
2015 – Paris Agreement	Legally binding climate accord committing nations to limit warming to 1.5–2 °C	Net-zero emissions and energy transition as central strategies	Institutionalised decarbonisation targets for oil, gas, and power industries
2015—UN 2030 Agenda for Sustainable Development (SDGs)	Adopted 17 SDGs, including SDG 7 on clean energy	Universal and integrated sustainability agenda	Made access to affordable and clean energy a global development priority

(continued)

Table 3.1 (continued)

Year/initiative	Sustainable development milestone	Key environmental or energy principle	Implications for the energy sector and this research
2019—European Green Deal (EU)	Comprehensive plan for climate neutrality by 2050	Circular economy and just transition principles	Accelerated renewable-energy investments and stricter emission standards
2021—COP26 (Glasgow)	Global momentum on phasing down coal and fossil fuels	Commitment to net-zero pathways and adaptation funding	Set new targets for renewable-energy expansion and fossil fuel reduction
2022—COP27 (Sharm el-Sheikh)	Introduced "Loss and Damage Fund" for vulnerable nations	Climate justice and financial equity	Strengthened funding for climate adaptation in developing energy economies
2022—Nigeria's Energy Transition Plan	National strategy for achieving net-zero by 2060	Integration of energy access, industrialisation, and decarbonisation	Demonstrates Global South participation in the global energy transition
2022—U.S. Inflation Reduction Act	Major legislative commitment to renewable energy and low-carbon innovation	Green incentives and domestic clean energy production	Reshaped the global renewable energy-investment landscape
2023—COP28 (Dubai)	First global agreement to "transition away from fossil fuels."	Tripling of renewable capacity and doubling energy efficiency by 2030	Marks decisive global shift towards renewable and low-carbon energy systems
2024—UNEP and IEA Sustainability Reports	Emphasis on systemic transformation for net-zero and biodiversity recovery	Integrative governance and climate–energy–nature nexus	Highlights need for cross-sectoral collaboration across oil, gas, electricity, and renewables

3.3 Theoretical Perspectives on Environmental Sustainability

Understanding environmental sustainability requires more than describing its goals; it calls for a look at the theories that explain *why* sustainability matters and *how* societies can actually achieve it. Theoretical perspectives help connect ideas, values, and actions, providing the frameworks through which policies and practices take shape. They also help explain why progress has been uneven across nations and sectors, and why sustainability is as much a social challenge as it is an environmental one.

Several major theories have guided the way scholars, governments, and industries think about sustainability. Each offers a unique lens for interpreting the relationship between humans and nature, and together they form the backbone of modern sustainability thinking.

3.3.1 Sustainability Science

At its core, sustainability science seeks to bridge the gap between knowledge and action. It is built on the understanding that environmental problems cannot be solved by one discipline alone; they require integrated approaches that combine ecology, economics, engineering, and social sciences. Sustainability science has evolved into a vibrant, problem-driven field focused on linking human and natural systems through transdisciplinary learning (Spangenberg, 2011).

In the energy context, this perspective encourages innovation that aligns ecological limits with human development needs. It asks practical questions: how can clean energy solutions be scaled up while maintaining equity and resilience? How can research and policy work together to create lasting change?

3.3.2 Systems Theory

Environmental sustainability is also deeply informed by systems theory, which views the world as a set of interconnected parts that influence one another. Energy, water, food, and climate are all part of a single system, and a change in one inevitably affects the others. Systems theory reminds policymakers that sustainability cannot be achieved by addressing issues in isolation (Berkes & Folke, 1998). For example, expanding renewable energy may reduce emissions but could also affect land use and biodiversity if poorly managed. The systems approach therefore calls for balance, feedback, and coordination across sectors, shifting attention from individual projects to the larger web of relationships that determine whether societies can remain within planetary boundaries.

3.3.3 Resilience Thinking

Closely linked to systems theory is resilience thinking the idea that social and ecological systems must be able to absorb shocks, adapt, and still function. It highlights the need for flexibility, diversity, and continuous learning (Folke, 2016). Rather than focusing only on preventing crises, resilience thinking emphasises; preparation and recovery. In the energy sector, this translates to building infrastructure and governance systems that can withstand disruptions such as price shocks, natural disasters, or technological failures. It also means involving communities in planning and decision-making, since resilience grows strongest when it is shared at the local level.

3.3.4 *Stakeholder Theory*

Stakeholder theory brings the human element to the forefront of sustainability. It argues that decisions about the environment should consider the interests of *all* who are affected not only shareholders or government bodies, but also workers, local communities, consumers, and future generations. Research shows that stakeholder pressures strongly influence firms' environmental actions and sustainability outcomes (Saleem et al., 2020).

In practice, this translates into participation, dialogue, and accountability. It challenges the assumption that environmental protection is solely the responsibility of the state, and instead promotes partnership among governments, businesses, and citizens. Within the energy transition, stakeholder theory has helped redefine what "responsibility" means, turning sustainability from a compliance exercise into a shared moral and strategic commitment.

3.3.5 *Ecological Modernisation Theory*

Another influential perspective is ecological modernisation theory (EMT), which suggests that economic growth and environmental protection do not have to be opposing forces. Rather, modern societies can innovate their way out of environmental problems by redesigning technologies, institutions, and industries to be more efficient and less wasteful. EMT argues that industrial transformation, policy reform, and technological innovation can jointly advance both economic and environmental goals (Setyari & Kusuma, 2021).

This theory underlies many of today's sustainability strategies from circular economy models to clean energy investments. It offers a pragmatic message: with the right incentives and governance, environmental responsibility can go hand in hand with industrial competitiveness. However, modernisation without social inclusion risks reproducing old inequalities under a new, "green" label (York & Rosa, 2003).

3.3.6 *Environmental Justice Theory*

Finally, no discussion of sustainability is complete without the principle of environmental justice the belief that environmental benefits and burdens should be distributed fairly. This perspective emerged from recognising that pollution, resource depletion, and climate impacts often fall most heavily on the poor and marginalised (Agyeman et al., 2016). Environmental justice extends the meaning of sustainability beyond ecological protection to include fairness, dignity, and human rights. It insists that true sustainability cannot exist in a world where some communities bear the costs while others enjoy the rewards.

Together, these theories form the ideas that link ethics, governance, and science. They remind us that sustainability is not a single path but a collective journey that combines knowledge, cooperation, and compassion. Each framework offers a piece of the puzzle: sustainability science connects research to practice; systems theory explains interdependence; resilience thinking prepares societies for change; stakeholder theory fosters inclusion; ecological modernisation aligns progress with responsibility; and environmental justice anchors it all in fairness.

These perspectives continue to shape how nations and corporations approach environmental sustainability particularly in the energy sector, where every decision carries both local and global consequences. Understanding them strengthens the theoretical foundation of sustainability and helps translate ambition into action in a world that must learn to live within its limits.

3.4 The Economic Aspect of Sustainability

The economic side of sustainability is about how societies can maintain long-term prosperity without eroding the social or environmental foundations that support it. The word "economy" comes from the Greek *oikos* (household) and *nomos* (law or management), which together suggest the responsible management of limited resources for the good of all. In this sense, economic sustainability is the ability of an economy to keep improving living standards while preserving the natural capital on which all production depends (Goodland, 1995).

For a long time, traditional economic thinking assumed that growth could continue indefinitely and that nature's resources were effectively limitless. By the late twentieth century, this belief had become impossible to defend. Studies such as *The Limits to Growth* (Meadows et al., 1972) showed that unchecked consumption and industrial expansion could push humanity beyond the planet's capacity to cope. Since then, economists and policymakers have worked to reconcile growth with efficiency, conservation, and regeneration trying to build systems that create prosperity without destroying the environment that sustains it.

In the energy sector, this challenge takes on a particularly clear form. Economic sustainability now means moving away from short-term profit goals towards long-term value creation based on innovation, diversification, and circular use of resources. Fossil fuels, long the foundation of industrial economies, are increasingly seen as transitional. In their place, renewable-energy sources such as solar, wind, and hydropower are becoming central to sustainable development (IEA, 2024). Global investment in renewables now surpasses spending on fossil fuels, driven by both market dynamics and deliberate policy shifts (World Bank, 2023). Together, these trends show that the economies of the future will rest on clean energy systems, low-carbon technologies, and resilient supply chains.

To make this transformation work, economic systems must account for environmental costs such as carbon emissions and pollution in the prices of goods and services. Instruments like carbon pricing, emissions trading, and green bonds have become important tools for aligning economic incentives with environmental outcomes (OECD, 2022). The circular economy model adds another layer, promoting reuse, recycling, and energy recovery to reduce waste and extend the life of resources (Ellen MacArthur Foundation, 2021). These approaches encourage efficiency and innovation while keeping growth within the limits of what ecosystems can sustain.

In developing countries, the economic aspect of sustainability is inseparable from broader development goals such as energy access, poverty reduction, and job creation. Nations like Nigeria and Kenya are using renewable mini-grids and public–private partnerships to expand electricity access while supporting local enterprise (Federal Government of Nigeria, 2022). The principle of a "just transition", which is now widely recognised in global climate governance, stresses that the shift to low-carbon economies must protect workers, communities, and livelihoods. Balancing growth, equity, and environmental responsibility is particularly critical for resource-dependent economies.

Finance is another major force shaping this transition. By 2023, global sustainable finance assets had exceeded USD 30 trillion, largely through the growth of environmental, social, and governance (ESG) investments and green credit instruments (McKinsey & Company, 2023). Development banks, institutional investors, and sovereign wealth funds are increasingly directing capital towards renewable infrastructure, climate adaptation, and biodiversity conservation. These movements show that sustainability has moved from the margins of economics to its very center, it now defines competitiveness, resilience, and long-term value.

The economic dimension of sustainability marks a shift from extractive, consumption-driven models to more regenerative and inclusive systems of prosperity. In the energy sector, it means building financial and industrial frameworks that make the low-carbon transition both feasible and fair. Achieving this balance requires active coordination among governments, businesses, and communities, and a shared recognition that sustainability is not only good ethics, it is sound economics.

3.5 The Social Aspect of Sustainability

At its core, the social dimension of sustainability is about people. It reminds us that no matter how efficient an economy becomes or how green our technologies are, development means little if it fails to improve people's lives. This side of sustainability deals with fairness, dignity, and inclusion, the things that make a society whole. While economic and environmental indicators can often be measured and compared, the social aspects are harder to capture. They involve questions of equity, participation, human rights, culture, and trust in institutions (Ezeani, 2010). In other words, a community cannot call itself sustainable if it leaves some of its members behind or if progress comes at the cost of justice.

In the energy world, these questions take on a very practical form. *Energy justice* and *energy equity* have emerged as guiding principles, insisting that everyone should have access to clean, affordable, and reliable energy, and that no group should carry an unfair share of the environmental burden (Heffron & McCauley, 2017). For decades, this has not been the case. Many oil-producing regions, for example, have seen huge revenues flow outward while local people live with pollution and declining livelihoods. It is no surprise that such patterns have led to growing calls for more inclusive decision-making, where community voices and local knowledge help shape energy policy.

Global frameworks now reflect this shift. The United Nations Global Compact (UNGC) places human rights and fair labour practices at the centre of responsible business (UN Global Compact, 2020). In practice, this means energy companies are expected to ensure that their growth does not come at the expense of workers' safety or the well-being of host communities. Other international guidelines like the Equator Principles and the OECD's standards for multinational enterprises reinforce this expectation by requiring social impact assessments and genuine engagement before major projects begin.

At the local level, social sustainability often comes down to resilience and empowerment. Resilience, in this sense, is the ability of people and communities to adapt to shocks whether environmental, social, or economic (Renschler et al., 2010). Access to diverse energy sources, strong community networks, and responsive institutions all make a difference. Research shows that communities directly involved in small-scale energy projects such as village solar cooperatives or community-owned wind farms tend to be more stable and better organised than those that are excluded from the process (Magis, 2010).

Magis (2010) identifies eight overlapping areas that shape community resilience, including resource access, engagement, collective action, and fairness. The key message is clear: communities thrive when they are part of the change, not just observers of it. This idea is slowly taking root. Across Africa and Europe, for instance, energy transition platforms and stakeholder councils are bringing together local governments, civil society groups, and indigenous representatives to plan energy projects. These partnerships are sometimes slow, but they build trust, and trust is what long-term sustainability depends on.

Social innovation is another powerful tool. Off-grid renewable systems, pay-as-you-go solar kits, and flexible financing schemes have allowed millions of low-income households to gain access to clean energy on their own terms (IEA, 2024). When designed with people's realities in mind, such initiatives do more than provide power, they create jobs, improve health and education, and give families a sense of control over their futures.

Gender and generational equity are also part of this story. Women and young people, once seen mostly as beneficiaries, are now leading many renewable-energy initiatives. Women, in particular, bear the brunt of energy poverty but have also become some of the most active innovators and entrepreneurs in the clean energy space (UN Women, 2022). Including gender perspectives in energy planning is not just about fairness; it makes policies more realistic and effective because they reflect the daily lives of the people they are meant to serve.

Social aspect of sustainability reminds us that the energy transition is not only a technical or economic project, it is a human one. Policies and investments will only succeed if they are grounded in participation, fairness, and trust. Without that foundation, even the best environmental or economic goals risk falling apart, because real sustainability begins and ends with people.

3.6 The Environmental Aspect of Sustainability

The environmental dimension of sustainability is about safeguarding the health and resilience of the planet's natural systems. It reminds us that economies and societies are not separate from the environment but entirely dependent on it. The air we breathe, the water we use, and the energy we consume all come from ecosystems that have limits. Environmental sustainability, therefore, means using natural resources at a rate that allows them to renew themselves, while keeping waste and pollution within the Earth's capacity to absorb them (Goodland, 1995).

In the energy sector, this translates into a simple but difficult goal: reducing the industry's ecological footprint while keeping the lights on. Energy remains the single largest contributor to global greenhouse gas emissions, roughly three-quarters of the total come from it (IEA, 2024). That fact alone makes transforming how we produce and use energy central to climate stability and long-term development. Fossil fuels, which have powered growth for over a century, continue to damage ecosystems, pollute air and water, and drive global warming. Renewable sources such as wind, solar, hydro, and geothermal, by contrast, offer a chance to meet energy needs without depleting the planet's natural capital.

The idea of environmental sustainability has deep roots in the growing recognition of planetary limits. Early works such as *The Limits to Growth* (Meadows et al., 1972) and the *World Conservation Strategy* (1980) laid the groundwork for understanding that the Earth's resources are finite. Later, the Planetary Boundaries framework (Rockström et al., 2009) quantified just how far humanity can safely push ecological systems before risking collapse. These milestones marked an important shift: sustainability came to mean not just conserving what is left, but actively restoring the health of the ecosystems we depend on.

Recent science has added another layer to this picture, the link between climate, energy, and biodiversity. The Intergovernmental Panel on Climate Change (IPCC, 2023) warns that current emission trends are incompatible with the 1.5 °C target set by the Paris Agreement. Despite advances in clean energy technologies, emissions from coal and oil continue to rise. This not only accelerates climate change but also undermines biodiversity and the ecosystem services that support agriculture, water supply, and human health. The challenge, therefore, is not simply to reduce emissions but to rethink the entire system: how energy is produced, distributed, consumed, and ultimately recycled.

Environmental sustainability in the energy sector also calls for better resource management. Cleaner production, energy efficiency, and reduced waste are now core elements of responsible practice. Technologies such as carbon capture, utilisation and storage (CCUS), green hydrogen, and battery recycling show how innovation can help align industry with ecological resilience. Modern electricity grids increasingly integrate renewables with storage and digital management systems, making it possible to balance supply and demand with less environmental strain.

Of course, even renewable energy is not impact-free. Expanding solar and wind capacity can create new environmental pressures, from land-use conflicts to the mining of rare minerals for batteries and turbines (UNEP, 2023). True sustainability means facing these trade-offs honestly. It requires assessing the environmental impact of energy systems across their full life cycle, from resource extraction to disposal, and designing circular systems where materials are reused rather than wasted.

Adaptation and ecosystem restoration are becoming equally important parts of the sustainability picture. The 2023 UNEP report stresses that adaptation finance must double by 2030 if countries are to protect vulnerable ecosystems and communities from rising climate risks. Reforestation, wetland restoration, and coastal protection do more than safeguard nature, they also make societies more resilient to climate shocks and energy disruptions.

In the end, the environmental dimension gives meaning to the whole idea of sustainability. It is the foundation on which social well-being and economic stability rest. For the energy sector, that means designing systems that respect ecological limits, protect biodiversity, and build resilience against shocks. Achieving this will require cooperation at every level, governments setting strong standards, companies investing in cleaner technologies, and citizens adopting more responsible consumption patterns.

Environmental sustainability is about moving from extraction to regeneration. It is not just about controlling pollution; it is about rebuilding our relationship with the natural world. Whether humanity can make that shift will determine not only the stability of the climate but also the survival of our civilisation within the planet's fragile boundaries.

3.7 Strategies for Environmental Sustainability

Talking about environmental sustainability is easy. Living it, and making it work across nations, companies, and communities is much harder. The truth is, keeping our planet healthy while trying to grow our economies and improve lives demands intentional, well-thought-out strategies. It is not just about passing green policies; it is about connecting people, power, and priorities at every level from small rural communities to global institutions.

The energy sector tells this story clearly. Energy drives everything we do, but it also drives most of the world's carbon emissions. How we handle energy, therefore, shows whether sustainability is just a word or a real commitment.

3.7.1 Stakeholder Collaboration and Governance

If there is one lesson from decades of environmental work, it is that no one can do it alone. Governments, corporations, civil society, and ordinary citizens all share responsibility for protecting the planet (Freeman, 1994; Weimeth, 2020).

Since the 1990s, *stakeholder theory* has reminded policymakers and companies that people who are affected by a decision should have a say in it. That sounds obvious but in practice, it changes everything. When people are part of designing policies and projects, they tend to believe in them more.

Take Denmark and Germany: local cooperatives own shares in wind and solar projects there, turning climate policy into something neighbours talk about with pride. In Kenya and Nigeria, community mini-grids have helped villages access electricity without destroying their surroundings. These examples show that when people are part of the process, solutions stick.

But engagement has to be real, not cosmetic. Too often, "consultation" means gathering feedback that no one intends to use. As Eaton et al. (2021) note, that kind of tokenism does more harm than good. The European Commission's, 2022 governance guidelines made this clear; if engagement does not start early, and if people do not actually share power, sustainability efforts will lose credibility before they even begin.

3.7.2 Policy Frameworks and International Cooperation

The big environmental agreements; the Paris Agreement (2015), the 2030 Agenda for Sustainable Development, and the annual COP meetings may seem far removed from everyday life, but they set the tone for how countries move forward. The COP28 Declaration (2023), for instance, was a breakthrough: world leaders finally agreed to begin moving *away* from fossil fuels and triple renewable-energy capacity by 2030 (UNFCCC, 2023).

These global commitments then find shape at home. The European Green Deal (2019), the U.S. Inflation Reduction Act (2022), and Nigeria's Energy Transition Plan (2022) all try to turn ambition into action. Each combines regulations with incentives, carbon pricing, green bonds, tax credits to push innovation and cleaner industry. Many of these plans also weave in biodiversity and circular economy goals so that growth does not come at nature's expense.

It is not perfect, but it is some progress and it shows how cooperation between countries and regions can set the stage for a more balanced global economy.

3.7.3 Technological Innovation and Industrial Transition

Technology is not the whole answer, but it is impossible to imagine sustainability without it. The transition to clean energy depends on new ideas: better batteries, smarter grids, cleaner fuels, and ways to capture carbon before it harms the atmosphere.

Right now, renewable energy is growing faster than anyone predicted. The International Energy Agency (IEA, 2024) notes that renewables make up over 90% of new global power capacity. That is an astonishing shift in just a decade.

Yet, innovation does not thrive in isolation. Governments must back research, protect inventors, and make it easier for poor and developing countries to access new technology. Initiatives like Mission Innovation and the Global Energy Alliance for People and Planet show that collaboration public and private can scale good ideas much faster than competition alone.

3.7.4 Market-Based Mechanisms and Financial Strategies

Money can either fuel destruction or drive change. Economic tools like carbon pricing, cap-and-trade systems, and green finance are ways to make the market work for the planet instead of against it (OECD, 2022).

The green bond market, for example, is booming over USD 500 billion in 2023. Investors are finally realising that sustainability is not charity; it is smart economics. Many banks now demand strong ESG (Environmental, Social, and Governance) records before releasing funds, which forces companies to act responsibly.

For developing countries, financing remains a hurdle. But mechanisms like blended finance and credit guarantees help attract private investors to renewable projects by lowering risks. The emerging Just Transition Fund adds something more humane: it ensures that people whose livelihoods depend on fossil fuels are not abandoned but retrained, supported, and given a stake in the new economy.

3.7.5 Education, Capacity Building, and Behavioural Change

You can build the best solar panels in the world, but without education and awareness, real change would not happen. Sustainability is not just a policy, it is a mindset. People need to understand why their daily choices matter, from how they use energy to how they dispose of waste.

For leaders and policymakers, capacity building means more than training; it is about learning to balance competing priorities; development, growth, and environmental protection without losing sight of the long-term picture. The UNEP

Report (2023) calls education and institutional learning the "missing link" in most climate strategies. It is indeed right since behaviour changes only when people truly understand the stakes.

3.7.6 Integrating Local and Indigenous Knowledge

For centuries, local and indigenous communities have practised sustainability long before the term became fashionable. They understand the rhythm of nature the patience of rotational farming, the wisdom in conserving water, the shared care in community forestry.

Modern policymakers are beginning to see this. In Canada and New Zealand, renewable-energy projects involving indigenous groups have seen higher success and stronger community buy-in. These experiences prove a simple truth: people protect what they feel connected to. Sustainability is not just about science; it is about respect for culture, for history, and for the land itself.

3.8 Challenges of Environmental Sustainability

For decades, the world has talked about sustainability; set goals, signed agreements, and written policies. Yet, in practice, the world still struggles to live up to those promises. Climate change continues to intensify, biodiversity keeps shrinking, and millions still lack access to clean energy. These failures show that the gap between vision and reality remains wide. Environmental sustainability faces a web of obstacles; political, institutional, financial, and behavioural, all pulling in different directions within a global system still heavily dependent on fossil energy.

3.8.1 Fragmented Global Governance

One of the biggest obstacles is the scattered nature of global environmental governance. The United Nations Environment Programme (UNEP), created back in 1972 to lead the charge, has always faced limits it does not have the power, budget, or independence needed to truly enforce change (Ivanova, 2021). It answers to the UN General Assembly, not as a full specialised agency, which means it operates more as a coordinator than a regulator.

Over the years, the number of environmental treaties has exploded more than 1,300 multilateral and 2,200 bilateral agreements (IEA Database, 2023). This may sound like progress, but in practice it often creates chaos: overlapping rules, conflicting priorities, and wasted effort. Different conventions handle biodiversity (CBD), climate change (UNFCCC), and desertification (UNCCD), yet they rarely align neatly, leaving countries juggling separate commitments that compete for attention and resources.

Many scholars have called for a more unified global structure, perhaps even a single Global Environmental Organisation but the politics of power and sovereignty have kept that idea out of reach.

3.8.2 National Sovereignty and Policy Inconsistency

At the national level, the problem shifts from fragmentation to conflict of interest. Countries naturally want to protect their sovereignty and push for growth. But environmental goals often clash with those ambitions. For developing nations especially, poverty reduction and economic expansion are immediate priorities, while sustainability tends to feel like a long-term luxury (Ivanova, 2011).

The result is policy inconsistency. A country might pledge carbon neutrality at the UN, yet continue subsidising fuel consumption at home. In West Africa, for instance, environmental laws exist on paper but enforcement often falters. Undermined by corruption, weak institutions, or political interference. The outcome is a familiar pattern: lofty goals, limited follow-through, and an ever-widening gap between what is promised and what is done.

3.8.3 Financing and Economic Constraints

Money remains the hardest nut to crack. The transition to sustainable energy systems is enormously expensive. The International Energy Agency (2024) estimates that reaching global net-zero by 2050 would require over USD 4 trillion in clean energy investments every year a number that dwarfs current spending levels.

Developing countries, in particular, struggle to attract affordable financing. High borrowing costs, unstable currencies, and limited access to global capital markets make clean energy projects risky. Funds like the Green Climate Fund and the Loss and Damage Fund were created to help, but the money trickles out too slowly, and not nearly enough. The UNEP Adaptation Gap Report (2023) warns that climate adaptation funding will need to at least double by 2030 to meet even the most basic needs.

Private investors, meanwhile, hesitate to put money into regions they see as politically uncertain or poorly regulated. Without new financing ideas like blended capital, carbon markets, or scaled-up green bonds the global transition risks leaving poorer countries behind altogether.

3.8.4 *Technological and Infrastructure Gaps*

There is the technology gap, a quieter but equally serious divide. Wealthier nations are racing ahead with renewables, hydrogen, and carbon capture systems, while much of the developing world still relies on old, carbon-heavy infrastructure. Access to new technologies is often blocked by high costs, weak grids, and strict intellectual property rules.

In sub-Saharan Africa, for example, solar and wind potential is immense, but electricity still fails to reach many rural areas. Transmission systems are underdeveloped, and markets remain small and fragile (World Bank, 2023). Closing that gap means more than just shipping equipment; it requires real investment in technical skills, fairer technology transfer, and international cooperation that treats developing countries as partners, not customers.

3.8.5 *Climate Change and Environmental Degradation*

Climate change itself has become the biggest threat to sustainability. Rising temperatures, floods, wildfires, and desertification are no longer distant forecasts, they are daily realities. The IPCC (2023) calls the impacts "widespread, rapid, and intensifying", and the description fits.

For the energy sector, the risks are growing: coastal power plants face flooding, hydropower output drops during droughts, and extreme heat strains electricity systems. Environmental degradation also deepens social suffering; reducing farm yields, displacing families, and worsening poverty. Each environmental shock ripples through economies, eroding both trust and stability.

3.8.6 *Weak Institutional Coordination*

Even within countries, sustainability often falters because of how governments are organised. Ministries work in silos: the environment is handled in one corner, the economy in another, and energy policy somewhere else. These walls make it nearly impossible to create policies that reinforce each other.

Coordination across ministries and regions is usually weak, and reliable environmental data are often missing. Without solid information, governments cannot track progress or adjust their strategies. Building stronger institutions, ones that share information, plan across sectors, and make evidence-based decisions, is essential if sustainability goals are to move beyond rhetoric.

3.8.7 Corporate Accountability and Greenwashing

The private sector carries huge influence both as part of the problem and as part of the solution. But here too, appearances can be deceiving. Many corporations talk a good game about "going green" while continuing business as usual. *Greenwashing*, painting a surface of sustainability over old habits is rampant.

Sustainability reports are published everywhere now, but many are vague, unverified, or selectively transparent. Without standardised reporting rules, comparing one company's impact to another's is nearly impossible. The International Sustainability Standards Board (ISSB) is trying to change this by harmonising reporting requirements, yet global adoption remains patchy. To make real progress, companies need to face tighter accountability mandatory ESG disclosures, independent audits, and penalties for misleading claims.

3.8.8 Social Inequality and the "just Transition"

Finally, no discussion of sustainability is complete without talking about fairness. The global shift away from fossil fuels, though necessary, threatens jobs and livelihoods in industries that millions depend on. If handled carelessly, it could deepen inequality and social unrest.

The principle of a *just transition*, now recognised in the Paris Agreement, insists that climate policies must also protect people through retraining, social support, and inclusive development. But turning that principle into practice is far from simple. In countries where oil and gas revenues fund public budgets, the transition can feel like an economic cliff. Ensuring justice in the process making sure no one is left behind is one of the hardest challenges sustainability faces today.

3.9 Benefits of Environmental Sustainability

Environmental sustainability offers far-reaching rewards that extend beyond environmental protection. It enhances social welfare, drives economic growth, and strengthens competitiveness across industries. In today's world where nations and corporations are aligning with global net-zero and green growth goals, sustainability has evolved from a moral obligation into a strategic and financial necessity.

Within the energy sector, which has long been viewed as both a driver of progress and a contributor to environmental degradation, embracing sustainability delivers tangible benefits that promote long-term success and societal well-being.

3.9.1 Enhanced Corporate Reputation and Market Value

Companies that integrate sustainability into their core strategies tend to perform better in both reputation and profitability. Research indicates that firms with strong environmental, social, and governance (ESG) practices enjoy higher investor confidence, lower risk exposure, and improved access to capital (Eccles et al., 2014).

According to McKinsey & Company (2023), sustainability has become a key driver of corporate value creation. Increasingly, executives regard sustainability as essential for long-term competitiveness, brand resilience, and stakeholder trust. Organisations that embed sustainability into their governance and day-to-day operations are more effective at managing risk, attracting investors, and achieving operational efficiency.

In the energy industry, companies that proactively manage environmental risks by cutting emissions, improving transparency, and investing in renewable technologies consistently outperform peers in valuation and stakeholder confidence. Conversely, environmental neglect can be catastrophic. The Deepwater Horizon disaster of 2010, for instance, demonstrated how weak sustainability practices can erase decades of brand equity and shareholder value, costing BP billions in penalties and clean-up expenses.

3.9.2 Operational Efficiency and Cost Reduction

Environmental sustainability often translates into greater operational efficiency and lower costs. By adopting energy-efficient technologies, reducing waste, and promoting circular resource use, companies can minimise input costs while increasing productivity.

Digital innovations such as smart grids, predictive maintenance, and automation allow energy producers to optimise operations and reduce losses. Between 2010 and 2023, for example, the cost of solar photovoltaic power dropped by more than 80%, while onshore wind fell by nearly 60% (International Energy Agency [IEA], 2024). Similarly, industrial redesigns that focus on waste heat recovery, recycling of drilling fluids, and closed-loop water systems have improved profitability while reducing environmental impact. These examples show that environmental stewardship can coexist with, and even enhance, commercial success.

3.9.3 Innovation and Technological Leadership

Sustainability drives innovation by encouraging companies to rethink processes, develop cleaner technologies, and explore new business models. The shift towards green hydrogen, energy storage, bioenergy, and carbon capture has created new markets and high-skilled employment opportunities.

The clean energy sector, for instance, employed over 35 million people in 2023, surpassing fossil fuel jobs for the first time (International Renewable Energy Agency [IRENA], 2024). Advances in materials science, such as recyclable solar panels and second-life battery systems, further demonstrate how sustainability fuels industrial transformation and energy security, reducing dependence on volatile fossil fuel markets.

3.9.4 Access to Finance and Investment Opportunities

The global financial landscape increasingly rewards sustainability-oriented companies. ESG-linked investments now represent more than one-third of total global assets under management, exceeding USD 30 trillion (Organisation for Economic Co-operation and Development [OECD], 2023). Financial institutions and sovereign wealth funds are redirecting capital away from carbon-intensive industries towards renewable and low-carbon projects.

Instruments such as green bonds, sustainability-linked loans, and transition finance mechanisms provide companies with lower-cost capital while incentivising measurable environmental outcomes. In developing economies, access to blended finance and carbon markets supports the rollout of renewable-energy infrastructure and climate adaptation initiatives. Thus, environmental sustainability enhances both environmental performance and financial inclusion.

3.9.5 Societal and Public Health Benefits

At the societal level, sustainability directly improves human health and overall quality of life. Cleaner air, reduced pollution, and responsible waste management lessen the burden of respiratory and waterborne diseases. The World Health Organisation (WHO, 2023) estimates that air pollution contributes to over seven million premature deaths annually, many of which could be prevented through cleaner energy transitions.

Expanding renewable energy and phasing out coal-fired power plants reduce harmful emissions such as sulfur dioxide, nitrogen oxides, and particulate matter, yielding enormous public health benefits. Furthermore, access to clean and reliable energy empowers communities: renewable mini-grids enable rural populations to access education, healthcare, and business opportunities, fostering economic and social inclusion.

3.9.6 Resilience and Long-Term Competitiveness

Sustainability strengthens resilience by equipping businesses and economies to better withstand environmental and market shocks. Climate-resilient infrastructure, diversified energy portfolios, and sustainable supply chains reduce vulnerability to extreme weather events, policy shifts, and resource scarcity.

Organisations that integrate sustainability into risk management are more adaptable in volatile markets, while nations investing in renewable energy gain long-term competitive advantages. Countries leading in clean energy innovation, such as China, the United States, and members of the European Union are now shaping industrial standards and influencing global trade. For developing economies, sustainability provides an opportunity to leapfrog outdated technologies and achieve inclusive, future-oriented growth.

The benefits of environmental sustainability are wide-ranging and mutually reinforcing. For governments, sustainability promotes policy stability and social welfare. For corporations, it enhances profitability, efficiency, and market value. For societies, it ensures cleaner environments and healthier lives.

In the energy sector, sustainability is no longer optional it defines resilience, credibility, and future relevance. The next chapter builds on these insights by exploring how governments, corporations, and communities are translating sustainability commitments into practical action across the oil, gas, electricity, and renewable-energy industries.

3.10 Conclusion

Environmental sustainability sits right at the meeting point of theory and real-life practice. It is not just a concept that belongs in policy papers or academic debates; it is a living, evolving challenge that touches how we live, work, and build our economies. As this chapter has shown, sustainability cannot be limited to protecting nature alone; it is about transforming the entire way societies think about growth, fairness, and responsibility to the future. The theories that frame this transformation sustainability science, systems theory, resilience thinking, stakeholder theory, ecological modernisation, and environmental justice remind us that achieving sustainability requires both knowledge and empathy, innovation and inclusion.

The review of different ideas and approaches makes it clear that sustainability is both a duty and an opportunity. Economically, lasting prosperity depends on recognising that natural resources are not endless. Models built around green growth, renewable energy, and circular economies reflect the logic of ecological modernisation, showing that innovation and economic progress can move hand in hand when guided by sound environmental principles. This aligns with the essence of sustainability science, which seeks to translate knowledge into tangible, balanced development outcomes.

Socially, sustainability is about people. It reminds us that progress loses meaning if it leaves some groups behind or destroys the foundations that future generations depend on. The principles of stakeholder theory and environmental justice reinforce this truth: genuine sustainability demands inclusion, fairness, and shared decision-making. Policies must therefore ensure that communities are active participants in shaping their futures, not passive recipients of top-down interventions. When participation and equity are at the centre of energy and environmental planning, sustainability becomes more than an aspiration it becomes a lived reality.

Environmentally, the message remains straightforward: societies must live within the planet's limits, reduce emissions, and restore what has been damaged. Systems theory and resilience thinking highlight how every component of the environment, economy, and society is interconnected. They remind policymakers that resilience depends on diversity, adaptability, and collective learning. The capacity to respond to shocks whether ecological or economic defines the true strength of a sustainable system.

While global efforts such as the Paris Agreement, the European Green Deal, and national transition plans have pushed the agenda forward, the road ahead is still full of obstacles. Fragmented governance, poor coordination, and unequal access to finance continue to slow progress, especially in developing regions. Meeting these challenges will take more than technology it will require honesty, cooperation, and political will. Sustainability, viewed through its theoretical lenses, is therefore not a fixed goal but a continuous process of balancing complexity, adapting to change, and building shared trust.

In the end, environmental sustainability offers a chance to rebuild our economies and societies on stronger, fairer, and cleaner foundations. Its rewards healthier communities, resilient economies, and a safer planet show that the effort is worth it. Sustainability science gives the roadmap, systems theory and resilience thinking supply the structure, stakeholder theory and environmental justice provide the ethics, and ecological modernisation offers the tools to make progress possible. Together, they frame a vision of a world that grows within its limits and prospers through cooperation.

But the key question remains: how do we turn all these ideas and strategies into real, practical actions that people can see and measure in their daily lives?

That question forms the starting point for the next chapter, which looks at how governments, businesses, and local communities are putting sustainability into action turning broad goals into everyday change.

References

Agyeman, J., Schlosberg, D., Craven, L., & Matthews, C. (2016). Trends and directions in environmental justice: From inequity to everyday life, community, and just sustainabilities. *Annual Review of Environment and Resources, 41*(1), 321–340. https://doi.org/10.1146/annurev-environ-110615-090052

Barbier, E. B. (2012). *The green economy post Rio+20. Science, 338*(6109), 887–888. https://doi.org/10.1126/science.1227360

Berkes, F., & Folke, C. (1998). *Linking social and ecological systems: Management practices and social mechanisms for building resilience.* Cambridge University Press. https://doi.org/10.1017/CBO9780511541957

Bendtsen, E., Clausen, L. P., & Hansen, S. F. (2021). A review of the state-of-the-art for stakeholder analysis with regard to environmental management and regulation. *Journal of Environmental Management, 279,* Article 111773. https://doi.org/10.1016/j.jenvman.2020.111773

Biesbroek, R., Peters, G., & Tosun, J. (2018). Public bureaucracy and climate change adaptation. *Review of Policy Research, 35*(5), 776–791. https://doi.org/10.1111/ropr.12316

Brodhag, C., & Taliere, S. (2006). Sustainable development strategies: Tools for policy coherence. *Natural Resources Forum, 30*(2), 136–145. https://doi.org/10.1111/j.1477-8947.2006.00166.x

Campagnolo, L., Carraro, C., Eboli, F., Farnia, L., Parrado, R., & Pierfederici, R. (2017). The ex-ante evaluation of achieving sustainable development goals. *Social Indicators Research, 136*(1), 73–116. https://doi.org/10.1007/s11205-017-1572-x

Desai, B. H. (2000). Revitalizing international environmental institutions: The UN Task Force Report and beyond. *Indian Journal of International Law, 40*(2), 253–276.

Eccles, R. G., Ioannou, I., & Serafeim, G. (2014). The impact of corporate sustainability on organisational processes and performance. *Management Science, 60*(11), 2835–2857. https://doi.org/10.1287/mnsc.2014.1984

Eaton, W. M., Brasier, K. J., Burbach, M. E., Whitmer, W., Engle, E. W., Burnham, M., Quimby, B., Kumar Chaudhary, A., Whitley, H., Delozier, J., & Weigle, J. (2021). A conceptual framework for social, behavioral, and environmental change through stakeholder engagement in water resource management. *Society & Natural Resources, 34*(8), 1111–1132. https://doi.org/10.1080/08941920.2021.1936717

Ellen MacArthur Foundation. (2021). *Completing the picture: How the circular economy tackles climate change.*

European Commission. (2022). *Environmental governance reforms for sustainability: Strengthening transparency and stakeholder participation under the European Green Deal.* European Union Publications. Retrieved from https://environment.ec.europa.eu/law-and-governance_en

Ezeani, E. C. (2010). *The WTO and its development obligation: Prospects for global trade.* Anthem Press.

Federal Government of Nigeria. (2022). *Nigeria's Energy Transition Plan.*

Folke, C. (2016). Resilience (Republished). *Ecology and Society, 21*(4), 44. https://doi.org/10.5751/ES-09088-210444

Freeman, E. R. (1994). The politics of stakeholder theory: Some future directions. *Business Ethics Quarterly, 4*(4), 409–421. https://doi.org/10.2307/3857340

Goodland, R. (1995). The concept of environmental sustainability. *Annual Review of Ecology and Systematics, 26*(1), 1–24. https://doi.org/10.1146/annurev.es.26.110195.000245

Heffron, R. J., & McCauley, D. (2017). The concept of energy justice across the disciplines. *Energy Policy, 105,* 658–667. https://doi.org/10.1016/j.enpol.2017.03.018

International Energy Agency (IEA). (2024). *World Energy Outlook 2024.*

International Renewable Energy Agency (IRENA). (2024). *Renewable energy and jobs: Annual review 2024.*

Ivanova, M. (2011). *Global governance in the 21st century: rethinking the environmental pillar.*

Ivanova, M. (2021). The untold story of the world's leading environmental institution: UNEP at fifty. *MIT Press.* https://doi.org/10.7551/mitpress/12373.001.0001

Magis, K. (2010). Community resilience: An indicator of social sustainability. *Society & Natural Resources, 23*(5), 401–416. https://doi.org/10.1080/08941920903305674

McKinsey & Company. (2023). *ESG report: Accelerating sustainable and inclusive growth for all.* McKinsey & Company. Retrieved from https://www.mckinsey.com/~/media/mckinsey/about%20us/social%20responsibility/2023%20esg%20report/mckinsey-and-company-2023-esg-report-executive-summary.pdf?utm_source=chatgpt.com

Meadows, D. H., Meadows, D. L., Randers, J., & Behrens, W. W. (1972). *The limits to growth.* Universe Books.
Organisation for Economic Co-operation and Development (OECD). (2022). *Investing in climate, investing in growth: Mobilising financing for the transition.* OECD Publishing. https://doi.org/10.1787/9789264273528-en
Renschler, C. S., Frazier, A. E., Arendt, L. A., Cimellaro, G. P., Reinhorn, A. M., & Bruneau, M. (2010). *Framework for defining and measuring resilience at the community scale: The PEOPLES resilience framework (MCEER-10–0006).* Multidisciplinary Center for Earthquake Engineering Research (MCEER), University at Buffalo, State University of New York.
Reed, M. S., Vella, S., Challies, E., De Vente, J., Frewer, L., Hohenwallner-Ries, D., Huber, T., Neumann, R. K., Oughton, E. A., Sidoli del Ceno, J., & Fazey, I. (2017). A theory of participation: What makes stakeholder and public engagement in environmental management work? *Restoration Ecology, 26*(1), 7–17. https://doi.org/10.1111/rec.12541
Rockström, J., Steffen, W., Noone, K., Persson, Å., Chapin, F. S., Lambin, E., Lenton, T. M., Scheffer, M., Folke, C., Schellnhuber, H. J., & Foley, J. A. (2009). A safe operating space for humanity. *Nature, 461*(7263), 472–475. https://doi.org/10.1038/461472a
Setyari, N. P. W., & Kusuma, W. G. A. (2021). Economics and environmental development: testing the environmental kuznets curve hypothesis. *International Journal of Energy Economics and Policy, 11*(4), 51–58 https://doi.org/10.32479/ijeep.11156
Saleem, M. A., Kumar, V., & Shahid, Z. (2020). The role of stakeholder pressure and green dynamic capabilities in environmental sustainability. *Sustainability, 12*(20), 8751. https://doi.org/10.3390/su12208751
Spangenberg, J. H. (2011). Sustainability science: A review, an analysis, and some empirical lessons. *Environmental Conservation, 38*(3), 275–287. https://doi.org/10.1017/S0376892911000270
UN Global Compact. (2020). *The ten principles of the UN Global Compact.*
United Nations Environment Programme (UNEP). (2023). *Emissions Gap Report 2023.*
United Nations Environment Programme (UNEP). (2024). *Global environment outlook 7: Systems transformation for a sustainable future.*
United Nations Framework Convention on Climate Change (UNFCCC). (2015). *Paris agreement.*
United Nations Framework Convention on Climate Change (UNFCCC). (2023). *Conference of the parties: COP28 outcome document.*
United Nations Women (UN Women). (2022). *Gender equality and the energy transition.*
World Bank. (2023). *Scaling up to phase down: Financing energy transition in developing countries.* World Bank Group. Retrieved from https://www.worldbank.org/en/news/press-release/2023/04/20/scaling-up-to-phase-down-financing-energy-transition-in-developing-countries
World Commission on Environment and Development (WCED). (1987). *Our common future.*
Weimeth, H. (2020). Stakeholder engagement for environmental innovations. *Journal of Business Research, 119*, 310–320. https://doi.org/10.1016/j.jbusres.2018.12.054
York, R., & Rosa, E. A. (2003). Key challenges to ecological modernisation theory: Institutional efficacy, case study evidence, and policy implications. *Organisation & Environment, 16*(3), 273–288. https://doi.org/10.1177/1086026603256299

Chapter 4
Initiatives for Environmental Sustainability

4.1 Introduction

The initiatives for environmental sustainability under regional and global dimensions have been a major theme in environmental policy and strategy for the past half-century. The rapid degradation of the natural global environment and the resultant biodiversity loss ignited these efforts, as people became increasingly aware of the links between the exponential growth of the human population and rising resource demands (Brundtland Report 2021). The awareness of the need to balance progress with planetary health has led organisations, governments, and regions to undertake initiatives designed for environmental sustainability.

To critically appraise these initiatives, this chapter attempts to identify those optimal trends by analysing environmental sustainability initiatives at international and regional levels. It achieves this objective by analysing both the theoretical and the practical application of key strategies available for the implementation of environmental sustainability. The fundamental drive of this analysis is to promote successful sustainability efforts by illuminating the wide range of practical approaches worthy of consideration when utilising effective strategies for environmental sustainability.

4.2 Regional Initiatives for Environmental Sustainability

Many of the complex social, economic, and environmental issues plaguing municipal areas may be resolved by adopting a regional approach to sustainability. When regions engage with and actively promote environmental technology-related sectors such as renewable energy, they not only benefit the environment but also enhance regional unity and stability while gaining economic advantages.

There are efforts in various states to promote environmental sustainability at the national level but these face certain criticisms. Firstly, political ideologies and interest

J. A. Debski, *Corporate Social Responsibility in the Energy Sector*, CSR, Sustainability, Ethics & Governance, https://doi.org/10.1007/978-3-032-17748-3_4

groups may not necessarily prioritise environmental sustainability in governments, be they centralised or federal (McCright & Dunlap, 2011). Secondly, not only are state governments frequently too massive and introverted to grasp regional issues and concerns (Howard, 2012), environmental issues transcend national borders and a collective effort reduces duplication whilst increasing efficiency.

International initiatives for the enhancement of environmental sustainability, on the other hand, might need to consider grassroots applications and adaptations of their policies to fit into the regional context. Given that regions face similar environmental challenges, regional policies tailored to the needs, peculiarities, and realities of the region are best suited. This applies particularly to developing countries and vulnerable groups, especially fragile states which contribute little to the global challenges but bear the environmental brunt of the consequences.

There are numerous methodologies to assess regional environmental sustainability policies and their outcomes, and regional indicators are becoming a growing concern in academia (Ramos, 2009). It is noteworthy that there is no optimal or recognised strategy for developing an indicator or a consensus on which design/approach is the best. Hence, this chapter is restricted to the analysis of existing and potential strategies used to achieve environmental sustainability, and an assessment of their performance through the available sustainability index indicators available in UN reports as well as through national indicators (Wilson et al., 2007). In the regions assessed, focus is placed on major oil-producing and consuming areas to examine the efforts of major contributors to climate change to combatting it.

4.2.1 Environmental Sustainability Initiatives and Strategies in Asia: People's Republic of China (PRC)

Asia is undergoing more rapid industrial development than any other part of the globe. The International Energy Agency (2025a, 2025b, 2025c) reported that three-fifths of the total global energy demand growth in 2024 took place in Developing Asia, with the growth in China alone greater than the increase in demand in all advanced economies combined. While the region is investing heavily in and expanding its renewable-energy sector, there's still a heavy reliance on fossils to meet the growing demand. By a wide margin, China is the region's largest oil producer in the region. It accounts for an estimated 50% of Asia's total production with approximately 5 million barrels of oil per day(b/d). In 2024, the country produced an average of 4.3 million b/d and had to import about 11.3 million b/d to meet its energy demand It is also the largest consumer of liquid fuels as the Energy International Administration (2025) estimates that the country's consumption of petroleum and other liquid fuels in 2024 was 16.3 million b/d, second only to the United States globally. Fossil fuels constitute a substantial proportion of their overall energy mix and supply. This reliance on fossil fuels places the region's climate goals and global net-zero aspirations at risk.

Asides fossils, China is also one of the largest producer and consumer of metallic minerals, increasing significantly the country's carbon emissions. The energy transition requires clean-energy-critical minerals, but the extraction process poses significant risks of habitat destruction, soil erosion and releasing pollutants (Sun et al., 2024). Undoubtedly, China's oil and gas and mineral sectors have propelled the country forward by fostering urbanisation and industrialisation (Qin et al., 2024). Nevertheless, the environmental consequences of this expansion are significant, necessitating the country, and the region at large to develop sustainable environmental initiatives.

There are significant efforts in China to mitigate the efforts of climate change. Pivotal to this is the Energy Conservation Law of 1997 which was formulated in order to promote energy conservation throughout society, improve the efficiency of energy utilisation, achieve economic benefits, protect the environment, secure national economic and social development, and meet the requirement everyday life of people. There are also series of climate action plan formulated and implemented as part of the Country's commitment to environmental sustainability, the most recent being the 14th five-year plan for 2021–2025 which aims for carbon neutrality by 2060. Another pillar of China's climate change initiatives is carbon capture, utilisation, and storage (CCUS) technology which captures of carbon dioxide emissions produced from large sources, such as power plants and industrial facilities, preventing them from entering the atmosphere. Since the 12th five-year plan, China has included this technology as part of its national carbon mitigation strategies (Jiang et al., 2020).

Following the adoption of the Sustainable Development Goals (SDGs) by all member states of the UN in 2015, the Asian Development Bank (ADB) has been (i) working with its developing member countries to deliver on the SDGs, (ii) direct financing of member countries and the private sector in support of the SDGs, (iii) mobilising additional finance for the SDGs from a wide range of sources and (iv) providing knowledge, data and policy dialogue on SDG progress and implementation (ADB, 2024). Through the activities in these four areas, ADB aims to increase implementation and achievement of the SDGs in DMCs, and contribute to realising its vision for a prosperous, inclusive, resilient, and sustainable Asia and the Pacific. In 2016, the ADB approved a technical assistance project titled the Supporting Implementation of Environment-Related Sustainable Development Goals in Asia and the Pacific (ADB, 2016). The document provides the context and background of the project, and provide information on impacts and outcomes, key activities, estimated costs, financing, and implementation arrangements.

To serve the changing needs of its DMCs more effectively, in 2023, ADB launched a New Operating Model to increase its capacity as Asia and the Pacific's climate bank; spur private sector engagement and investment; provide a wide range of integrated and innovative development solutions; and modernise how ADB works. These four shifts, together with an ongoing decentralisation process that will strengthen country offices and empower decision-making closer to clients, will lead to more innovative solutions and greater mobilisation of finance for ADB members to reignite progress towards the SDGs (ADB, 2025).

From a global perspective, Asia's statistics from the ADB brief show that various factors, from poor governance to a lack of incentives and funding to act, hinder environmental sustainability (ADB, 2016). For instance, many developing member countries (DMCs) in the region face degraded marine and terrestrial ecosystems, along with resource-intensive consumption and production patterns (ADB, 2016).

However, governments alone cannot overcome the effects of the connection between growth, resource usage and pollution (Shin, 2005). As a result of the severity of environmental deterioration, demands have been made for the private sector as well to supply the technology and finance required to counteract these effects. In 2003, India passed the Companies Act which mandates companies to spend a portion of their profit on corporate social responsibility. Although it neither sanctions nor makes provision specifically for environmental sustainability, this represents a good example of how government can work with firms to achieve the goal of environmental sustainability. A further instance of a nation utilising commercial processes to tighten environmental rules on companies is the Environmental Label, created by the PRC in 1993 as a signalling tool for firms seeking public procurement contracts. Additionally, the Singapore Stock Exchange has required that all listed firms must account for their environmental, social, and governance practices, and has created new indices for assessing sustainability that investors may utilise (Shin, 2005). Although these initiatives are promising, more initiatives to address significant regional problems are to be encouraged.

In line with these initiatives, the Carbon Disclosure Project (CDP), despite a growing number of participating firms, has revealed that many companies are neither reporting their emission levels nor establishing aggressive objectives within the 2030 timeframe (Simpson, 2017). The CDP data reflect that businesses are using internal carbon pricing to manage climate risks and make investment decisions, but only a handful of these have set objectives for growing renewable-energy output or utilisation. The project further disclosed that 68% of respondents identified underlying physical, regulatory and/or other climate change-related potential which were required to modify company operations, income or expenditures (Simpson, 2017).

However, a far lower number of companies identified strategies to improve water efficiency or reduce water usage, as well as ways to minimise energy use by improving water efficiency. Compulsory reporting is more likely to encourage companies to participate. This approach further allows companies and stakeholders to monitor the progress of businesses, therefore promoting environmental sustainability gradually over time.

4.2.2 Environmental Sustainability Initiatives and Strategies in Africa: The African Union (AU)

Africa holds 30% of the world's mineral reserves, 8% of its natural gas, and 12% of its oil (UNEP, 2024). In comparison with other areas, Africa's nations do not consume a large amount of fossil fuels on a per capita basis (World Bank, 2002). The region's per capita emissions are far lower than any other as it is responsible for only 3.7% of carbon emissions from the burning of fossil fuels (Ford, 2025). The region's primary contributions to global carbon emissions come from natural gas flaring resulting from oil and gas production in several African nations, primarily Nigeria, combined with the large-scale and widespread burning of grasslands and forests. Nevertheless, Africa is the most vulnerable to climate change impacts under all climate scenarios above 1.5 degrees Celsius (ADBG, 2024). The region has been warming at a slightly faster rate (+0.3C per decade) than the global average, with the environment deteriorating faster than in other regions (WMO, 2024).

The first-ever comprehensive assessment of air pollution and climate change for the continent, titled the Integrated Assessment of Air Pollution and Climate Change for Sustainable Development in Africa (IAAPCCSDA) represents a solid scientific foundation for guaranteeing clean air in Africa (UNEP 2022). The Assessment's recommendations are closely aligned with Agenda 2063's top priorities (AU, 2022) and the SDGs' objectives and ambitions. Nearly all of the proposals are presently acknowledged as contributing significantly to at least one African Nationally Determined Contribution, as articulated in Article 4, paragraph 2 of the 2015 Paris Agreement. The recommendations for implementing sustainability are based on the concept of partnerships between international institutions, local governments and rural communities. There is no specific strategy delineated, per se, in the IAAPCCSDA to achieve environmental sustainability. It is the author's considered view, however, that to make the IAAPCCSDA more impactful vis-a-vis the attainment of environmental sustainability, it would be crucial to provide more detailed guidelines on the actual implementation and enforcement strategies, along the lines of the EU Commission's Environmental Implementation Review (EIR).

The AU Africa Ocean Governance Strategy and Implementation Plan (2025–2035) was also developed in 2025 to address existing governance gaps, enhance coordination and implementation of existing frameworks, as well as promote sustainable economic opportunities of Africa's aquatic and marine resources. Another notable strategy, indeed a missed opportunity, for implementing environmental sustainability, has been identified in the Report on the Implementation of Agenda 2063 (AU and AUDA, 2022). The report explicitly links the implementation of environmental sustainability to the social economy in Africa and gives funding a major role in achieving environmental sustainability. Financial support can be leveraged by key actors, such as the African Development Bank (AU and AUDA, 2022). Disappointingly, the report focuses largely on the progress of social and economic flagship projects. Regarding the objectives of achieving an environmentally sustainable climate, there is no mention of advancing environmental sustainability, for example, in the context of the oil and gas industries and their undoubted links to climate change. Notwithstanding this, the AU Climate Change and Resilient Development Strategy and Action Plan for 2022–23, (AU, 2022) which is aligned to the implementation of Agenda 2063, acknowledges the crucial requirement for financial mobilisation. Again however, while it acknowledges the need for the energy transition to enhance the generation of renewable energy, there are no discernible strategies proposed.

It would appear though that, at a national level, African countries are making individual efforts to achieve environmental sustainability in their oil and gas producing regions. (McKenzie, 2022) For example, in Egypt, there are incentives e.g. the National Initiative for Smart Green Projects, National Green Building Strategy, etc. for companies that are set up with the goal of achieving sustainable development. These initiatives are strengthened by key legislations and regulations, which contain modalities for the design and specifications for such projects, and is subject to constant reviews.

In Ghana, there is a procurement strategy to ensure a market-competitive price for renewable energy-generated power, rooted in the Renewable Energy (Amendment) Act 2020 (Act 1045). In its Renewable Energy Master Plan of 2019 (which is currently under review) the government provided substantial tax reliefs and proposes exemptions on import duties and VAT on materials for manufacturing or assembling renewable-energy equipment, such as solar panels or wind turbines. The Sustainable Use of Natural Resources and Energy Financing Programme, an initiative of the country's Energy Commission, provides financing for sustainable energy projects and technical support to both industry and individuals.

Nigeria has also demonstrated its commitment to achieving environmental sustainability by recently empowering the NNPC LTD to engage in renewable-energy businesses via the Petroleum Industry Act of 2021. It further enacted a Climate Change Act in 2021 to provide an enabling framework to achieve low greenhouse emissions and has submitted its third Nationally Determined Contribution (NDC) under the Paris Agreement in 2025.

In Kenya, there's a policy-enabling environment which has resulted in combined governmental efforts (e.g. Renewable Energy and Climate Technologies programme (REACT) and private sectors efforts (e.g. the Sustainable Inclusive). The resultant effect is the country having one of the cleanest electrical networks in the world (ITA, 2022) and being on track to achieving universal electricity access by 2030 (IEA, 2025). In 2024, the largest source of energy consumed in the country was generated from biofuels and waste and the largest source of energy generation being geothermal.

From this brief survey of initiatives relating to the attainment of genuine environmental sustainability in the AU, it is apparent that there currently exists a lot of room for fairly radical changes in the mindsets of many African nations, and more joined-up regional approaches.

4.2.3 Environmental Sustainability Initiatives and Strategies in South America: Brazil

A range of South American nations have signed numerous bilateral and multilateral treaties related to environmental issues. It is pertinent to note that environmental protection laws and regulations are subject to wide institutional and regional variations throughout South America. Some countries have relatively complex procedures, with a central environmental agency in charge of all regulations. In others, there is no central authority in charge, and the infrastructure of institutions is more malleable (Wagner, 1998). For precision, this section will focus on sustainability initiatives and strategies adopted by a major oil-producing country, Brazil.

Over half of South America's total population lives in Brazil, making it the continent's most populated country. Also, Brazil has emerged in the last few decades as the major regional power, producing more than half of the continent's GDP (Statista, 2025). In 2024, the average annual production of oil and gas in Brazil reached 4.322 million barrels of oil equivalent per day with extraction rates of oil 3.559 million barrels per day and natural gas being 153 million cubic meters per day (BEI, 2025). In July 2025, an all-time high was reached as country produced above 5 million barrels of oil and natural gas per day for the first time ever (BEI, 2025). Apart from Petrobras, which is the Brazilian state oil company, 47 local and 50 foreign companies hold oil exploration and appraisal areas in Brazil. The Organisation of America States Charter states that all foreign transnational enterprises and foreign private investments shall be subject to the legislation of the host countries, to the jurisdiction of their competent courts, and to the international treaties and agreements to which the said countries are parties, and should conform to the recipient countries' development policies.

The recent legislation for the Brazil oil and gas industry includes the new Gas Law 2021(Law No. 14,134/21) and Decree No. 12,153/24 which amended the Gas Decree (Decree No. 10,721/21) of 2021. These new regulations are expected to boost the deliverability of LNG and natural gas, perceived as an appealing transition fuel, to complement the expanding market for renewable-energy sources and encourage the use of intermittent renewable-energy output which is becoming increasingly important in Brazil (Clyde & Co, 2021).

In environmental terms, Brazil is focused on bringing its policies and practices in line with the Organisation for Economic Co-operation and Development (OECD) established norms (OECD 2021). The notion of "polluter pays" is codified in Brazilian law. Brazil has a strict civil liability regime that makes proof of blame or negligence unnecessary in imposing a legal duty for remediating environmental harm. To be held liable, however, the operator's conduct must be shown to be a substantial factor in bringing about the undesirable outcome (OECD, 2021).

Regarding the recommendation of the Council on Improving the Environmental Performance of Government and in accordance with Recommendation OECD/LEGAL/0283, Brazil has implemented a number of programmes to encourage public institutions to adopt more effective and environmentally friendly policies. This includes initiatives such as the 2011 Environmental Agenda in the Public Administration (A3P) programme, aimed at disseminating effective policies and procedures in areas such as water protection and energy efficiency, as well as separate solid waste collection and recycling, throughout the various tiers of government.

A nationwide forum, an award for exemplary practices, labelling, and pilot projects are all also key components of this initiative. An "agreement on terms of adherence" is signed between the Ministry of the Environment and each participating institution. (A3P, 2022) Since its inception in 2010, the number of participating government agencies has increased to over 1,000. Importantly, according to OECD, there is a positive correlation between participation in the programme and the adoption of sustainability measures (OECD, 2016). Furthermore, as part of the national energy efficiency initiative, there is a specific component aimed at improving public sector energy efficiency via the creation of guidelines and training for service providers.

All public procurement must take into account the products' and services' long-term viability, as mandated by the 2021 Public Bidding and Administrative Contracts Law. Public bids are required to promote innovation, and mandate that the selection process takes the product's lifetime cycle into account. The Federal Government must also adhere to sustainability standards as set out in Decree 7746/2012. This Decree also established a federal government advisory organisation named the *Comisso Interministerial de Sustentabilidade na Administraço Publica* (CISAP), to coordinate sustainability efforts across departments. But according to the OECD implementation report, the CISAP Commission has been dormant since its inception, with its most recent meeting occurring in 2018.

Overall, the CISAP framework represents an innovative approach to enhance the role of the Brazilian Government's policy towards environmental sustainability. However, in line with the OECD 2021 recommendations, it needs, in order to achieve more purpose and coherence in its approach to achieving environmental sustainability, to establish clearer requirements and objectives, and an effective monitoring system to promote better performance.

4.2.4 Environmental Sustainability Initiatives and Strategies in Europe: European Union

The European Union is regarded as a global leader in environmental governance as it has implemented a wide range of policies aimed at promoting environmental protection and addressing climate change. EU environmental law comprises literally of hundreds of directives, regulations rules, and decisions. However, it is national, regional, and local implementation of EU environmental policy that determines its success. The region's environmental policy is based on the principles of precaution, prevention, rectifying pollution at source and the "polluter pays" principles (Kurrer, 2022). This mandate has been expanded several times to encompass issues such as the care for geological storage facilities, the security of offshore oil and gas activities, and the disposal of waste from the extraction process.

Environmental monitoring and environmental legislation compliance in the EU is thorough and crucial. In 2001, the European Parliament and the Council set (non-binding) basic requirements for environmental inspections to address the considerable gap in implementation across member states. Effective, appropriate, and dissuasive criminal punishments for the most serious environmental offences were to be applied to member states in order to strengthen the implementation of EU environmental law. This strategy ensures enforcement by providing a forum for policymakers, environmental inspectors and enforcement officers to exchange ideas and best practices. Named the European Union Network for the Implementation and Enforcement of Environmental Law (IMPEL), it comprises an international network of environmental authorities of EU Member States, accession and candidate countries, as well as Norway.

The European Commission further facilitates the monitoring and reporting of environmental regulations and obligations through a strategic, comprehensive approach known as the Environmental Implementation Review (EIR) 2022. The EIR is inclusive and participative of major stakeholders. Its aim is to be flexible enough to consider a member state's challenges and then allow it to adopt the relevant environmental policy in a timely and appropriate manner. The EIR is conducted by a dedicated commission which designs support for member states, improving the effectiveness and efficiency of delivering environmental policy and legislation and its direct links with environmental sustainability (EU, 2012). If a member state fails to comply with EU legislation, the Commission may initiate a formal infringement case against the state concerned. Before initiating a formal procedure, the Commission may initially consult with the member state to conduct an investigation.

In late 2020, the European Commission proposed the 8th Environment Action Programmes (EAPs) for 2021–2030 to implement EU climate and environment policy. The 8th Environment Action Programme's headline indicators were agreed by the Commission on 26 July 2022, to track EU environment and climate targets (EAP). Underpinned by the EU's 2030 Agenda and SDGs, the EAP urges stakeholder participation at all levels. The European parliament proposed 2027 as a deadline to phase out all environmentally harmful subsidies, with comprehensive evaluations to be issued by 2029. If necessary, the next environmental action programme will be proposed by 31 December 2029.

4.2.5 Environmental Sustainability Initiatives and Strategies in North America: US

All North American countries have federal systems of government, yet the authority to make energy policy differs in each federalist system (Mildenberger & Leah, 2019). In Canada, the provinces have nearly complete sovereignty over Canadian energy policy as energy matters are allocated to these provinces under the Canadian constitution (Harrison, 1997). Federal efforts to design and harmonise Canadian energy policy would thus necessitate provincial negotiations and coordination.

In the United States, the federal government has a greater degree of authority over energy planning than the central government of Canada. Nonetheless, the states still retain significant energy sovereignty compared to other countries, and indeed to some governments worldwide. As a result, energy policy in the United States is typically a synthesis of federal and state legislations, regulations, and initiatives (Byrne et al., 2007). As an example, the Obama administration's proposed Clean Power Plan intended to use its powers under the 1990 amended federal Clean Air Act to establish requirements for carbon intensity at state-level energy outputs. However, the proposal required individual states to submit plans to the federal government outlining how they planned to implement the new federal standards. This power dichotomy is reflected in many energy policies in the United States, enabling individual states to have significant subnational flexibility (Lutsey & Sperling, 2008).

In terms of the enhancement of environmental sustainability in federal systems, it seems apparent that such collaboration is more likely to be a positive factor. On the ground, state voices and stakeholders are acknowledged, listened to, and their views factored in and acted upon by federal authorities. Examining more closely the offshore oil and gas industry in the US, the federal government's role in regulating exploration and production is concerned, among other matters, with environmental protection and sustainability.

On 19 May 2010, in a post Deepwater Horizon Disaster context, the Secretary of the Interior, Ken Salazar, signed a secretarial order dividing the Minerals Management Service (MMS) into three independent entities, to better carry out its three missions:

i. ensuring the balanced and responsible development of energy resources on the Outer Continental Shelf (OCS).
ii. ensuring safe and environmentally responsible exploration and production and enforcing applicable rules and regulations.
iii. ensuring a fair return to the taxpayer from offshore royalty and revenue collection and disbursement activities.

Under Salazar's direction, the previous MMS (Mineral and Mining Service) was renamed the Bureau of Ocean Energy Management, Regulation and Enforcement (BOEMRE) to more accurately describe the scope of the organisation's oversight. The creation of BOEMRE was essentially a comprehensive reform of the federal government's regulation of offshore energy development and the institutions responsible for it. Following on from this, in 1 October 2011, the new Bureau of Safety and Environmental Enforcement (BSEE) was created to enforce safety and environmental regulations. Its functions include supervision of all field operations including Permitting and Research, Inspections, Offshore Regulatory Programs, Oil Spill Response, and newly formed Training and Environmental Compliance functions (Bureau of Safety and Environmental Enforcement, 2022).

In broader terms, under the authority of the Clean Air Act 1970, the Clean Water Act 1972, the Safe Drinking Water Act, 1974 and the Environmental Protection Agency strict drinking water and air quality standards have already been enforced. Here again, obvious forward links to environmental sustainability can be discerned.

In addition, a range of regulatory schemes have been initiated to reduce growth in GHG emissions from automobiles, appliances and equipment, and buildings. For example, the National Highway Traffic Safety Administration's (NHTSA) Corporate Average Fuel Efficiency (CAFE) standards establish fuel economy targets in miles per gallon for newly produced passenger automobiles and light trucks marketed in the United States. Importantly, and of high significance in enhancing environmental sustainability, the Energy Conservation and Production Act, 2021, among other provisions, established federal performance standards for new residential and commercial buildings and encouraged state and local governments to adopt and enforce standards through building codes. The Act also authorises the federal programme to create minimum energy conservation requirements for consumer products and industrial equipment. These have had, and will continue to have, a growing impact on lowering GHG emissions, as rules have tightened over time (U.S Climate Change Policy, 2021).

It is also worth noting that since the 1970s, the US Congress has passed a vast range of energy-related policy measures, including support for energy conservation and efficiency. Of high significance in enhancing environmental sustainability is the Energy Conservation and Production Act 2021, which among other features, established federal performance standards for new residential and commercial buildings and encouraged state and local governments to adopt and enforce standards through building codes. The Energy Policy and Conservation Act further authorises the federal programme to create minimum energy conservation requirements for consumer products and industrial equipment.

However, somewhat disappointingly, and in contrast to Europe, North America has not built strong international institutions to handle continental energy and environmental policies. While oil, natural gas and electricity are traded throughout the region, energy policies remain the responsibility of national and subnational governments in Canada, Mexico, and the United States. Thus, integration and independence are two competing forces driving the region's energy strategy. It is contended that a more holistic approach would be desirable, to enhance the cause of environmental sustainability.

4.3 Global Initiatives for Environmental Sustainability

Since the United Nations Conference on the Human Environment in 1972, environmental protection has been a major topic of international politics and governance. Over 900 international environmental treaties are currently in existence. Regrettably, these initiatives have failed to impact the general patterns of human-induced environmental degradation over past decades. Thus, the following sections will discuss a range of major strategies and approaches adopted by several notable international institutions.

4.3.1 The United Nations Right of Indigenous Peoples Declaration (UNDRIP)

This declaration was adopted by the General Assembly of the United Nations in 2007 with a majority of 144 states in its favour, 11 abstentions, while Australia, Canada, the US, and New Zealand voted against it (UN, 2022). It is noteworthy that the four states have since then changed their position and now support the Declaration. The Declaration details and establishes a universal framework of minimum standards for the rights of the world's indigenous people. Indigenous peoples' rights are commonly referred to as development actions in indigenous communities. They are the first victims in the pursuit of land, done frequently without regard to guarantees such as the right to freely provide permission after receiving all relevant information, which is the key tenet of the Declaration.

The Declaration employs the use of the term "Free, Prior and Informed Consent" which in essence provides the basis of relations between Indigenous people and those who have competing interests in their lands and resources. The FPIC guidance provides a context for business adoption of the FPIC. For businesses, it means securing the agreement of local communities and indigenous peoples before engaging in any action that would damage their rights to land and resources or their ability to live comfortably and eat and drink safely.

Various international treaties which are also part of international law, support this principle (ICCPR, 2022). Numerous additional efforts and voluntary standards for ethical supply chains are also compatible. New laws and institutions for communication with indigenous peoples have been influenced by this highly important declaration at national and international levels. Despite these encouraging signals, the Declaration relating to the Rights of Indigenous Peoples is still very far from being realised on a global scale. (Pillay, 2013).

4.3.2 The United Nations Global Compact Environmental Stewardship Strategy Report 2010

The United Nations' Global Compact is the world's largest corporate sustainability initiative. The initiative encourages businesses to link their strategies and operations to universal principles on human rights, labour, the environment, and anti-corruption. Based on their environmental mandate, the UN Global Compact Office collaborated with Duke University to develop an Environmental Stewardship Strategy (ESS) and related Resource (in the form of a website and CD-ROM). These were designed to assist companies to prepare for an increasingly challenging environmental landscape, and to further express the UN Global Compact's three core environmental principles (UN, 2010).

For organisations at the top of the corporate ladder, the ESS is a valuable tool for establishing an all-encompassing environmental approach. The core model of the ESS translates into the core elements of environmental sustainability. The four pillars of environmental stewardship management include:

a. **Embed**—All aspects of the business should be integrated with environmental stewardship.
b. **Balance**—Short-term aims and long-term goals should be balanced to ensure the firm's long-term success.
c. **Diffuse**—By working with and engaging stakeholders, they diffuse best practices across value chains and business networks.
d. **Translate**—Translation of best practices into processes and procedures that may be used across a wide range of locations.

As part of the overall strategy, companies were expected to upload current information relating to how they have adapted in order to embed, balance, diffuse, and translate approaches on to the website, as well clarifying all information about this process. This is similar to the approach of the international oil and gas producers' association (IOGP), where members are expected to produce a report on their practices to resolve environmental issues (IOGP, 2022).

Over the years, the UN Global Compact has catalysed corporate action. From the coinage of the concept of Environmental, Social, and Governance (ESG) in 2004, the CEO Water Mandate of 2007, Caring for Climate in 2008, the Science-Based Targets Initiative of 2015, to the recent Forward Faster initiative launched in 2023, it is evident that the UNGC has accelerated corporate action on environmental sustainability at a global scale.

4.3.3 International Standards Organisation (ISO) 26000:2010 Guidance on the Compatibility of Social Responsibility with Environmental Sustainability

The social responsibility standard, applicable to all companies, is ISO 26000, released in 2010 by the International Organisation for Standardisation (ISO). It provides guidelines on social responsibility in policies, strategies and initiatives to organisations. It guides the organisations on what social responsibility entails, what type of concern a business should address, and the best practices for putting social responsibility into effect with regard to the environment.

The ISO 26000 agrees and states that measuring an organisation's overall performance and its capacity to continue functioning successfully now includes looking at how well it performs in relation to the society in which it works and how it impacts the environment. Hence it could be inferred that a company needs to consider its impact on the environment to be ISO compliant. In addition to affecting a company's ability to attract and retain employees, customers, clients, and users, it may also impact the perception of investors, owners, donors and sponsors and the financial community's perception of a company's social responsibility performance.

It is noteworthy that the ISO 26000 is not a management system standard. It is not intended or appropriate for certification purposes or regulatory or contractual use. As a result, ISO 26000's ability to be used as a means of indicating a company's CSR pledges and performance may be hindered (Moratis, 2016a, 2016b). However, it aids in the transformation of good intentions into positive outcomes for companies. Companies wishing to comply with ISO 26000 might find the aid of national guidelines established by, for example, Germany and Italy useful. State-owned firms are also being made ISO 26000-compliant in various Nordic nations, and the Nordic area is working assiduously to promote these concepts (Moratis, 2016a, 2016b).

The ISO 26000 addresses the relevance and significance of the social responsibility's "core themes" and "problems". It also examines legal and other requirements, such as, international standards of conduct, possible abuses of human rights, behaviours that might risk life or health, and actions that could gravely harm the environment. ISO 26000 requires companies to do "due diligence"; the process of determining the social, environmental, and economic consequences of an organisation's actions and operations, and to prevent and mitigate such consequences (Pojasek, 2011).

An increasing number of standards and certifications intersect and, in certain aspects, overlap with ISO 26000. Special agreements have been made between the ISO and organisations such as the International Labour Organisation (ILO), the United Nations Global Compact and the Global Reporting Initiative (GRI), to assure uniformity in this regard (EU, 2014). However, it should not be considered a redundant replication of earlier standards or a distinct alternative to UNGC, GRI or other standards. These tools complement one another since they serve diverse purposes and are valuable in different sections of a company's CSR policy in the areas of environmental sustainability (Moratis, 2016a, 2016b). These sustainability standards have been designed for three purposes: to raise a company's transparency to its stakeholders, strengthen internal governance, and involve its stakeholders. ISO 26000 seems to be more focused on encouraging corporate executive leadership to conduct a thematic reflection on its management and associated outcomes. (Idowu et al., 2018).

4.3.4 Environmental, Social and Governance (ESG) Initiatives

Environmental, Social and Governance is a set of standards that is used to assess an organisation's environmental and social impact using environmental, social, and governance factors. Although the term was first coined by the United Nations Global Compact in a 2004 report titled "Who Cares Wins", the concept of ESG can be traced to as early as the 1950's in Howard Bowen's book "Social Responsibilities of the Businessman", which initiated discussions on corporate accountability. The concept however began to gain traction in the 1970's and in the 1990s, ESG considerations started to appear in mainstream investment strategies. In 1995, the U.S Social Investment Forum (SIF) Foundation took inventory of all the sustainable investments in North America. The total of USD 639 billion, shed light on how shareholders were starting to invest out of principle versus strictly profit (Krantz, 2023).

Slowly but surely, institutional investors started to recognise that companies could potentially improve financial performance and risk management by focusing on ESG issues like greenhouse gas emissions. In response, asset managers began to develop ESG strategies and metrics to measure the environmental and social impact of their investments. In 1997, the Global Reporting Initiative (GRI) was founded with the aim of addressing environmental concerns, though it soon broadened its scope to also focus on social and governance issues (Krantz, 2023).

ESG is no longer a fringe concept as there are efforts to make it mandatory for businesses. The European Union's Corporate Sustainability Reporting Directive (CSRD) requires businesses to report on the environmental and social impact of their business activities, and on the business impact of their ESG efforts. In North America, the Securities and Exchange Commission (SEC) is considering mandatory ESG reporting for public companies, with similar efforts in Canada, Brazil, India, Australia, and Japan. Environmental, Social, and Governance initiatives are crucial for businesses striving for sustainability and ethical governance. The initiatives focus on creating a positive impact on the environment, society, and enhancing governance standards.

The implementation of ESG standards however faces certain problems. It is not a concept in itself as it lacks a clear definition due to it being a coinage of three different terms. This translates to it having no uniform measurement or reporting standards. Companies and investors measure different things and report in different ways. It gets confusing fast, especially when investors try and de-code whether their money has made a difference or not.

Also, a significant issue is the prevalence of "greenwashing", in which symbolic reporting and selective disclosure engineers the obscurity a company's true environmental impact, creating a facade of sustainability without substantive change (Berg et al., 2022). The lack of standardised, mandatory metrics further complicates this issue, as it makes meaningful cross-company comparisons difficult and allows for a "check-the-box" compliance mentality as against driving genuine operational transformation. For the energy sector, this can manifest in continued investment in fossil fuels under vague "transition" narratives, whereas marginal, high-profile green projects receive disproportionate attention.

4.3.5 Global Reporting Standards (GRI)

The GRI Standards represent global best practice for reporting publicly on a range of economic, environmental and social impacts, to give insight on an organisation's positive or negative contributions to sustainable development. The Standards is an amalgam of interconnected standards which are the GRI Universal Standards, the GRI Sector Standards, and the GRI Topic Standards. Corporations are under growing scrutiny to demonstrate their ethical practices and decision-making credentials. When choosing a company for investment, potential investors are increasingly taking environmental, social, and governance factors into account. Through the GRI standards, corporations may improve strategic decision-making, risk mitigation, opportunity recognition, and stakeholder interactions by better understanding, managing, and providing transparency on the effects of their activities.

Sustainability reporting, variously known as non-financial reporting, corporate social responsibility (CSR) reporting, or environmental, social, and governance (ESG) reporting, is a growing discipline; the GRI Standards provide the most frequently used and accepted framework in this area. The largest companies in the world have embraced it, and it has been cited in international policy documents and stock markets.

The GRI guidelines framework defines well-structured and detailed guidelines for the construction of a social and environmental report, (Fig. 4.1), the issues to be considered, the elements and Key Performance Indicators (KPIs) necessary for proper disclosure, the involvement of stakeholders, and the correct and broad application of the principle of materiality; however, their actual impact still remains unclear (Moratis & Brandt, 2016).

Given the significance of these guidelines and the fact that previous studies have failed to clarify the actual effect they have on the quality of disclosure and the efficient application of several key reporting principles and stakeholder engagement for environmental sustainability, a number of researchers have called for the GRI Standards to be made mandatory and for the use of external assurance to expand their role

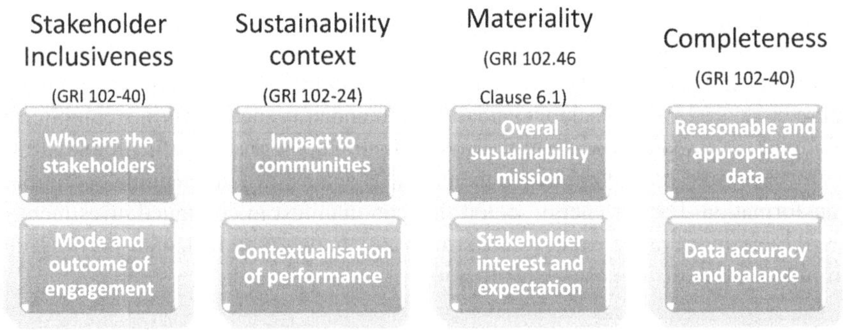

Fig. 4.1 Summative guidelines for sustainability reporting

(Carol Adams, 2019). The requirement for governments to enforce compliance on companies to adequately adhere to GRI guidelines is essentially driving the necessity for a multi-stakeholder strategy.

4.3.6 IOGP and Ipieca: Report 254 on Environmental Management in the Upstream Oil and Gas Industry, 2020

The Guide to Best Practices for Environmental Management Throughout the Life-cycle of Upstream Oil and Gas Projects was initially released in 1997 by the E&P Forum (IOGP's predecessor) and UNEP (E & P Forum, 1997). Staff from the secretariats of the IOGP, Ipieca, and UNEP, as well as volunteers from oil and gas firms (representing Ipieca and IOGP membership), worked together to create this new version, known as the 254 Report (Brown et al., 2020).

The 254 report (IOGP, 2022) analysed the existing and potential role of the oil and gas industry in meeting global energy demand, factoring in the Sustainable Development Goals (SDG). The 254 report was aligned with the IOGP's Operating Management System (OMS) framework and the ISO14001:2015 EMS standard. (*IMSM GB*, 2022) Another notable major change was the incorporation of the SDGs into the 254 Report.

In the 254 Report, a review of over fifty environmental components of offshore and onshore oil and gas operations, as well as their environmental implications, are analysed. The report can justifiably be regarded as a guide to providing a GRI type sustainability report, very comprehensive and with a range of implications for stakeholders. A range of the oil and gas industry's environmental impacts are supplemented by environmental mitigation and management strategies, as well as a "callout box" containing supplementary information, such as relevant frameworks, guidance papers, and/or technical information connected to that particular aspect.

One salient issue the report identifies is that many nations have a wide range of relevant authorities at various levels (e.g. federal, state, provincial, and municipal), and frequently, many of these agencies have overlapping jurisdiction. Consequently, oil and gas companies have to integrate meticulous preparation and organisation to meet sometimes complex national legislation in host countries.

It is abundantly clear therefore that oil and gas companies must have a very good grasp of the national regulatory regimes and requirements of their host nations. It is also critical that their activities are carried out in accordance with national, regional and international law. This necessitates in-depth due diligence and organisation, both in the field and within their corporate structures.

4.3.7 *The Human Right to a Clean, Healthy and Sustainable Environment*

A clean, healthy, and sustainable environment is widely regarded as a necessary precondition for the enjoyment of many long-established and universally recognised human rights, such as the right to life and the right to the highest standard of living (McClymond, 1992). Despite this international agreement on the close relationship between human rights and a healthy environment, no global agreement on the precise legal status of the environment emerged until recent times. In 2021, the Council on Human Rights adopted a resolution on the human right to have a clean, healthy, and sustainable environment. Subsequently, the General Assembly on 28 July 2022 adopted the Resolution. (UNGA, 2022).

An important part of the resolution is the reaffirmation of the duties of states and businesses in achieving environmental sustainability (UNGA, 2018). States have a duty to respect, protect, and promote human rights in all efforts, to address environmental challenges, and to take measures to protect the human rights of all; as recognised by various international instruments. Additionally, special attention should be paid to the rights of those who are most at risk from environmental degradation. On the other hand, businesses and other relevant stakeholders are required to adopt policies, strengthen international cooperation, build capacity, and continue to share best practices in order to scale up efforts to ensure a clean, healthy and sustainable environment for all (UNGA, 2011).

Subsequent to the UN Council and General Assembly resolution, many countries have started to integrate the right into their constitutional and national legislation and regional agreements. The general implication is that the right to a clean and healthy environment is now a universally recognised right. More than eighty percent % (156 out of 193) of UN Member States (including those bound by a treaty) recognise this right to a safe, clean, healthy, and sustainable environment (UNGA, 2020). More specifically, where these rights are relevant to the research is the call for vulnerable regions to take additional measures to combat degradation in order to achieve environmental sustainability.

4.4 Conclusion

The foundations of effective governance for environmental sustainability include efficient administrative entities, institutions, and supportive legislative and regulatory frameworks which allow governments, at federal, state or municipal levels, to undertake and implement crucial environmental protection actions to enhance sustainability. In order to achieve environmental sustainability, it is now generally accepted that both economic growth and environmental stewardship are necessary.

Regional institutions play a critical role in the formulation and implementation of government strategies, policies, and programmes. Their role in achieving environmental sustainability is becoming increasingly important, as it entails translating a new and uncharted approach to development planning and policy, as well as reorienting existing institutional paradigms and relationships. This will achieve that vital paradigm: the integration of environmental concerns into development processes which must embrace the concept of environmental sustainability.

The big picture of the global and regional entities critically surveyed in this chapter undoubtedly shows a modest but steady improvement in institutional capacity, as the prominence of environmental issues in the overall development policies of many regions, governments, cities and in the commercial sector continues to grow. While regional and global initiatives for environmental sustainability are crucial for addressing the pressing environmental challenges facing our global environment, the input of corporate organisations is also required to mitigate the impact of climate change, protect biodiversity and ensure sustainable future for generations yet unborn.

References

Accountancy Europe. (2019). *Interconnected standard setting for corporate reporting*. https://www.accountancyeurope.eu/publications/interconnected-standard-setting-for-corporate-reporting/

Adams, C., Alhamoon, A., He, X., Tian, J., Wang, L., & Wang, Y. (2022). The development and implementation of GRI Standards: practice and policy issues. *Handbook of Accounting and Sustainability*. https://doi.org/10.4337/9781800373518.00009

African Development Bank Group. (2025). *Climate change in Africa*. https://www.afdb.org/en/cop25/climate-change-africa

African Union, & Africa Union Development Agency (AUDA). (2022). *Second continental report on the implementation of agenda 2063*. https://au.int/sites/default/files/documents/41480-doc-2nd_Continental_Progress_Report_on_Agenda_2063_English.pdf

African Union. (2022a). *Goals & priority areas of agenda 2063*. https://au.int/en/agenda2063/goals

African Union. (2022b). *African Union climate change and resilient development strategy and action plan (2022–2032)*. https://au.int/en/documents/20220628/african-union-climate-change-and-resilient-development-strategy-and-action-plan. African Union.

Agência Nacional do Petróleo, Gás Natural e Biocombustíveis. (2020). *Oil and gas production in Brazil exceeds 4 million Boe/d for the first time*. https://web.archive.org/web/20200220091405/http://www.anp.gov.br/noticias/5628-producao-de-petroleo-e-gas-no-brasil-ultrapassa-4-milhoes-de-boe-d-pela-primeira-vez

Asia Development Bank. (2016). *Supporting implementation of environment-related sustainable development goals in Asia and the Pacific*. https://www.adb.org/sites/default/files/project-documents/50158/50158-001-tcr-en.pdf

Asia Development Bank. (2024). *Pillars of progress: ADB's contributions to the sustainable development goals*. https://www.adb.org/multimedia/sdg/wp-content/uploads/2024/07/Pillar-of-Progress_Web.pdf

Brazil Energy Insight. (2025). *ANP - Brazil 2024 annual oil & gas production*. https://brazilenergyinsight.com/2025/02/03/anp-brazil-2024-annual-oil-gas-production/

Brazil Energy Insight. (2025). *Brazil hits record oil and gas production in July*. https://brazilenergyinsight.com/2025/09/01/brazil-hits-record-oil-and-gas-production-in-july/

Brown, W., Kostareli, A., & Sealy, I. (2020). *Environmental management in the oil & gas industry, a guide to environmental management good practices in the upstream oil & gas industry – second edition.* https://doi.org/10.2118/199456-MS
Bureau of Safety and Environmental Enforcement. Organisational History. Retrieved 15 December, 2022 from https://www.bsee.gov/about-bsee/our-organisation/organisational-history
Byrne, J., Hughes, K., Rickerson, W., & Kurdegelashvili, L. (2007). American policy conflict in the greenhouse: Divergent trends in federal, regional, state, and local green energy and climate change policy. *Energy Policy, 35*(9), 4555–4573. https://doi.org/10.1016/j.enpol.2007.02.028
Christmann, P., & Taylor, G. (2006). Firm self-regulation through international certifiable standards: Determinants of symbolic versus substantive implementation. *Journal of International Business Studies, 317*, 863–878.
Congressional Research Service. (2019). *Department of Energy appliance and equipment standards program* (CRS In Focus IF11354). https://www.congress.gov/crs_external_products/IF/PDF/IF11354/IF11354.1.pdf
E&P Forum & United Nations Environment Programme. (1997). *Environmental management in oil and gas exploration and production: An overview of issues and management approaches.* Joint E&P Forum/UNEP Technical Publication. https://www.laohamutuk.org/OilWeb/RDTLdocs/303Conf/Dunster/Refs/13%20E%26P-UNEP%201997.pdf
Energy Commission Ghana. (2019). *Ghana renewable energy master plan.* https://energycom.gov.gh/index.php/reports
Energy Information Administration. (2024). *Frequently asked questions (FAQs).* https://www.eia.gov/tools/faqs/faq.php?id=709&t=6
Energy Information Administration. (2025). *Today in energy - China's crude oil imports decreased from a record as refinery activity slowed.* https://www.eia.gov/todayinenergy/detail.php?id=64544
European Commission. (2014). *Corporate social responsibility, national public policies in The European Union (Compendium 2014).* https://ec.europa.eu/newsroom/dae/document.cfm?doc_id=7377
European Commission. "Legal Enforcement" (*Environment*) https://environment.ec.europa.eu/law-and-governance/legal-enforcement_en
European Parliament. (1997). Treaty of Amsterdam amending the treaty on European Union, the treaties establishing the European communities and certain related acts. *Official Journal of the European Union, C340*, 1–144. https://eur-lex.europa.eu/eli/treaty/ams/sign/eng
European Parliament. (2004). Directive 2004/35/EC of the European Parliament and of the Council of 21 April 2004 on environmental liability with regard to the prevention and remedying of environmental damage. *Official Journal of the European Union, L143*, 56–75. https://eur-lex.europa.eu/eli/dir/2004/35/oj/eng
European Parliament. (2008). Directive 2008/99/EC of the European Parliament and of the Council of 19 November 2008 on the protection of the environment through criminal law. *Official Journal of the European Union, L328*, 28–37. https://eur-lex.europa.eu/eli/dir/2008/99/oj/eng
European Parliament. (2021). *Fact sheets on the European Union.* European Parliament. https://www.europarl.europa.eu/factsheets/en/home
Eurostat. (2025). *Shedding light on energy in Europe.* https://ec.europa.eu/eurostat/web/interactive-publications/energy-2025
Global Reporting Initiative. (2025). *GRI Standards by language - English.* https://www.globalreporting.org/how-to-use-the-gri-standards/gri-standards-english-language/
Hanson, E. UN Declaration on the Rights of Indigenous Peoples. https://indigenousfoundations.arts.ubc.ca/un_declaration_on_the_rights_of_indigenous_peoples/
Harrison, K. (1997). *Passing the buck: Federalism and Canadian environmental policy.* UBC Press
Hirs, E. (2019). China is betting big on increasing oil production. *Forbes.* https://www.forbes.com/sites/edhirs/2019/06/06/china-is-betting-big-on-increasing-oil-production/?sh=5a2a5aa6371e
Howard, P. (2012, March 3). The U.S. government is too big to succeed. *The Atlantic* https://www.theatlantic.com/politics/archive/2012/03/the-us-government-is-too-big-to-succeed/253920/

Idowu, S., Sitnikov, C., & Moratis, L. (2019). *ISO 26000 - A Standardized View on Corporate Social Responsibility – Practices, cases and controversies.* Springer International Publishing.

Industrial Trade Administration. (2025). Kenya – Energy - Electrical power systems. https://www.trade.gov/country-commercial-guides/kenya-energy-electrical-power-systems

International Energy Agency. (2025). *Global energy review 2025.* https://www.iea.org/reports/global-energy-review-2025/global-trends

International Energy Agency. (2025). *Kenya's energy sector is making strides toward universal electricity access, clean cooking solutions and renewable energy development.* https://www.iea.org/news/kenyas-energy-sector-is-making-strides-toward-universal-electricity-access-clean-cooking-solutions-and-renewable-energy-development

International Energy Agency. (2025). *Where does Kenya get its energy?* https://www.iea.org/countries/kenya/energy-mix

International Federation of Accountants. (2020). *Enhancing corporate reporting: The way forward.* https://www.ifac.org/knowledge-gateway/contributing-global-economy/publications/enhancing-corporate-reporting-way-forward

International Organisation for Standardisation. (2015). *ISO 14000 Family — Environmental management.* https://www.iso.org/iso-14001-environmental-management.html

International Standard Organisation. (2010). *ISO 26000 - Guidance on social responsibility.* www.iso.org/standard/42546.html

Jiang, K., Ashworth, P., Zhang, S., Liang, X., Sun, Y., & Angus, A. (2020). China's carbon capture, utilisation and storage (CCUS) policy: A critical review. *Renewable and Sustainable Energy Reviews,* 119. https://doi.org/10.1016/j.rser.2019.109601

Kaledzi, I. (2023). Energy transition policies and regulatory developments light up across Africa. *Africa Feeds.* https://africafeeds.com/2023/02/08/energy-transition-policies-and-regulatory-developments-light-up-across-africa/

Khanna, M. (2020). Growing green business investments in Asia and The Pacific Asian Development Bank Sustainable Development Working Paper Series. No. 72. https://doi.org/10.22617/WPS200357-2

Krantz, T. (2025) The history of ESG: A journey towards sustainable investing. *IBM Think.* https://www.ibm.com/think/topics/environmental-social-and-governance-history

Leech, S., & Medeiros, D. (2021). The new Brazilian gas law: Opportunities for international investors. Lexology. Retrieved December 11, 2022 from https://www.lexology.com/library/detail.aspx?g=c019c557-5106-4219-82d8-83cc685e372bc

Lutsey, N., & Sperling, D. (2008). America's bottom-up climate change mitigation policy. *Energy Policy, 36*(2), 673–685. https://doi.org/10.1016/j.enpol.2007.10.018

McClymond, J. (1992). The Human right to a healthy environment: An international legal perspective. *The New York Law School Law Review, 37*, 583–634.

McCright, A. M., & and Dunlap, R. E. (2011). Cool Dudes: The denial of climate change among conservative white males in the United States. *Global Environmental Change, 21*(4), 1163–1172. https://doi.org/10.1016/j.gloenvcha.2011.06.003

Mildenberger, M., & Stokes, L. (2021). The energy politics of North America. In K. Hancock, & J. Allison (Eds.), *The Oxford handbook of energy politics* (pp. 406–428). Oxford University Press.

Moratis, L. (2016a). Out of the ordinary? Appraising ISO 26000's CSR definition. *International Journal of Law and Management, 58*(1), 26–47. https://doi.org/10.1108/IJLMA-12-2014-0064

Moratis, L. (2016b). Signalling strategies for ISO 26000: A firm-level approach. *International Journal of Operations & Production Management, 36*(5), 512–531. https://doi.org/10.1108/IJOPM-08-2014-0402

Moratis, L., & Brandt, S. (2016). Corporate stakeholder responsiveness? Exploring the state and quality of GRI-based stakeholder engagement disclosures of European Firms. *Corporate Social Responsibility and Environmental Management, 24*(4), 312–325.

National Highway Traffic Safety Administration. Corporate average fuel economy. Retrieved October 14, 2025, from https://www.nhtsa.gov/laws-regulations/corporate-average-fuel-economy

Organisation for Economic Co-operation and Development. (1996). *Recommendation of the Council on Improving the Environmental Performance of Government Legal/0283*. https://legalinstruments.oecd.org/public/doc/43/43.en.pdf
Organisation for Economic Co-operation and Development. (2017). *OECD due diligence guidance for meaningful stakeholder engagement in the extractive sector*. https://mneguidelines.oecd.org/stakeholder-engagement-extractive-industries.htm
Organisation for Economic Co-operation and Development. (2021). *Evaluating Brazil's progress in implementing Environmental Performance Review recommendations and promoting its alignment with OECD core acquis on the environment*. https://one.oecd.org/document/ENV/EPOC/WPEP(2021)6/FINAL/en/pdf
Pojasek, B. (2011). ISO 26000 guidance on social responsibility. *Environmental Quality Management, 20*(3), 85–93. https://doi.org/10.1002/tqem.20292
PolSci Institute. (2024). *Sustainable development – Issues and challenges - Effective regional environmental initiatives: Lessons from the EU, NAFTA, and ASEAN*. https://polsci.institute/sustainable-development/effective-regional-environmental-initiatives/
Qin, P., Wang, J., Xu, A., & Hussain, S. (2024). China's green energy growth: Economic policies, environmental economics, and strategies for resilience in the global economy. *Energy Strategy Reviews, 54*. https://doi.org/10.1016/j.esr.2024.101475
Ramos, T. (2009). "Development of regional sustainability indicators and the role of academia in this process: The Portuguese practice. *Journal of Cleaner Production, 17*(12), 1101–1115. https://doi.org/10.1016/j.jclepro.2009.02.024
Schenoni, L. L. (2015). Unveiling the South American balance. *Estudos Internacionais, 2*(2), 215–232.
Shahidur, T. (2018). Pursuing sustainability: A case for regional approach. *Community Change, 2*(1), 4. https://doi.org/10.21061/cc.v2i1.a.14
Shin, S. (2005). The role of the government in voluntary environmental protection schemes: The case of ISO 14001 In China. *Issues & Studies, 41*(4), 141–173.
Statista. (2025). *Gross domestic product (GDP) of South America in 2023, by country*. https://www.statista.com/statistics/1537029/gdp-south-america-by-country/
Stokes, L. (2015). Electoral backlash against climate policy: A natural experiment on retrospective voting and local resistance to public policy. *American Journal of Political Science, 60*(4), 958–974. https://doi.org/10.7910/DVN/SDUGCC
Sun, L., Yu, H., Chen, B., Han, Z., Dai, M., Zhang, L., Sun, M., & Wang, Y. (2024). Safeguarding biodiversity from critical mineral mining in China. *Nexus, 1*(4). https://doi.org/10.1016/j.ynexs.2024.100042
Tachev, V. (2022). Oil and gas in Asia - Current state and what lies ahead for the industry. *Energy Tracker Asia*. https://energytracker.asia/the-oil-and-gas-industry-in-asia-current-state-and-what-lies-ahead/
Tambunlertchai, K., Kontoleon, A., & Khanna, M. (2013). Assessing participation in voluntary environmental programmes in the developing world: The role of FDI and export orientation on iso14001 adoption in Thailand. *Applied Economics, 45*(15), 2039–2048. https://doi.org/10.1080/00036846.2011.648320
The International Oil & Gas Producers. (2020). *Environmental management in oil and gas exploration and production*. https://www.iogp.org/bookstore/product/environmental-management-in-the-upstream-oil-and-gas-industry/
U.S. Senate. (2010). *Minerals management service reorganisation*. https://www.govinfo.gov/content/pkg/CHRG-111shrg57214/html/CHRG-111shrg57214.htm
UN General Assembly A/HRC/37/59 of 23rd March 2018: Report of the Special Rapporteur on the issue of human rights obligations relating to the enjoyment of a safe, clean, healthy and sustainable environment and the UN Special Rapporteur on Human Rights and the Environment, "Framework Principles on Human Rights and The Environment" (2018).

UN General Assembly A/HRC/43/53 of 20th March 2020 Right to a healthy environment: good practices Report of the Special Rapporteur on the issue of human rights obligations relating to the enjoyment of a safe, clean, healthy and sustainable environment.

UN General Assembly Resolution A/RES/76/300 of 28 July 2022 The Human Right to A Clean, Healthy, and Sustainable Environment.

UN General Assembly. Report of the Special Representative of the Secretary-General on the issue of human rights and transnational corporations and other business enterprises, John Ruggie: Guiding principles on business and human rights: Implementing the United Nations "protect, respect and remedy framework". Retrieved October 14, 2025, from https://digitallibrary.un.org/record/705860?v=pdf

UN Global Compact and Duke University, 'Environmental Stewardship Strategy Overview and Resource for Corporate Leaders' (United Nations 2010).

UN, "Paris Agreement" (Climate Change Conference, Paris, November 2015)2015.

UNEP, "GEO-6 Regional Assessment for Africa" (UNEP, 2016).

UNEP, CCAC and AU "Integrated assessment of air pollution and climate change for sustainable development in Africa summary for decision makers" (UNEP, 2022).

United Nations Conference on the Human Environment, Stockholm 5–16 June 1972.

United Nations Declaration on the Rights of Indigenous Peoples (A/RES/61/295).

United Nations Digital Library System" (*United Nations*) https://digitallibrary.un.org/?ln=en accessed February 25, 2022.

United Nations Environment Program. (2024). *Our work in Africa*. https://www.unep.org/regions/africa/our-work-africa

United Nations Global Compact. (2010) *Environmental stewardship strategy- overview and resource for corporate leaders*. https://kss.unglobalcompact.org/library/331

Van Dyke, B. (1994). A proposal to introduce the right to a healthy environment into the European convention regime. *Virginia Environmental Law Journal, 13*(3), 323–373.

Wachira, G. (2022, August 18). Energy white paper provides the spark for revitalising power sector. *Business Daily*. https://www.businessdailyafrica.com/bd/opinion-analysis/columnists/energy-white-paper-provides-the-spark-for-revitalising-sector-3919204

Wagner, J. P. (1998). Oil and gas operations and environmental law in Latin America. *Journal of Energy & Natural Resources Law, 16*(2), 153–185. https://doi.org/10.1080/02646811.1998.11433134

Wilson, J., Tyedmers, P., & Pelot, R. (2007). Contrasting and comparing sustainable development indicator metrics. *Ecological Indicators, 7*(2), 299–314. https://doi.org/10.1016/j.ecolind.2006.02.009

World Bank. (2002). *Building a sustainable future: The Africa region Environment strategy*. http://documents1.worldbank.org/curated/en/834421468742154792/pdf/multi0page.pdf

World Meteorological Organisation. (2024). *Extreme weather and climate change impacts hits Africa hard*. https://wmo.int/news/media-centre/extreme-weather-and-climate-change-impacts-hit-africa-hard

Berg, F., Kölbel, J. F., & Rigobon, R. (2022). Aggregate confusion: The divergence of ESG ratings. *Review of Finance, 26*(6), 1315–1344. https://doi.org/10.1093/rof/rfac033

Chapter 5
Corporate Social Responsibility and Environmental Sustainability in Energy Sector

5.1 Introduction

Over the years, corporate social responsibility (CSR) has grown far beyond its early image as a voluntary act of philanthropy. It has become a central element of modern corporate governance and a key instrument in advancing sustainability within the global energy sector (Carroll, 1991; Idowu et al., 2013). As the world shifts towards cleaner energy and grapples with the realities of climate change, CSR now serves as a practical framework for ensuring that companies in oil, gas, power, renewables, and mining remain accountable for the social and environmental footprints of their operations (OECD, 2023a; UNIDO, 2021a).

The ongoing energy transition has also reshaped what CSR means in practice. It is no longer confined to compliance or charity but increasingly tied to how businesses engage with long-term sustainability goals. Contemporary CSR thinking emphasises openness, ethical behaviour, and meaningful inclusion of stakeholders. These ideals resonate strongly with global sustainability agendas such as the Paris Agreement (2015) and the United Nations Sustainable Development Goals, particularly Goals 7, 12, and 13, as well as with regional frameworks like the EU Green Deal and Africa's Agenda 2063 (European Commission, 2024; UN Global Compact, 2023). In Nigeria, the *Energy Transition Plan* (2022) similarly reflects this approach by embedding CSR in a broader, inclusive effort to reach net-zero emissions while promoting social equity.

This chapter explores how CSR theories and practices, particularly those derived from Carroll's (1991) hierarchy of corporate responsibilities, Elkington's (1994) *Triple Bottom Line*, and Freeman's (1984) *Stakeholder Model*, intersect with the pursuit of environmental sustainability across various segments of the energy industry. It examines how firms integrate ethical values, social concerns, and environmental stewardship into their core strategies, and how these efforts shape both competitiveness and community relations (Aklin, 2021, Visser, 2010).

J. A. Debski, *Corporate Social Responsibility in the Energy Sector*, CSR, Sustainability, Ethics & Governance, https://doi.org/10.1007/978-3-032-17748-3_5

The analysis draws on theory, policy review, and recent case illustrations to capture current trends and emerging challenges in the sector. The discussion proceeds by first tracing the historical development of CSR, then unpacking its major theories and guiding principles, before turning to its role in promoting environmental sustainability and maintaining a social licence to operate. The chapter concludes by linking these insights to the next discussion, which narrows the focus to CSR practices specific to the oil and gas industry.

5.2 Evolution and Definitions of CSR Across Energy Industries

The concept of Corporate Social Responsibility (CSR) has deep intellectual roots and a long history of practical evolution. Its origins can be traced to the mid-twentieth century when scholars and policymakers began to question the social obligations of business beyond profit-making. Howard Bowen (1953), often described as the "father of CSR", argued that business leaders have an ethical duty to pursue actions and policies that align with the broader values and objectives of society. Two decades later, the Committee for Economic Development (CED, 1971) observed that the link between business and society was being redefined. It suggested that corporations were no longer expected to focus solely on economic returns but also on meeting the growing social needs of the communities within which they operate.

As global economies expanded, CSR gradually evolved from the charitable acts of benevolent corporations to a more structured notion of corporate accountability and stakeholder inclusion. Carroll's (1991) influential four-tier pyramid comprising economic, legal, ethical, and philanthropic responsibilities was among the earliest attempts to connect moral expectations with corporate practice. Freeman's (1984) *Stakeholder Theory* broadened this thinking, proposing that the interests of employees, customers, communities, and the environment are as important as those of shareholders. Elkington (1994) later introduced the *Triple Bottom Line* framework, which called on companies to measure success not only in financial terms but also through their social and environmental performance captured in the idea of "people, planet, and profit." Together, these perspectives established CSR as a multidimensional field that integrates ethics, governance, and sustainability (Visser, 2013) (Table 5.1).

In recent years, the scope of CSR has widened to reflect the realities of the global energy transition. The urgency of climate action and the demand for sustainable resource management have led energy firms from renewables to electricity and mining to embed CSR directly into corporate strategy. Renewable-energy companies now adopt sustainability standards inspired by the International Renewable Energy Agency's (IRENA, 2023) principles of inclusive stakeholder participation and ecosystem protection. Likewise, mining corporations, responding to the surge in demand for transition minerals, are implementing responsible sourcing

Table 5.1 Summary of key definitions and interpretations of corporate social responsibility (CSR)

Source / Institution	CSR Definition or Interpretation	Conceptual Contribution / Research Impact
Bowen (1953)	CSR refers to the obligations of businesspersons to pursue policies, make decisions, and follow actions desirable in terms of society's values and objectives	Recognised as the foundation of modern CSR thought; established the idea of corporate obligations to society
Committee for Economic Development (CED, 1971)	CSR acknowledges that business functions within a changing social contract and must balance economic goals with social needs	Highlighted business–society interdependence and the evolution of corporate accountability
Freeman (1984)	CSR involves managing for stakeholders; recognising the interests of all parties affected by corporate decisions	Shifted CSR from shareholder focus to stakeholder inclusion, shaping contemporary governance models
Carroll (1991)	CSR comprises four layers of responsibility: economic, legal, ethical, and philanthropic	Provided the most enduring framework for categorising corporate responsibilities
Elkington (1994)	CSR requires a triple bottom line: people, planet, and profit	Integrated sustainability into CSR and introduced measurable dimensions of performance
European Commission (2006)	CSR is the voluntary integration of social and environmental concerns in business operations and stakeholder interactions	Formalised CSR within EU policy, emphasising voluntary but strategic corporate action
International Organisation for Standardisation (ISO, 2010)	CSR, as defined in ISO 26000, is responsibility of an organisation for the impacts of its decisions and activities on society and the environment, through transparent and ethical behaviour	Standardised CSR within global management systems and linked it to ethical governance
United Nations Industrial Development Organisation (UNIDO, 2021b)	CSR is a management concept whereby companies integrate social and environmental concerns into business concerns operations and stakeholder relations	Recast CSR as a management tool for sustainable industrial performance

(continued)

Table 5.1 (continued)

Source / Institution	CSR Definition or Interpretation	Conceptual Contribution / Research Impact
Organisation for Economic Co-operation and Development (OECD, 2023a)	CSR is responsible business conduct that contributes to sustainable development while addressing social and environmental challenges	Positioned CSR as an operational pathway towards sustainability in global value chains
International Renewable Energy Agency (IRENA, 2023)	CSR in the energy transition involves inclusive engagement, environmental protection, and responsible value-chain practices in renewables	Extended CSR to the broader energy context, connecting it to clean-energy governance and transition ethics

Source Compiled by the author from Bowen (1953), CED (1971), Freeman (1984), Carroll (1991), Elkington (1994), European Commission (2006), ISO (2010); UNIDO (2021b); OECD (2023a); IRENA (2023)

mechanisms and local-content policies that encourage community participation and environmental conservation (OECD, 2023a).

Across Africa, these shifts are visible in policy frameworks such as Nigeria's *Energy Transition Plan* (2022) and South Africa's *Just Energy Transition Investment Plan* (2023), both of which emphasise fairness, equity, and broad access to clean energy. In Europe, the 2024 *Corporate Sustainability Due Diligence Directive* (CSDDD) moves CSR further into the realm of enforceable corporate obligation by requiring large energy companies to identify and address social and environmental risks across their supply chains (European Commission, 2024).

CSR in the modern energy sector can therefore no longer be understood as a matter of goodwill or compliance alone. It now functions as a strategic governance tool, an ethical and operational framework through which companies pursue long-term environmental stewardship, maintain their social licence to operate, and align business objectives with the global agenda for sustainable development (Aklin, 2021; UN Global Compact, 2023).

5.3 CSR Theories

The practice of Corporate Social Responsibility (CSR) in its modern form rests on several key theoretical foundations that explain why and how companies pursue socially and environmentally responsible behaviour. Among the most cited are Carroll's Pyramid of CSR, Elkington's *Triple Bottom Line* (TBL), and Freeman's *Stakeholder Theory*. Each framework offers a distinct yet complementary way of understanding corporate responsibility, particularly within the energy sector where sustainability, ethics, and economic imperatives are deeply intertwined (Carroll, 1991; Elkington, 1994; Freeman, 1984).

Fig. 5.1 Carroll's Pyramid

5.3.1 Carroll's Pyramid of CSR

Carroll (1991) conceptualised CSR as comprising four interrelated levels of economic, legal, ethical, and philanthropic responsibility. In this model, financial performance forms the foundation of business responsibility, while compliance with the law, adherence to ethical norms, and voluntary philanthropy represent progressively higher expectations. The model remains a cornerstone of CSR theory, yet it has been criticised for oversimplifying the complex ethical and environmental realities facing today's industries (Carroll, 2016; Visser, 2013) (Fig. 5.1).

Within the energy sector, Carroll's framework requires some rethinking. For companies engaged in oil, gas, and mining, legal and ethical responsibilities such as pollution prevention, resource management, and meaningful community engagement are no longer secondary obligations but central to corporate survival and legitimacy. Even renewable-energy firms face their own ethical questions, including land-use conflicts, biodiversity protection, and equitable access to clean power (IRENA, 2023). Consequently, many scholars now argue that ethical and environmental stewardship should form the *core* of CSR, while profitability emerges as a result of responsible and sustainable practices rather than their foundation (Visser, 2013).

5.3.2 The Triple Bottom Line Theory

Elkington (1994) advanced a new way of thinking about business success, one that moves beyond financial profit to include social well-being and environmental care. The *Triple Bottom Line* (TBL) encourages firms to measure performance across three dimensions: *people*, *planet*, and *profit*. This approach fits neatly with today's global energy transition, where companies are expected to contribute simultaneously to economic growth, social inclusion, and environmental protection (Elkington, 2018) (Fig. 5.2).

Energy companies increasingly use the TBL as a reporting framework, often combining it with Environmental, Social, and Governance (ESG) metrics. Electricity utilities, for example, now include indicators of affordability and access in their performance reports, while renewable-energy developers disclose their efforts in

Fig. 5.2 John Elkington's triple bottom line

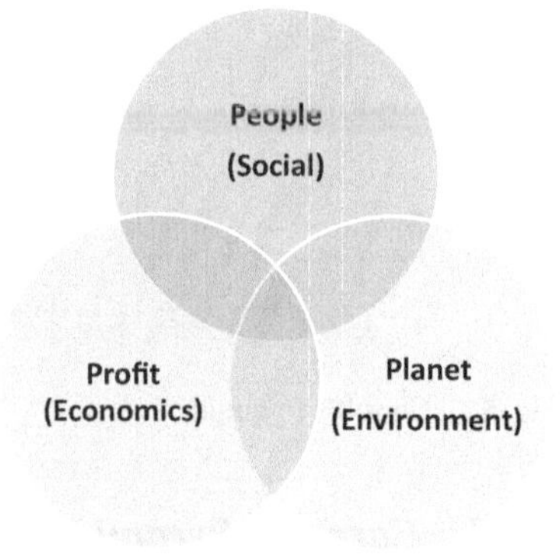

carbon reduction, biodiversity conservation, and community empowerment (OECD, 2023a; UN Global Compact, 2023). In extractive industries, the TBL has evolved into a practical benchmark linking financial investment to sustainability outcomes. Regulatory developments such as the European Union's *Corporate Sustainability Due Diligence Directive* (CSDDD, 2024) now make these linkages more explicit by requiring firms to disclose and manage environmental and social risks throughout their supply chains.

5.3.3 *The Stakeholder Theory*

Freeman's (1984) *Stakeholder Theory* shifted the conversation about corporate responsibility away from shareholders alone and towards all groups affected by a company's activities. This perspective is particularly relevant for the energy industry, where operations intersect with governments, local communities, investors, employees, consumers, and environmental systems (Freeman et al., 2010).

In oil and gas, stakeholder engagement has traditionally focused on host communities and environmental justice. In renewable energy, it often extends to indigenous land rights, participatory ownership, and fair benefit distribution. Electricity providers face pressure to ensure fair pricing and energy access, while mining corporations navigate complex networks involving regulators, advocacy groups, and supply-chain auditors (Brin & Nehme, 2019; Mancini, 2018).

The stakeholder approach now underpins many sustainability frameworks, including the *Global Reporting Initiative (GRI)* and the *United Nations Guiding Principles on Business and Human Rights (UNGPs)*, both of which promote transparency, participation, and inclusivity in corporate governance (Idowu et al., 2013; OECD, 2023a). Across developing regions, particularly in Africa, this model supports equitable energy development by ensuring that investments enhance both environmental protection and community well-being (AU Agenda, 2063; Nigeria Energy Transition Plan Update, 2024).

5.3.4 Integrating ESG and Contemporary Sustainability Frameworks

In recent years, CSR has become increasingly aligned with Environmental, Social, and Governance (ESG) standards, which operationalise CSR principles through measurable indicators. ESG metrics allow companies and their investors to evaluate corporate performance on issues such as climate risk, diversity, transparency, and ethical governance (UN Global Compact, 2023). The integration of CSR and ESG has redefined corporate accountability in the energy sector, making sustainability performance a matter not only of ethics but of financial and reputational viability.

Global initiatives such as the *International Sustainability Standards Board (ISSB,* 2023) and the EU's *Sustainable Finance Disclosure Regulation (Regulation* 2019/ *2088)* have moved CSR reporting into the heart of corporate finance. Together, they demonstrate a shift from voluntary responsibility to structured, data-driven sustainability governance (Camilleri, 2017).

Thus, CSR theories today do more than outline what responsible business behaviour should look like; they define how energy companies must operate to remain legitimate and resilient in a rapidly decarbonising global economy. Taken together, Carroll's hierarchical model, Elkington's tripartite framework, and Freeman's participatory approach provide a coherent foundation for understanding how corporate ethics, environmental responsibility, and sustainable governance converge in the energy transition.

5.4 Fundamental Principles of CSR and Environmental Accountability

The strength of Corporate Social Responsibility (CSR) lies in a set of foundational principles that define how corporations interpret and fulfil their social, ethical, and environmental duties. Whether articulated through the *Global Reporting Initiative (GRI)*, the *OECD Guidelines for Multinational Enterprises*, or similar international standards, these principles consistently emphasise accountability, transparency, legitimacy, creativity, and inclusivity (Idowu et al., 2013; Visser, 2013). Although these ideas have long shaped responsible business conduct, they have taken on renewed significance in the era of sustainability-driven governance and the global energy transition.

5.4.1 Accountability

Accountability stands at the heart of CSR and environmental governance. It requires companies not only to monitor and report their environmental and social impacts but also to take clear responsibility for addressing them. Crowther and Aras (2008) describe accountability as the obligation to explain and justify corporate actions that affect society and the environment. In the energy sector, this expectation has evolved far beyond compliance; it now encompasses proactive climate strategies, transparent communication, and measurable commitments to decarbonisation.

Recent policies reinforce this shift. The European Union's *Corporate Sustainability Due Diligence Directive* (CSDDD, 2024) obliges energy corporations to identify, prevent, and remediate human rights and environmental harms across their value chains. Similarly, Nigeria's *Energy Transition Plan* (2022) expects both domestic and international operators to contribute to national emission-reduction goals through verifiable sustainability reporting. Accountability, therefore, functions not only as a regulatory requirement but as a moral compass ensuring that business models operate within the limits of social legitimacy and ecological responsibility (OECD, 2023a; UN Global Compact, 2023).

5.4.2 Transparency

Closely linked to accountability is transparency, which ensures that stakeholders can access accurate, timely, and relevant information about a company's performance and decision-making processes. Idowu et al. (2013) describe transparency as removing the barriers that obscure public understanding of corporate behaviour. In the energy sector, especially in extractive industries such as oil, gas, and mining, this principle has been institutionalised through initiatives like the *Extractive Industries Transparency Initiative* (EITI) and the *GRI Standards* (2021), both of which promote disclosure of emissions, payments, and community investments.

The growing integration of *Environmental, Social, and Governance (ESG)* reporting frameworks has made transparency an indispensable part of energy governance. Regulators and investors now expect full disclosure of climate-related risks, resource efficiency, and carbon accounting (ISSB, 2023). However, transparency must be genuine rather than performative. As the GRI (2021) warns, sustainability disclosure is not a branding exercise; it is a tool for reflection, accountability, and continuous improvement. A transparent company builds trust; one that conceals or manipulates data risks losing credibility and its social licence to operate.

5.4.3 Legitimacy

Legitimacy refers to the moral and social acceptance of corporate power. As Palazzo and Scherer (2006) argue, legitimacy stems from society's consent and must therefore be exercised responsibly. Davis's (1973) *Iron Law of Responsibility* captures this principle succinctly: those who fail to use corporate power responsibly will ultimately lose it. Within the energy sector, legitimacy often takes shape through the "social licence to operate", the informal yet essential approval granted by host communities and the wider public.

Companies that ignore social and environmental expectations risk losing this licence. The long-standing case of Shell in the Niger Delta is an instructive example: neglecting community welfare and environmental protection eroded both public trust and corporate reputation (Hennchen, 2014; Vidal, 2011). By contrast, renewable and electricity firms that engage openly with communities tend to enjoy greater acceptance and enduring partnerships. Legitimacy, therefore, depends on consistent ethical behaviour, stakeholder participation, and responsiveness to evolving social values (Freeman et al., 2010).

5.4.4 Creativity and Innovation

Visser (2013) identifies creativity as one of the defining attributes of modern CSR. True responsibility, he suggests, goes beyond compliance; it involves innovation and problem-solving that produce tangible social and environmental value. This idea is increasingly visible in the global energy transition, where companies are investing in carbon capture, renewable-energy systems, and circular-economy models to mitigate climate impacts while creating shared prosperity.

The *International Renewable Energy Agency* (IRENA, 2023) highlights how innovation has enabled affordable renewable solutions in developing regions through hybrid energy systems, digital grids, and decentralised microgeneration. These creative approaches not only reduce emissions but also expand energy access in underserved communities. In this sense, creativity aligns with the notion of *shared value,* where business success is directly linked to societal benefit (Camilleri, 2017).

5.4.5 Inclusivity and Multi-Stakeholder Engagement

Inclusivity gives CSR its participatory dimension. It ensures that all relevant voices—employees, communities, regulators, and civil society—are represented in corporate decision-making. Freeman's (1984) *Stakeholder Theory* laid the foundation for this principle, later strengthened by frameworks such as the *GRI Standards* and the *UN Global Compact* (2023), both of which call for collaborative approaches to sustainability.

In the energy transition, inclusivity is fundamental to achieving what is often referred to as a *just transitional* process that ensures the move towards clean energy does not exclude or disadvantage vulnerable populations. Mining firms engaged in the extraction of transition minerals are now expected to follow *Free, Prior, and Informed Consent (FPIC)* principles when dealing with local communities, while renewable-energy developers increasingly adopt participatory planning and benefit-sharing mechanisms (OECD, 2023a). Inclusivity transforms CSR from a corporate pledge into a shared social contract, one that ties sustainable development to fairness, dialogue, and collective responsibility.

Together, these five principles form the moral and operational backbone of CSR in today's energy industries. Accountability ensures responsibility; transparency builds trust; legitimacy secures social acceptance; creativity drives innovation; and inclusivity promotes fairness and shared progress. Within the modern energy transition, these principles define how corporations can uphold environmental stewardship while sustaining the confidence of investors, governments, and the communities they serve. The next section builds on these foundations to explore how CSR is operationalised in advancing environmental sustainability across the oil, gas, renewable, electricity, and mining sectors.

5.5 CSR, Environmental Sustainability, and the Energy Transition

Environmental sustainability lies at the very centre of contemporary Corporate Social Responsibility (CSR). It is grounded in the classic Brundtland Commission (1987) definition, which describes sustainable development as meeting the needs of the present without compromising the ability of future generations to meet theirs. Within the energy sector, this idea has evolved from a peripheral concern of environmental management into a core element of strategic planning, corporate regulation, and stakeholder dialogue. Today, CSR provides the principal framework through which energy companies confront challenges of climate change, biodiversity loss, and ecological degradation associated with industrial growth (Idowu et al., 2013; OECD, 2023a).

5.5.1 CSR as a Driver of Environmental Sustainability

CSR functions as a bridge between corporate governance and environmental stewardship. The Organisation for Economic Co-operation and Development (OECD, 2023a) defines responsible business conduct as the integration of social and environmental considerations into decision-making and value-chain management. Likewise, the *International Chamber of Commerce's Business Charter for Sustainable Development* (2010) calls for resource efficiency, pollution prevention, and precautionary environmental action. Applied to the energy sector, these principles demand that corporations move beyond basic compliance and take proactive steps to mitigate environmental harm.

In the oil and gas industry, CSR initiatives now encompass gas-flaring reduction, ecosystem restoration, and carbon-offsetting programmes. Chevron's *2023 Sustainability Report*, for example, sets emission-intensity reduction targets aligned with the Paris Agreement. Renewable-energy companies such as Ørsted, Vestas, and Enel Green Power are integrating CSR into innovation through biodiversity protection, recycling of wind-turbine blades, and community grid projects (IRENA, 2023). Electricity utilities increasingly embed CSR in their energy-access programmes and "just transition" measures to ensure that the shift to cleaner systems does not deepen social inequalities (UN Global Compact, 2023).

5.5.2 CSR and Climate Change Mitigation

The *Intergovernmental Panel on Climate Change* (IPCC, 2023) underscores that reaching global carbon neutrality depends on meaningful corporate participation. CSR offers the structure for such engagement by linking emission reduction with ethical accountability and long-term governance. Under the *Corporate Sustainability Due Diligence Directive* (CSDDD, 2024), large energy companies within the European Union must identify and mitigate climate-related risks across their operations and supply chains.

In developing economies, CSR supports the implementation of Nationally Determined Contributions (NDCs) under the Paris Agreement. Nigeria's *Energy Transition Plan* (2022), for example, calls for active collaboration between the government and the private sector to expand renewable electrification, reduce gas emissions, and curb methane release. In this regard, CSR has become both a moral and practical response to climate imperatives, ensuring that corporations contribute not only to profitability but also to global and national sustainability targets.

5.5.3 CSR and Biodiversity Conservation

Beyond the question of carbon, CSR now extends to protecting the ecosystems upon which human and industrial survival depend. Energy projects, particularly in mining and hydroelectric sectors, can threaten biodiversity through habitat destruction and water pollution. To address such risks, companies increasingly align with global frameworks like the *Global Biodiversity Framework* (Convention on Biological Diversity and the *Taskforce on Nature-related Financial Disclosures* TNFD).

Leading mining corporations such as Anglo American and Rio Tinto now integrate biodiversity management plans and post-extraction land restoration into their CSR policies. Renewable-energy developers have also begun to adopt site-selection guidelines that avoid sensitive habitats and migratory corridors (IRENA, 2023). Through these efforts, CSR operates as both an ethical and a governance tool merging environmental science with corporate responsibility to balance economic returns with ecological integrity.

5.5.4 CSR, the Circular Economy, and Resource Efficiency

The transition to sustainable energy systems requires moving away from the traditional "take-make-dispose" production model towards a circular economy that values resource efficiency and waste reduction. CSR frameworks are increasingly adopting circular-economy principles to minimise environmental footprints across supply chains (UN Global Compact, 2023; Visser, 2013).

In renewable and electricity sectors, circularity manifests in the recycling of solar panels, repurposing of lithium-ion batteries, and recovery of materials from decommissioned turbines. Companies such as Siemens Gamesa and General Electric have invested in recycling technologies that reclaim rare components, demonstrating how CSR can drive operational innovation. Similarly, oil and gas firms are diversifying into cleaner technologies—bioenergy, hydrogen, and carbon capture—as part of their transition strategies. These initiatives not only conserve resources but also extend product life cycles and improve energy efficiency, showing how CSR can link profitability with sustainability outcomes.

5.5.5 CSR and the "Just Energy Transition"

A defining dimension of CSR in the current energy landscape is its contribution to what is often termed the *just transition*, a shift towards clean-energy systems that is equitable, inclusive, and socially protective. The *International Labour Organisation* (ILO, 2015) and the *UN Global Compact* (2023) both emphasise that sustainability must incorporate decent work, fair compensation, and participation for all affected communities.

Renewable-energy developers increasingly embed social equity into their CSR programmes through workforce retraining and community ownership initiatives. In South Africa and Kenya, for instance, wind and solar projects have introduced local equity schemes that allow communities to co-own energy assets. In Nigeria and Ghana, electricity companies use CSR to fund technical education for young people entering green industries (Nigeria Energy Transition Plan, 2022). Through such efforts, CSR becomes not an optional gesture but a governance mechanism that connects economic transformation to social justice.

5.5.6 Cross-Sectoral Integration of CSR and Sustainability Reporting

The integration of CSR into environmental sustainability has been reinforced by a convergence of global reporting standards. Frameworks such as the *Global Reporting Initiative* (GRI, 2021), the *Sustainability Accounting Standards Board (SASB, 2021)*, and the *International Sustainability Standards Board (ISSB,* 2023*)* now provide consistent benchmarks for assessing corporate environmental and social performance. Energy companies increasingly rely on these frameworks to report progress on emissions, resource efficiency, and pollution control.

This standardisation has strengthened the link between CSR and strategic management, turning sustainability into a measurable and enforceable component of corporate governance. By embedding environmental accountability within financial and ethical reporting, firms demonstrate that sustainable operations are not peripheral ideals but the foundation of long-term competitiveness and investor confidence.

In essence, CSR has evolved from a voluntary ethical code into a systemic framework that guides the environmental responsibilities of the energy industry. It compels corporations to internalise the social and ecological costs of production, invest in cleaner technologies, and drive the transition towards low-carbon, resource-efficient, and inclusive energy systems. The next section builds on this foundation by examining how CSR and environmental accountability influence stakeholder relations through the concept of the *Social Licence to Operate (SLO)—the* moral legitimacy granted by communities and societies to companies whose activities affect their environment.

5.6 CSR and the Social Licence to Operate (SLO)

The *Social Licence to Operate* (SLO) has emerged as one of the most practical and visible expressions of Corporate Social Responsibility (CSR) in the relationship between business and society. It refers to the ongoing acceptance or approval of a company's operations by its stakeholders, especially host communities, regulators, and the wider public (Boutilier, 2014; Gunningham et al., 2004). Although it carries no legal force, the SLO functions as a moral and social contract that determines a company's legitimacy and stability. In the energy sector, where environmental and social impacts are often direct, visible, and long-term, the SLO has become a crucial measure of corporate accountability, trust, and sustainability performance.

5.6.1 Origins and Meaning of the SLO

The term *social licence to operate* first appeared in the 1990s as a response to rising community resistance to mining and oil operations, particularly in developing countries (Thomson & Boutilier, 2011). What began as an informal expectation quickly evolved into a normative framework of legitimacy, requiring corporations to earn and sustain public consent through responsible conduct, openness, and equitable benefit-sharing. The concept is rooted in both Freeman's (1984) *Stakeholder Theory* and Palazzo and Scherer's (2006) *Legitimacy Theory*, which together emphasise that corporate endurance depends on societal approval.

In contemporary sustainability governance, the SLO is now embedded in global frameworks such as the *OECD Guidelines for Multinational Enterprises* (2023a) and the *UN Global Compact* (2023). These frameworks reinforce the idea that meaningful community consultation, environmental impact assessment, and grievance redress mechanisms are central to responsible business practice. Within the energy industry, obtaining an SLO has become an essential prerequisite for financing, permitting, and long-term operational success.

5.6.2 CSR as the Pathway to Securing SLO

CSR provides the most tangible pathway for companies to build and sustain their social licence. By aligning business strategies with ethical and environmental expectations, CSR transforms potential sources of tension into opportunities for collaboration (Visser, 2013). Initiatives such as local employment, environmental restoration, transparent revenue sharing, and infrastructure support help corporations demonstrate good faith and foster trust among stakeholders.

Nigeria's *Energy Transition Plan* (2022), for instance, highlights the importance of CSR in cultivating social legitimacy through rural electrification, renewable-energy partnerships, and community development agreements in extractive regions. Similarly, the *International Renewable Energy Agency* (IRENA, 2023) identifies sustained dialogue and benefit-sharing as decisive factors in the success of renewable-energy projects. In this sense, CSR is not merely a public-relations exercise but a sustained process through which companies earn acceptance anchored in accountability, inclusivity, and transparency.

5.6.3 Legal and Regulatory Dimensions of the SLO

While the SLO remains a moral construct, its principles increasingly shape legal and regulatory frameworks. Many jurisdictions now embed CSR obligations that effectively give legal force to the spirit of the SLO. The European Union's *Corporate Sustainability Due Diligence Directive* (CSDDD, 2024) mandates stakeholder consultation, disclosure of environmental and social risks, and remediation of harms across corporate supply chains. In Nigeria, the *Petroleum Industry Act* (PIA, 2021) institutionalises *Host Community Development Trusts (HCDTs)—legally* binding mechanisms that require oil and gas companies to invest directly in community development.

Similarly, environmental impact assessment (EIA) laws and renewable-energy regulations increasingly demand evidence of local consultation and benefit-sharing before project approval. These developments blur the boundary between voluntary and statutory responsibility, transforming the SLO from a purely ethical expectation into an enforceable dimension of sustainable governance (OECD, 2023a).

5.6.4 The SLO Across Energy Subsectors

Although its application differs across industries, the ethical foundation of the SLO mutual respect, participation, and trust remains consistent.

a. **Oil and Gas:** The long history of environmental degradation and social unrest in areas such as Nigeria's Niger Delta illustrates the cost of losing an SLO. Years of poor engagement led to litigation, protests, and production disruptions (Hennchen, 2014). The *Petroleum Industry Act* (2021) represents a structural response, compelling firms to embed CSR through community trusts and legally defined social obligations.
b. **Renewable Energy:** Even clean-energy projects can face opposition related to land use, cultural disruption, or aesthetic concerns. Research shows that projects with early stakeholder engagement and shared ownership enjoy far greater acceptance (IRENA, 2023; UN Global Compact, 2023). CSR in this context enables developers to align environmental goals with local realities.
c. **Electricity Utilities:** Power providers must maintain public confidence through fair tariffs, reliable supply, and equitable access. CSR initiatives such as rural electrification, consumer education, and investment in grid resilience are key to sustaining that trust.
d. **Mining and Critical Minerals:** As global demand for transition minerals increases, extractive companies face renewed scrutiny. The OECD (2023a) and World Bank (2023) promote responsible sourcing standards and supply-chain due diligence to safeguard communities and ecosystems. Many firms now adopt CSR-based certification schemes, such as the *Responsible Mining Initiative*, to maintain social legitimacy and investor confidence.

5.6.5 The Dynamics of Trust and Legitimacy

Securing and maintaining an SLO is not a single achievement but an ongoing process shaped by trust, performance, and responsiveness. Boutilier (2014) describes four levels of social licence: withdrawal, acceptance, approval, and psychological identification, reflecting the evolving depth of community consent. When corporations act with consistency, openness, and integrity, their relationships with stakeholders often progress from cautious tolerance to genuine partnership.

However, this trust is fragile. Perceived insincerity, environmental harm, or lack of transparency can quickly erode legitimacy. The *Intergovernmental Panel on Climate Change* (IPCC, 2023) warns that superficial or delayed corporate climate action may fuel public scepticism and weaken societal support for the energy transition. Conversely, firms that sustain authentic CSR practices through fair compensation, inclusive reporting, and co-created local benefits tend to maintain both stability and goodwill (Visser, 2013).

The SLO, in essence, mirrors the moral reputation of a corporation. In the energy sector, where operations touch directly on ecosystems and livelihoods, the SLO redefines success beyond efficiency or profit; it gauges the moral standing of the enterprise within society. CSR remains the most reliable route to achieving and maintaining that standing, ensuring that corporate influence operates within the bounds of ethical legitimacy and social expectation.

The next section builds on these dynamics, examining how governments, corporations, and host communities can collaborate to advance environmental sustainability and shared governance across the wider energy sector.

5.7 Effective Multi-Stakeholder Strategies: Roles of Government, Corporations, and Host Communities Across the Energy Sector

The sustainability challenges confronting the global energy sector are far too complex for any single actor to manage alone. Achieving environmental sustainability now depends on a coordinated partnership among governments, corporations, host communities, and civil society each performing complementary functions within a shared governance framework. Corporate Social Responsibility (CSR), both as a principle and as a practice, provides the ethical foundation and operational logic for such collaboration (Freeman, 1984; Idowu et al., 2013). When these actors work together, it becomes possible to align economic development with environmental protection, social inclusion, and long-term energy security.

5.7.1 The Role of Government: Regulator, Facilitator, and Enabler

Governments occupy a pivotal position in defining the legal and institutional architecture that shapes corporate conduct. As regulators, they establish environmental standards, emission limits, and disclosure obligations that convert CSR from a voluntary expression of goodwill into a concrete, enforceable responsibility. The *European Union's Corporate Sustainability Due Diligence Directive* (CSDDD, 2024) and the *EU Green Deal (2020)*, for instance, impose binding sustainability and climate-risk reporting duties on companies. In a similar vein, Nigeria's *Energy Transition Plan* (2022) embeds CSR principles into national policy, linking corporate responsibility directly to decarbonisation, community development, and energy-access objectives.

Beyond their regulatory function, governments also serve as facilitators creating enabling environments for sustainable investment and technological advancement. Policy tools such as tax incentives, feed-in tariffs, and green bonds reward innovation and responsible performance. The World Bank (2023) and the *International*

Renewable Energy Agency (IRENA, 2023) note that transparent and predictable policy frameworks tend to attract private capital into clean-energy markets, while participatory policymaking strengthens public trust.

Equally important, governments act as enablers of just and equitable transitions. Instruments such as just-transition funds and retraining schemes for workers in fossil-fuel industries (ILO, 2015) ensure that the shift towards low-carbon economies does not deepen inequality. In this sense, governments play a dual role, setting the rules for environmental governance while empowering citizens to participate in and benefit from the energy transformation.

5.7.2 The Role of Corporations: Implementers and Innovators

Corporations remain the central implementers of CSR across the energy value chain. Their day-to-day operations determine the sector's environmental footprint and its contribution to social welfare. As such, responsible firms are expected to integrate CSR objectives into their governance systems, risk management processes, and overall business strategies (OECD, 2023a; Visser, 2013).

Across oil, gas, electricity, and renewable industries, CSR-driven action typically takes several forms:

a. **Environmental stewardship:** Investing in cleaner technologies such as carbon capture, hydrogen energy, and advanced recycling to cut emissions and minimise waste.
b. **Sustainability reporting:** Adopting global frameworks like the *Global Reporting Initiative* (GRI, 2021), *International Sustainability Standards Board (ISSB,* 2023*)*, and *Sustainability Accounting Standards Board (SASB, 2021)* to ensure transparent disclosure of ESG performance.
c. **Community engagement:** Co-creating social programmes that expand education, healthcare, and energy access within host regions.
d. **Inclusive innovation:** Supporting local participation in renewable-energy supply chains and entrepreneurship in green technology sectors (UN Global Compact, 2023).

Forward-looking firms increasingly view CSR not as an expense but as a strategic investment that enhances reputation, attracts sustainability-minded investors, and preserves their social licence to operate. According to *IRENA* (2023), corporations that embed CSR within their innovation systems are better equipped to adapt to evolving policies, market dynamics, and climate-related risks.

5.7.3 The Role of Host Communities: Partners and Custodians

Host communities occupy a unique position as both beneficiaries and custodians of environmental resources. Their participation is indispensable to achieving legitimacy, trust, and long-term sustainability. Effective multi-stakeholder governance therefore depends on recognising communities as active partners rather than passive recipients of corporate benevolence (Boutilier, 2014; Freeman, 1984).

In extractive and infrastructure projects, community participation helps secure the social licence to operate through consultation, monitoring, and shared decision-making. Mechanisms such as *Community Development Agreements (CDAs)*, *Host Community Development Trusts (HCDTs)* under Nigeria's *Petroleum Industry Act* (2021), and *Free, Prior and Informed Consent (FPIC)* standards all promote this participatory approach (OECD, 2023a). Through these instruments, communities gain a voice in determining how CSR funds are allocated, how environmental impacts are managed, and how social investments are prioritised.

Within renewable-energy and electricity projects, host communities increasingly participate as co-owners or profit-sharing partners. Solar microgrid projects across East and West Africa exemplify this model, combining CSR with local equity participation to ensure both long-term sustainability and community empowerment (IRENA, 2023; World Bank, 2023). When communities share in the benefits of clean-energy development, CSR becomes not a form of corporate charity but a framework for genuine partnership built on mutual trust and shared prosperity.

5.7.4 Multi-Stakeholder Synergy and Policy Integration

Lasting progress in environmental sustainability depends on synergy between all the major actors. Governments, corporations, and communities must work through institutionalised platforms for dialogue, joint monitoring, and transparent accountability. *Public-private partnerships (PPPs)* have proven to be particularly effective in facilitating these collaborations, especially in renewable-energy deployment and grid-modernisation projects.

Initiatives such as the *UN Global Compact* (2023), the *Extractive Industries Transparency Initiative* (EITI, 2022), and the *Africa Renewable Energy Initiative* (AREI) demonstrate how coordinated multi-stakeholder action can translate shared commitments into measurable outcomes. These partnerships foster cross-sector innovation, knowledge exchange, and equitable distribution of sustainability benefits. The OECD (2023b) underscores that meaningful CSR implementation requires "policy coherence for sustainable development" that is, alignment among regulatory frameworks, corporate governance, and community participation.

Crucially, collaboration relies on trust and communication. As Freeman (1984) observed, genuine stakeholder engagement built on respect for local values and common interests produces more resilient governance structures. Where stakeholders act in isolation or suspicion, energy projects often face conflict, delay, or outright rejection.

5.7.5 *Institutionalising Collective Accountability*

For multi-stakeholder cooperation to endure, mechanisms of *collective accountability* must be institutionalised. This involves creating independent oversight bodies, transparent reporting frameworks, and shared indicators that measure tangible sustainability outcomes rather than mere intentions. Frameworks such as the *Global Reporting Initiative* (GRI, 2021) and the *International Sustainability Standards Board (ISSB,* 2023) advocate integrated ESG reporting as a foundation for accountability and public trust.

At the national level, initiatives like Nigeria's *Energy Transition Plan* (2022) and South Africa's *Just Energy Transition Investment Plan* (2023) illustrate how cross-sector coordination can advance low-carbon development. These examples demonstrate that sustainable energy governance is not simply a regulatory exercise; it is a shared moral enterprise grounded in mutual responsibility.

Ultimately, effective multi-stakeholder strategies transform CSR from a corporate obligation into a genuine societal partnership. Governments establish the policy and legal foundations, corporations drive innovation and implementation, and communities ensure legitimacy and stewardship. Together, they form a triadic model of governance essential for achieving an equitable, inclusive, and environmentally responsible energy future.

The next section will consolidate these insights within a developing-country context, using Nigeria as a focal case study for building an integrated framework of CSR and environmental sustainability across the energy sector.

5.8 Framework for Environmental Sustainability in Developing Countries: Nigeria as a Case Study

Developing countries face distinct structural and institutional challenges in achieving environmental sustainability within the energy sector. These include weak regulatory capacity, heavy dependence on fossil fuels, inadequate enforcement of environmental standards, and persistent socio-economic inequalities that limit effective governance. Nigeria Africa's largest oil producer and one of its most dynamic emerging economies offers a compelling case study of how Corporate Social Responsibility (CSR) can serve as a bridge between development imperatives and environmental protection under these constraints.

5.8.1 Context and Energy Landscape

Nigeria's energy system has historically been dominated by oil and gas, which contribute more than 90% of export revenue and a substantial share of government income (World Bank, 2023). This dependence, however, has come at a significant ecological and social cost: decades of oil spills, gas flaring, deforestation, and community displacement have undermined local ecosystems and livelihoods (UNEP, 2011).

In recent years, Nigeria has sought to re-orient its energy policy to align with sustainability and climate-resilience goals. The *Energy Transition Plan (ETP)* launched in 2022 envisions achieving net-zero emissions by 2060 while expanding access to affordable, clean energy (Nigeria ETP, 2022). The ETP embodies CSR principles by promoting inclusive growth, a just transition, and public-private collaboration. As IRENA (2023) observes, Nigeria's approach represents a hybrid model in which policy direction, corporate innovation, and community engagement converge towards a low-carbon future.

5.8.2 Legal and Institutional Frameworks

Nigeria's legal architecture for environmental governance has evolved considerably over the past decade. The *Petroleum Industry Act* (PIA, 2021) stands as a landmark reform, embedding CSR obligations directly into statute through the creation of *Host Community Development Trusts (HCDTs)*. These trusts require energy companies to allocate a fixed percentage of operating expenditure to community-driven development projects, ensuring participatory governance and transparent benefit distribution.

Complementing the PIA are environmental statutes such as the *Environmental Impact Assessment Act* (Cap E12, LFN 2004), the *National Oil Spill Detection and Response Agency (NOSDRA) Act* (2006), and policies under the Federal Ministry of Environment addressing renewable energy and climate adaptation. Together, these instruments form a multilayered framework for environmental accountability grounded in both legal obligation and social expectation.

At the regional level, Nigeria aligns with the *African Union's Agenda 2063* and the *African Energy Transition Framework* (2022), both of which prioritise clean energy, biodiversity conservation, and climate resilience. These frameworks reinforce the principle that CSR functions not only as corporate policy but also as a developmental strategy anchored in sustainability ethics (OECD, 2023a; UN Global Compact, 2023).

5.8.3 Corporate Practices and CSR Implementation

Corporate engagement with environmental sustainability in Nigeria has expanded markedly, driven by global norms and domestic reform. Multinational oil and gas companies such as Shell, Total Energies, and Chevron have integrated CSR into their Nigerian operations through biodiversity protection, gas-flaring reduction, and local capacity-building programmes. While these efforts have faced criticism for inconsistency and insufficient transparency (Hennchen, 2014), they mark a gradual transition from reactive philanthropy towards structured sustainability governance.

In the renewable and electricity sectors, local firms such as Lumos, Daystar Power, and private partners of the *Rural Electrification Agency* have embedded CSR within energy-access initiatives that deliver off-grid solar solutions to underserved communities merging social inclusion with environmental stewardship (IRENA, 2023). Similarly, mining companies are beginning to adopt international CSR benchmarks such as the *OECD Due Diligence Guidance for Responsible Mineral Supply Chains* to mitigate social and ecological risks associated with the extraction of critical minerals essential to the energy transition.

5.8.4 Institutional Challenges

Despite progress, Nigeria's CSR and sustainability landscape continues to face systemic obstacles. Weak regulatory enforcement, overlapping institutional mandates, and corruption often erode the impact of environmental laws. Many corporations still approach CSR as a reputational exercise rather than a strategic governance tool, resulting in tokenistic projects and persistent community distrust (Idowu et al., 2013; Visser, 2013).

Community participation remains another major weakness. Although the PIA institutionalises Host Community Trusts, disparities in capacity, awareness, and oversight mechanisms frequently limit equitable implementation. Financing constraints also persist, as renewable-energy and sustainability projects rely heavily on foreign capital and donor funding (World Bank, 2023).

Overcoming these barriers requires strengthened institutional capacity, clearer inter-agency coordination, and more robust public-private accountability systems. Adopting global sustainability-reporting standards such as the *GRI Standards* (2021) and the *ISSB Sustainability Disclosure Framework* (2023) could enhance transparency, comparability, and trust in corporate sustainability performance.

5.8.5 *Towards a Coherent Framework for Environmental Sustainability*

For Nigeria and other developing economies, a sustainable energy future demands an integrated framework that aligns legal, corporate, and community interests. Such a framework can be conceptualised around five interdependent pillars:

a. **Regulatory Integration**: Harmonising environmental and energy legislation to ensure clarity, consistency, and effective enforcement.
b. **Corporate Governance Reform**: Embedding CSR and ESG principles into board-level decision-making, risk management, and disclosure practices.
c. **Community Empowerment**: Institutionalising participatory planning and equitable benefit-sharing through HCDTs and local CSR councils.
d. **Technological Innovation**: Leveraging private-sector research and investment to promote renewable energy, efficiency, and low-carbon technologies.
e. **International Cooperation**: Strengthening partnerships with multilateral institutions to secure finance, knowledge exchange, and technology transfer.

When these pillars are combined, Nigeria can establish a CSR-driven sustainability model that balances economic growth with ecological preservation. As the *UN Global Compact* (2023) emphasises, genuine sustainability governance in developing countries depends not merely on regulation but on shared accountability, ethical leadership, and adaptive learning.

Nigeria's experience underscores that the pursuit of environmental sustainability in the energy sector is simultaneously a governance challenge and a moral obligation. CSR, when integrated with coherent legal frameworks and inclusive participation, becomes the bridge connecting corporate self-interest with collective well-being.

5.9 Conclusion

Corporate Social Responsibility (CSR) has evolved from a voluntary or philanthropic activity into a core pillar of corporate governance and sustainability across the global energy sector. As demonstrated throughout this chapter, CSR is not merely a moral gesture but a structured framework through which corporations, governments, and communities reconcile industrial growth with ecological preservation and social justice. In contemporary energy practice, CSR defines how firms embed environmental sustainability, transparency, and accountability within their operations, ensuring that economic advancement proceeds without undermining human welfare or planetary integrity.

The discussion traced CSR's intellectual foundations from Carroll's hierarchical model of responsibility and Elkington's *Triple Bottom Line* to Freeman's *Stakeholder Theory* and applied these to the evolving realities of global energy industries. It showed that CSR principles such as accountability, transparency, legitimacy, creativity, and inclusivity are not abstract ideals but practical standards guiding ethical decision-making across oil, gas, renewable, electricity, and mining sectors. Through theoretical analysis, policy review, and cross-sectoral examples, the chapter established CSR as both a moral compass and a governance mechanism for achieving environmental sustainability in an era defined by decarbonisation and climate urgency.

Furthermore, the examination of the *Social Licence to Operate (SLO)* and the dynamics of multi-stakeholder collaboration highlighted that sustainable energy governance depends on trust, mutual responsibility, and enduring partnerships between governments, corporations, and host communities. The Nigerian case study illustrated how developing economies can institutionalise CSR through regulatory innovation, participatory frameworks, and local empowerment, even in the face of infrastructural and economic limitations.

Ultimately, CSR provides the ethical and operational bridge between the global energy transition and the pursuit of environmental justice. It redefines corporate legitimacy at a time when sustainability is no longer aspirational but existential. Yet, critical questions remain: How effectively are CSR principles being implemented in the high-impact oil and gas sector? And to what extent do industry-specific CSR frameworks address persistent concerns about accountability, environmental degradation, and community trust?

These questions guide the discussion in the next chapter **"CSR in the Oil and Gas Industry: A Sector-Specific Review"** which builds upon the theoretical and policy insights developed here to evaluate how CSR is operationalised within one of the world's most economically vital yet environmentally contested energy subsectors.

References

African Union. (2022). *African Energy transition framework.* African Union Commission.

Aklin, M. (2021). Do high electricity bills undermine public support for renewables? Evidence from the European Union, *Energy Policy, 156*, 112400, ISSN 0301-4215, https://doi.org/10.1016/j.enpol.2021.112400

Boutilier, R. G. (2014). Frequently asked questions about the social licence to operate. *Impact Assessment and Project Appraisal, 32*(4), 263–272. https://doi.org/10.1080/14615517.2014.941141

Bowen, H. R. (1953). *Social responsibilities of the businessman.* Harper & Row.

Brin, P., & Nehme, M. (2019). Corporate social responsibility: Analysis of theories and models. *International Journal of Business and Management, 14*(5), 59–72. https://doi.org/10.21303/2504-5571.2019.001007

Brundtland Commission. (1987). *Our common future: Report of the World Commission on Environment and Development.* Oxford University Press.

Camilleri, M. A. (2017). Corporate sustainability, social responsibility, and environmental management: An introduction to theory and practice with case studies. *Springer*. https://doi.org/10.1007/978-3-319-46849-5

Carroll, A. B. (1991). The pyramid of corporate social responsibility: Toward the moral management of organisational stakeholders. *Business Horizons, 34*(4), 39–48. https://doi.org/10.1016/0007-6813(91)90005-G

Carroll, A. B. (2016). Carroll's pyramid of CSR: Taking another look. *International Journal of Corporate Social Responsibility, 1*(3), 1–8. https://doi.org/10.1186/s40991-016-0004-6

Committee for Economic Development (CED). (1971). *Social responsibilities of business corporations*. CED.

Crowther, D., & Aras, G. (2008). *Corporate social responsibility*. Ventus Publishing ApS.

Davis, K. (1973). The case for and against business assumption of social responsibilities. *Academy of Management Journal, 16*(2), 312–322. https://doi.org/10.2307/255331

Elkington, J. (1994). Towards the sustainable corporation: Win-win-win business strategies for sustainable development. *California Management Review, 36*(2), 90–100. https://doi.org/10.2307/41165746

Elkington, J. (2018). 25 years ago I coined the phrase "triple bottom line." Here's why it's time to rethink it. *Harvard Business Review*. https://hbr.org/2018/06/25-years-ago-i-coined-the-phrase-triple-bottom-line-heres-why-im-giving-up-on-it

European Commission. (2006). *Implementing the partnership for growth and jobs: Making Europe a pole of excellence on corporate social responsibility (COM/2006/0136 final)*. https://eur-lex.europa.eu/LexUriServ/LexUriServ.do?uri=CELEX:52006DC0136:EN:HTML

European Commission. (2024). *Corporate Sustainability Due Diligence Directive (CSDDD)*. European Union. https://commission.europa.eu

Freeman, R. E. (1984). *Strategic management: A stakeholder approach*. Pitman.

Freeman, R. E., Harrison, J. S., & Wicks, A. C. (2010). Stakeholder theory: The state of the art. *Cambridge University Press*. https://doi.org/10.1017/CBO9780511815768

Global Reporting Initiative (GRI). (2021). *GRI standards: Consolidated set of sustainability reporting standards*. GRI. https://www.globalreporting.org

Gunningham, N., Kagan, R. A., & Thornton, D. (2004). Social licence and environmental protection: Why businesses go beyond compliance. *Law & Social Inquiry, 29*(2), 307–341. https://doi.org/10.1111/j.1747-4469.2004.tb00338.x

Hennchen, E. (2014). Royal Dutch shell in Nigeria: Where do responsibilities end? *Journal of Business Ethics, 129*(1), 1–25. https://doi.org/10.1007/s10551-014-2142-7

International Labour Organisation (ILO). (2015). *Guidelines for a just transition towards environmentally sustainable economies and societies for all*. ILO.

International Renewable Energy Agency (IRENA). (2023). *Renewable energy and jobs: Annual review 2023*. IRENA. https://www.irena.org

Intergovernmental Panel on Climate Change (IPCC). (2023). *Seventh assessment report (AR7)*. IPCC. https://www.ipcc.ch/assessment-report/ar7/

International Sustainability Standards Board (ISSB). (2023). IFRS S2 Climate-related disclosures. *IFRS Foundation*. https://www.ifrs.org/content/dam/ifrs/publications/pdf-standards-issb/english/2023/issued/part-a/issb-2023-a-ifrs-s2-climaterelated-disclosures.pdf?bypass=on

ISO 26000:2010 Guidance on social responsibility.

Idowu, S. O., Capaldi, N., Fifka, M., Zu, L., & Schmidpeter, R. (Eds.). (2013). *Dictionary of corporate social responsibility*. Springer.

Mancini, L., & Sala, S. (2018). Social impact assessment in the mining sector: Review and comparison of indicators frameworks. *Resources Policy, 57*, 98–111. https://doi.org/10.1016/j.resourpol.2018.02.002

Nigeria. (2021). *Petroleum Industry Act, 2021 (No. 6)*. Federal Government Printer.

Nigeria. (2022). *Nigeria energy transition plan*. Federal Ministry of Environment. https://energytransition.gov.ng

Nigeria Energy Transition Plan Update. (2024). Nigeria energy transition investment plan Update. *Sustainable Energy For All.* https://www.seforall.org/system/files/2025-05/Nigeria-ETIP-u.pdf

OECD. (2023a). *OECD guidelines for multinational enterprises on responsible business conduct.* OECD. https://doi.org/10.1787/81f92357-en

Organisation for Economic Co-operation and Development (OECD). (2023b). *Policy coherence for sustainable development 2023: Empowering people and ensuring inclusiveness.* OECD.

Palazzo, G., & Scherer, A. G. (2006). Corporate legitimacy as deliberation: A communicative framework. *Journal of Business Ethics, 66*(1), 71–88. https://doi.org/10.1007/s10551-006-9044-2

Regulation (EU) 2019/2088 of the European Parliament and of the Council of 27 November 2019 on sustainability-related disclosures in the financial services sector, 2019 O.J. (L 317) 1 [15 pp.]. https://eur-lex.europa.eu/eli/reg/2019/2088/oj/eng

Thomson, I., & Boutilier, R. G. (2011). Modelling and measuring the social licence to operate: Fruits of a dialogue between theory and practice. *Social Licence Conference Proceedings.* Centre for Social Responsibility in Mining.

United Nations Environment Programme (UNEP). (2011). *Environmental assessment of Ogoniland: Update and implementation review.* UNEP.

United Nations Global Compact. (2023). *Principles of responsible business and the 2030 agenda.* United Nations. https://unglobalcompact.org

United Nations Industrial Development Organisation. (2021a). *Annual report 2021.* UNIDO. https://www.unido.org/sites/default/files/unido-publications/2023-02/UNIDO_AR2021_EN.pdf

United Nations Industrial Development Organisation (UNIDO). (2021b). *Corporate social responsibility: Guidelines for sustainable industrial performance.* UNIDO.

Visser, W. (2010). The age of responsibility: CSR 2.0 and the new DNA of business. *Journal of Business Systems, Governance & Ethics, 5*(3). https://doi.org/10.15209/jbsge.v5i3.185

Vidal, J. (2011, October 3). Shell accused of fuelling Nigeria conflict. *The Guardian.* https://www.theguardian.com/world/2011/oct/03/shell-accused-of-fuelling-nigeria-conflict

World Bank. (2023). *Nigeria country climate and development report.* World Bank Group.

Chapter 6
Corporate Social Responsibility in the Oil and Gas Industry: A Sector-Specific Review

6.1 Introduction

The oil and gas industry has long been at the heart of the global energy mix. For decades, it has powered economies, created jobs, and supported industrial growth. Yet, alongside these benefits, the sector has also been a source of deep environmental and social concern. Issues such as oil spills, gas flaring, and community displacement have sparked debates about the true cost of fossil fuel dependence. In today's world marked by the accelerating impacts of climate change, stricter energy transition policies, and heightened public awareness, these debates have become even more urgent.

Within this shifting environment, Corporate Social Responsibility (CSR) has taken on new significance. It is no longer viewed merely as a charitable extra, but as a strategic and ethical approach that allows energy companies to balance profit-making with sustainable development (Bonini and Swartz, 2014). For many oil and gas corporations, CSR has become a way to rebuild trust, demonstrate accountability, and contribute meaningfully to the societies and environments in which they operate (Husted & Allen, 2007).

In developing countries such as Nigeria, Brazil, and China, CSR assumes an especially important role. These are contexts where government oversight can be limited and local communities often rely heavily on the natural environment for their livelihoods. In such settings, CSR is expected to go beyond donations or short-term projects, it must address environmental protection, fair resource distribution, local participation, and alignment with international frameworks like the Sustainable Development Goals (SDGs) and the Paris Climate Agreement (UNDP, 2023). Recent reforms, including Nigeria's Petroleum Industry Act of 2021 and the global move towards stricter Environmental, Social, and Governance (ESG) standards, further highlight a growing demand for transparency, inclusivity, and long-term impact.

This chapter explores how CSR operates within the oil and gas sector, both as a theoretical concept and as a practical tool. It examines how companies design and

J. A. Debski, *Corporate Social Responsibility in the Energy Sector*, CSR, Sustainability, Ethics & Governance, https://doi.org/10.1007/978-3-032-17748-3_6

implement CSR initiatives, the challenges they face, and the legal and ethical questions that arise along the way. By comparing experiences across different countries and energy subsectors, including renewables and mining, the discussion aims to show how CSR can serve as a pathway towards environmental sustainability and social stability in developing economies. The chapter concludes by linking these insights to the broader energy transition, setting the stage for the next section's focus on CSR across the wider energy economy.

6.2 CSR and Environmental Sustainability in the Oil and Gas Industry

Corporate Social Responsibility (CSR) has gradually shifted from being a voluntary moral gesture to an essential part of how modern businesses operate, especially in industries that have significant environmental footprints, such as oil and gas. The idea behind CSR originally developed from the long-standing tension between the pursuit of profit and the responsibility companies owe to society. Friedman (1970) famously argued that the only responsibility of a business is to make profits for its shareholders. Over time, however, that narrow view of business responsibility has been challenged. Scholars like Carroll (1999) have argued that companies also have legal, ethical, and philanthropic obligations that go hand in hand with their economic goals. Within the energy sector, these responsibilities are particularly urgent, since the very activities that generate profits often come with environmental costs that can be felt for generations.

Today, CSR in the oil and gas industry is closely linked to the global push for environmental sustainability. The industry sits at the centre of the world's energy system but is also one of the largest sources of pollution and greenhouse gas emissions. Activities such as drilling, refining, and transportation can lead to serious environmental damage: oil spills, habitat destruction, air pollution, and the displacement of local communities. These realities have forced companies to rethink how they operate. More and more, firms are aligning their operations with international sustainability frameworks such as the United Nations Sustainable Development Goals (SDGs) and the Paris Climate Agreement (International Energy Agency [IEA], 2023). In this sense, CSR has become a strategic tool that helps companies respond to growing public pressure, government regulation, and the moral expectation that they should not destroy the environments in which they operate (Frynas & Yamahaki, 2016).

In practice, many oil and gas companies now incorporate CSR into their core governance systems. They adopt ESG standards, publish sustainability reports, and participate in external certification programmes designed to verify environmental performance. Beyond meeting legal requirements, these efforts help companies secure what is often called a "social license to operate" the acceptance and trust of host communities and the general public (Wilburn & Wilburn, 2014). Without that trust, operations in environmentally sensitive regions can become extremely difficult, both politically and socially.

From a business perspective, CSR is no longer seen as a cost, but as an investment in stability and reputation. Firms that demonstrate environmental responsibility tend to enjoy stronger relationships with regulators and local communities. They also find it easier to attract investors, since global markets are increasingly factoring sustainability into credit ratings and valuations. A 2023 report by McKinsey & Company shows that over 80% of institutional investors now take ESG disclosure seriously when deciding where to place their capital. Similar initiatives by organisations such as the United Nations Principles for Responsible Investment (UNPRI) and the Task Force on Climate-Related Financial Disclosures (TCFD) have reinforced this global trend towards transparency and accountability.

Still, the story of CSR in developing countries is not as optimistic. In places like Nigeria, Angola, and parts of Latin America, weak governance and poor enforcement of environmental laws limit the impact of CSR programmes. Communities in oil-producing areas often remain impoverished and environmentally degraded despite decades of corporate "development projects". Many companies still treat CSR as a form of public relations, building schools or clinics while continuing harmful extraction practices. Scholars have described this as "symbolic CSR", meaning initiatives that appear socially responsible on paper but fail to address the deeper structural issues driving inequality and environmental decline (Enabulele & Ekhator, 2022; Visser, 2016).

This has led to growing interest in what Porter and Kramer (2011) call "strategic CSR". Instead of treating sustainability as an add-on, strategic CSR weaves environmental and social concerns into the core of business strategy. In the oil and gas context, that might mean investing in cleaner technologies, improving waste management, reducing gas flaring, or supporting local suppliers to strengthen community economies. The goal is to create "shared value", where both the company and society benefit. For example, a firm that invests in renewable energy or biodiversity restoration may not only protect its operating environment but also open new market opportunities in a world shifting away from fossil fuels (Zhu & Zhang, 2015).

For developing economies, this evolution of CSR carries important developmental implications. When companies take environmental sustainability seriously, they can contribute to broader national goals such as reducing pollution, building infrastructure, and promoting community resilience against climate change. In Nigeria, for example, oil companies that engage in environmental CSR can help improve waste management systems, fund reforestation, and train local workers in sustainable practices. However, the success of these initiatives depends on government oversight, transparent reporting, and honest engagement with host communities. Without those, CSR risks remaining a slogan rather than a solution.

CSR in the oil and gas sector operates both as a form of risk management and as a pathway towards sustainable development. It helps companies maintain legitimacy, reduce conflict, and align their business models with global sustainability goals. Yet, for CSR to truly support environmental sustainability, especially in developing contexts, it must move beyond charity and become a genuine part of how companies plan, invest, and measure success. The next section examines the barriers that often prevent this shift, focusing on the institutional, regulatory, and social challenges that continue to shape CSR practice in resource-dependent economies.

6.3 Implementation Challenges and Institutional Barriers to CSR in Developing Countries

Although the principles of Corporate Social Responsibility (CSR) are widely accepted, putting them into practice remains a difficult task, especially in developing countries where weak institutions, dependence on natural resources, and political instability complicate sustainability governance (Enabulele & Ekhator, 2022; Jamali & Karam, 2018). The disconnect between what CSR promises in theory and what it delivers in practice often reflects a mix of internal corporate limitations and external environmental constraints that make consistent and accountable implementation hard to achieve.

6.3.1 Internal Organisational Barriers

At the company level, the success of CSR depends largely on leadership commitment, internal culture, and how resources are allocated. In many emerging economies, corporate leaders still see CSR as a charitable activity rather than a strategic business function. This attitude results in fragmented projects scholarships, boreholes, or community clinics that look good on paper but rarely connect to the company's broader environmental or social strategy (Hohnen, 2007; Pinto & Allui, 2020).

A lack of technical capacity also plays a major role. Managers and employees often have limited training in sustainability planning or stakeholder engagement, and CSR is sometimes handled by public relations departments instead of being embedded within risk management or operational divisions. In Nigeria, for example, many oil companies still treat CSR as an image-management exercise rather than as an instrument for long-term community development (Isallah, 2023). This internal separation means environmental and social concerns remain peripheral, not integral, to corporate decision-making.

Transparency is another internal weakness. Without consistent data collection and clear reporting frameworks, it becomes difficult to measure or verify CSR outcomes. Few firms align their reporting with global benchmarks such as the Global Reporting Initiative (GRI & Support the Goals, 2022) or the UN Guiding Principles on Business and Human Rights (United Nations, 2011). For smaller domestic companies, financial limitations add another layer of difficulty. Unlike large multinationals, they often lack the resources to sustain comprehensive CSR programmes or to obtain independent verification for sustainability reports (Jamali et al., 2017). Even when funds are available, poor alignment between corporate incentives and community outcomes discourages genuine, long-term environmental investment.

6.3.2 External Institutional and Regulatory Constraints

Externally, the effectiveness of CSR is heavily shaped by the legal and policy environment. Many developing countries have environmental laws that look strong on paper but are weakly enforced due to bureaucratic bottlenecks and political interference (Acheampong & Wang, 2021). This lack of enforcement allows companies to adopt what is sometimes called "compliance minimalism", doing just enough to satisfy formal requirements without committing to substantive reform.

In Nigeria, before the Petroleum Industry Act (PIA) 2021, company–community relations in the Niger Delta were largely managed through voluntary memoranda of understanding that lacked legal weight. The PIA's creation of Host Community Development Trusts (HCDTs) has provided a legal mechanism for channeling oil revenues directly into community development (NUPRC, 2022). Still, implementation has been uneven. Questions about governance structure, transparency, and fair representation have led to delays and disputes (Agbarakwe & Bredino, 2024). Similar problems are visible elsewhere in Brazil's Amazon Basin, Indonesia's resource corridors, and parts of Central Africa where fragmented environmental regulations and limited judicial capacity weaken accountability (Hilson, 2012).

Political instability and corruption further erode progress. The "resource curse" literature highlights how the concentration of resource wealth can empower elites who divert CSR or development funds for private gain (Kolstad & Wiig, 2009). In contexts where governments lack legitimacy, communities often view CSR projects as corporate propaganda rather than genuine development, fueling mistrust and occasional conflict.

6.3.3 Cultural and Stakeholder-Engagement Challenges

Cultural dynamics also influence how CSR unfolds on the ground. In many developing societies, community structures are complex, with competing ethnic, religious, or clan-based interests. Companies often struggle to navigate these layers of social identity when deciding how to distribute CSR benefits fairly (Visser, 2016). What one group sees as inclusion, another may perceive as exclusion.

Meaningful participation, too, is often more rhetoric than reality. Consultations are commonly conducted through local elites or political intermediaries rather than through broad-based dialogue with the people most affected by extractive activities (Ekhator & Iyiola-Omisore, 2021). The idea of a "social licence to operate", which depends on trust and ongoing communication, is rarely institutionalised as a continuing process. In much of sub-Saharan Africa and Southeast Asia, consultation tends to occur once at the start of a project, then fades away. Research has shown that this limited engagement often leads to disillusionment, protest, and reputational crises for companies operating in sensitive regions (Hilson & Maconachie, 2020).

6.3.4 Global Pressures and Emerging Compliance Regimes

Globalisation has introduced new layers of accountability for corporations. Policies such as the EU Corporate Sustainability Reporting Directive (Directive (EU) 2022/2464, 2022) and the OECD Due Diligence Guidance for Responsible Business Conduct (2023) have raised expectations for environmental and social disclosure, even for subsidiaries based in developing countries. These rules are reshaping how multinational oil and gas companies report their impacts, but they also create challenges. Compliance costs can be high, data infrastructure is often weak, and inconsistencies between national and international standards complicate enforcement.

For developing economies, the challenge is twofold: to strengthen domestic regulatory capacity and to ensure that global sustainability frameworks apply fairly across borders. Without both, CSR risks becoming performative rather than transformative, producing glossy sustainability reports but little change in the lives of the people most affected (Paiement, 2021).

CSR implementation in developing countries is held back by a web of internal and external barriers: limited managerial capacity, weak governance, financial constraints, cultural complexities, and fragmented regulation. Yet there are encouraging signs of progress. Legal reforms such as Nigeria's PIA 2021 and emerging regional sustainability directives point to a gradual institutionalisation of accountability in the energy sector. Overcoming these challenges requires more than policy design; it demands genuine corporate reform, empowered communities, and international cooperation that ensures CSR is not just a compliance requirement, but a real pathway towards equitable and sustainable development.

6.4 CSR Failures, Legal Accountability, and Environmental Liabilities in the Oil and Gas Industry

Despite the widespread adoption of Corporate Social Responsibility (CSR) frameworks, failures in implementation continue to produce serious environmental and social consequences. The oil and gas sector illustrates this contradiction clearly: while major firms increasingly promote their sustainability commitments, oil spills, gas flaring, and community displacement remain recurring realities in many developing regions. These persistent failures reveal the limits of voluntary self-regulation and highlight the need for more enforceable legal accountability mechanisms to complement CSR efforts (Isallah, 2023; Spence, 2011).

6.4.1 Environmental Disasters and Corporate Negligence

Perhaps the most striking example of corporate failure in environmental risk management is the **Deepwater Horizon** disaster in the Gulf of Mexico in 2010. The explosion on BP's offshore rig killed 11 workers and released nearly 4.9 million barrels of oil into the sea (U.S. Environmental Protection Agency [EPA], 2021). Despite operating in a highly regulated context, the incident exposed systemic flaws in both oversight and corporate culture. BP's pre-disaster sustainability reports had emphasised its "Beyond Petroleum" vision, yet subsequent investigations revealed cost-cutting measures and neglected safety systems that contradicted those claims (Freudenburg & Gramling, 2011). The disaster prompted major institutional reforms in the United States, including revisions to the Oil Pollution Act (OPA) 1990, and demonstrated that meaningful CSR requires legally binding obligations, not just voluntary promises (National Commission, 2011).

In contrast, similar disasters in developing countries often receive limited remediation due to weak governance structures. The Niger Delta remains one of the most affected regions globally. Since the 1950s, decades of extraction by companies such as Shell Petroleum Development Company (SPDC) and Chevron have caused chronic environmental degradation, biodiversity loss, and widespread health problems (Amnesty International, 2020). Ubani's (2022) study notes that the restoration of Ogoniland's ecosystem will take decades, given the extent of accumulated oil pollution and the inadequacy of clean-up efforts. While Shell's CSR initiatives since the 1990s have included community projects and social investments, the persistence of contamination has led to several domestic and international court actions against the company.

One of the most notable developments came in 2021, when the Court of Appeal of The Hague ruled in *Milieudefensie* et al. *v. Royal Dutch Shell plc*, ordering Shell to reduce its global carbon emissions by 45% by 2030 compared with 2019 levels (Rechtbank Den Haag, 2021). This landmark decision connected corporate emissions directly to human rights responsibilities, marking a critical shift in global climate litigation. It underscored that voluntary CSR commitments, however well-intentioned, cannot substitute for binding legal accountability.

In Nigeria, Shell's recent divestment from its onshore assets has sparked further debate. The company cited security concerns, yet many observers view the move as an attempt to transfer environmental liabilities to smaller domestic operators (Sahara Reporters, 2025). This pattern raises a new form of CSR risk: corporate exit strategies that externalise environmental damage without ensuring adequate remediation, thereby undermining commitments to sustainability and justice (Table 6.1).

Table 6.1 Selected Landmark Cases on Corporate Environmental Liability in the Oil and Gas Industry

Case / Year	Jurisdiction	Core Issue	Legal Outcome	Implication for CSR Accountability
Deepwater Horizon (BP), 2010	United States	Offshore rig explosion and catastrophic oil spill	Strengthened implementation of the Oil Pollution Act and large-scale compensation settlements	Demonstrated limits of voluntary self-regulation and the need for statutory compliance
Milieudefensie et al. *v. Royal Dutch Shell*, 2021	Netherlands	Corporate carbon emission obligations under international climate norms	Court ordered Shell to reduce global emissions by 45% by 2030 relative to 2019 levels	Established judicial enforcement of climate-related CSR obligations
Okpabi v. Royal Dutch Shell plc, 2021	United Kingdom	Environmental harm caused by foreign subsidiaries of a multinational parent company	UK Supreme Court held that parent companies can be held liable for the acts of subsidiaries	Expanded transnational corporate accountability under CSR frameworks
Bodo Community v. Shell, 2015	Nigeria	Oil spills and community compensation claims	£55 million settlement paid to affected Niger Delta communities	Strengthened local CSR claims and recognition of host community rights
Doe v. ExxonMobil Corp., 2021	United States	Alleged human rights abuses under the Alien Tort Statute	Case limited by jurisdictional scope but reinforced human rights due diligence debates	Reinforced integration of human rights into corporate CSR responsibilities

Note Table compiled by the author from multiple sources, including EPA (2021), Rechtbank Den Haag (2021), UK Supreme Court (2021), Amnesty International (2020), and secondary legal commentaries

6.4.2 Weak Enforcement and Institutional Capture

CSR failures are not only the product of corporate negligence but also of fragile regulatory environments. Agencies charged with environmental monitoring such as Nigeria's National Oil Spill Detection and Response Agency (NOSDRA) or the Brazilian Institute of the Environment and Renewable Natural Resources often lack adequate funding, technical expertise, and independence. Between 2015 and 2021, numerous oil spills in Nigeria went uninvestigated due to "logistical and institutional constraints" (Ukhurebor et al., 2021). This lack of capacity allows corporations to evade sanctions and encourages a culture of minimal compliance.

Moreover, the entanglement of politics and corporate interests weakens environmental enforcement. Acheampong and Wang (2021) note that across much of

Sub-Saharan Africa, informal networks of patronage frequently influence regulatory outcomes. In such contexts, CSR often becomes a substitute for state governance rather than a complement to it. Companies step in to provide social amenities—roads, schools, or water projects—but these efforts rarely address the root causes of environmental degradation (Omeje, 2020).

6.4.3 Human Rights and Transnational Litigation

The growing use of human rights litigation has started to reshape corporate accountability in the extractive sector. Courts in both the United Kingdom and the Netherlands have increasingly allowed claims by Nigerian communities against Shell and other multinationals (Isallah, 2023). The *2021 Okpabi v. Royal Dutch Shell plc* decision by the UK Supreme Court affirmed that parent companies can owe a duty of care for environmental harm caused by their overseas subsidiaries (UKSC 3, 2021). Similarly, cases under the U.S. *Alien Tort Statute (ATS),* such as *Doe v. ExxonMobil Corp.* (2021), continue to test the limits of corporate liability for human rights abuses abroad.

These cases mark a significant evolution from voluntary CSR to legally enforceable accountability. They demonstrate that while CSR frameworks may foster corporate awareness, meaningful behavioural change often depends on the real prospect of litigation. This development also signals a convergence between environmental law, corporate governance, and international human rights standards.

6.4.4 The Emerging ESG Accountability Framework

Recent global reforms show that the line between voluntary CSR and mandatory sustainability disclosure is increasingly blurred. The EU Corporate Sustainability Reporting Directive (CSRD, 2023) and the IFRS S2 Climate-Related Disclosures (2023) now influence multinational operations worldwide, including subsidiaries in developing regions. In Nigeria, the Securities and Exchange Commission (SEC) introduced an ESG disclosure framework in 2021 that requires listed companies to produce annual sustainability reports aligned with GRI and TCFD standards (SEC Nigeria, 2021).

These developments signal a major shift: environmental and social disclosures are no longer just ethical gestures but legal obligations. For oil and gas companies, CSR failure now carries tangible regulatory and financial consequences, not merely reputational harm. As investors integrate ESG metrics into their decision-making, firms with weak sustainability performance face restricted access to capital and higher financing costs (OECD, 2023).

6.4.5 Lessons for Developing Economies

The persistence of CSR failures in the oil and gas industry underscores the limitations of purely voluntary approaches. For developing countries, several lessons are clear. Effective CSR requires a combination of strong regulatory enforcement, transparent community participation, and credible cross-border accountability. Embedding principles such as "polluter pays" and mandatory environmental remediation into domestic law can help restore public trust and enhance the legitimacy of CSR frameworks. Equally, empowering host communities through participatory governance and local content initiatives can shift CSR from a reputational strategy towards a genuine tool for environmental justice and inclusive development.

6.5 Comparative Corporate Approaches to Environmental Sustainability in the Oil and Gas Industry

Corporate Social Responsibility (CSR) strategies in the oil and gas sector take shape within very different political, regulatory, and cultural settings. While multinational corporations (MNCs) often proclaim uniform global sustainability commitments, their actual practices on the ground are deeply influenced by local institutional realities and governance traditions. This section compares CSR and environmental sustainability approaches across five jurisdictions—Nigeria, Brazil, China, the Netherlands, and the United States—highlighting their distinct patterns and drawing lessons that may guide developing economies in refining their own frameworks.

6.5.1 Nigeria: Regulatory Reforms and Localised CSR Governance

Nigeria's oil and gas sector reflects both the opportunities and contradictions of CSR in a developing context. Decades of exploration in the Niger Delta have left behind a legacy of oil spills, gas flaring, and environmental degradation. For many years, CSR efforts were largely voluntary, shaped by corporate goodwill rather than binding obligations. Initiatives like Shell's Global Memoranda of Understanding (GMoUs) sought to fund community projects, but most focused on short-term welfare provision rather than long-term environmental recovery (Enabulele & Ekhator, 2022).

The Petroleum Industry Act (PIA) 2021 changed that landscape. It institutionalised CSR through the creation of Host Community Development Trusts (HCDTs), requiring oil firms to allocate 3% of annual operating expenses to community-driven projects (NUPRC, 2022). The Act also enhanced the authority of the National Oil Spill Detection and Response Agency (NOSDRA), giving it greater oversight powers. Yet, as scholars observe, translating these legal gains into practice has been uneven, hampered by bureaucratic delays, community rivalries, and weak institutional capacity (Agbarakwe & Bredino, 2024). Even so, Nigeria's model marks a shift from charity-based CSR to a legally defined and locally governed approach, a transition that other resource-dependent economies can learn from.

6.5.2 Brazil: State-Led Sustainability and the Energy Transition

Brazil offers a different picture, one where the state plays a central role in shaping corporate sustainability. The national oil company, Petrobras, operates under a strong public mandate, embedding CSR into its governance through adherence to the UN Global Compact, ISO 14001, and the Task Force on Climate-related Financial Disclosures (TCFD) (Petrobras, 2024). These measures are reinforced by national laws such as the Environmental Crimes Law (1998) and the National Policy on Climate Change (Law No. 12.187/2009), which hold corporations legally accountable for ecological harm.

Still, Brazil's regulatory system is far from flawless. Enforcement gaps and political instability have periodically undermined sustainability oversight. The 2019 Brumadinho dam disaster, though from the mining sector, reignited public debate about corporate responsibility and triggered new ESG disclosure rules (Hilson, 2012). Today, Brazilian energy firms are increasingly investing in biofuels, wind, and solar power, linking CSR to the country's broader low-carbon transition. The lesson from Brazil is that strong state involvement can drive sustainability forward, but lasting progress depends on consistent enforcement and political will.

6.5.3 China: Centralised Policy Direction and Institutional Experimentation

China's CSR approach is defined by its top-down structure and the close integration of corporate sustainability goals with national development policy. Since 2015, the Chinese government has actively embedded CSR into state planning, notably within the 14th Five-Year Plan (2021–2025), which sets the country's course towards carbon neutrality by 2060 (State Council of China, 2021). Major firms such as China National Petroleum Corporation (CNPC) and Sinopec now produce detailed sustainability reports aligned with the Global Reporting Initiative (GRI) and the UN Sustainable Development Goals (SDGs).

However, unlike in liberal democracies where CSR often arises from stakeholder advocacy, China's model remains predominantly state-driven. CSR performance tends to correlate with government priorities and regional regulatory incentives rather than voluntary community engagement (Ervits, 2023; Zhu & Zhang, 2015). This approach ensures policy coherence and rapid diffusion of environmental goals, but it can also restrict local participation and transparency, particularly in remote or ethnic-minority areas. Even so, China's example shows how a coordinated national strategy can mobilise large-scale corporate compliance in pursuit of sustainability targets.

6.5.4 The Netherlands: Judicial Activism and Corporate Accountability

The Netherlands stands out for its robust institutional oversight and an active judiciary that enforces environmental accountability. The 2021 *Milieudefensie* et al. *v. Royal Dutch Shell plc* ruling by the Hague District Court required Shell to cut its global carbon emissions by 45% by 2030 compared with 2019 levels (Rechtbank Den Haag, 2021). This unprecedented decision effectively turned CSR rhetoric into a binding legal obligation, setting a global precedent for climate litigation.

Dutch corporations also display a mature culture of CSR integration. The Dutch Corporate Governance Code (2022) mandates the disclosure of environmental risks and sustainability policies, while civil society organisations and environmental NGOs play an important watchdog role. The combination of judicial oversight, strong civic participation, and detailed ESG reporting has made the Netherlands a model for how institutional strength and citizen engagement can transform CSR into enforceable sustainability practice.

6.5.5 The United States: Market-Driven CSR and ESG Integration

In the United States, CSR has evolved largely through market forces and investor activism rather than state-led regulation. The U.S SEC has progressively tightened disclosure rules, and its Climate Disclosure Rule requires public companies to report emissions and climate-related risks in their filings (U.S. SEC, 2024).

American oil majors such as ExxonMobil and Chevron have embraced CSR frameworks focused on decarbonisation, energy efficiency, and carbon capture. However, scepticism remains widespread. Critics argue that many sustainability claims amount to "greenwashing", with little measurable environmental benefit (InfluenceMap, 2024). State-led lawsuits against ExxonMobil and other corporations suggest that voluntary initiatives are no longer sufficient. Yet, the growing influence of ESG investing, where sustainability metrics affect capital access, has begun to reshape corporate priorities. The U.S. experience shows how financial markets, even in the absence of stringent regulation, can exert significant pressure for environmental performance (Table 6.2).

Table 6.2 Comparative CSR and environmental sustainability approaches in the oil and gas sector

Country/Region	CSR Governance Framework	Key Legal/Policy Instruments	Institutional Strengths	Implementation Challenges	Emerging Trends/Lessons
Nigeria	Transition from voluntary CSR to mandatory Host Community Development Trusts (HCDTs)	Petroleum Industry Act (PIA) 2021; NOSDRA Act	Legal embedding of CSR; community participation structures	Weak local capacity; elite capture; governance disputes	Institutionalisation of CSR through legal mechanisms
Brazil	State-led CSR through Petrobras and hybrid ESG model	National Policy on Climate Change (2009); Environmental Crimes Law (1998)	Strong environmental legal base; active civil society engagement	Inconsistent enforcement and political volatility	Integration of CSR with energy transition planning
China	Government-driven CSR aligned with national development goals	14th Five-Year Plan; Green Development Strategy	Strong policy coherence; rapid regulatory implementation	Limited transparency and participatory inclusion	Alignment of CSR with state-led sustainability agenda
Netherlands	Judicially enforced environmental accountability	Dutch Corporate Governance Code (2022); *Milieudefensie v. Shell*	Strong rule of law; civic and NGO engagement	High compliance and reporting costs	Legalisation and standardisation of CSR obligations
United States	Market- and investor-driven CSR models	SEC Climate Disclosure Rule (2023); Sarbanes–Oxley Act	Robust ESG investor activism; financial incentives for sustainability	Fragmented federal–state regulation; risk of greenwashing	Mainstreaming of CSR through finance and litigation channels

Note Data compiled by the author from Enabulele and Ekhator (2022), Petrobras (2024), State Council of China (2021), Rechtbank Den Haag (2021), and U.S. Securities and Exchange Commission (2024)

6.5.6 Comparative Insights and Lessons for Developing Economies

Across these cases, a clear pattern emerges: CSR effectiveness depends less on corporate goodwill and more on institutional capacity and enforcement strength.

a. **Nigeria** illustrates a shift from voluntary CSR to statutory community-based governance, but implementation gaps persist.
b. **Brazil** demonstrates the potential of state leadership, especially when transparency and civic oversight reinforce corporate accountability.
c. **China's** centralised model achieves coherence and scale, though sometimes at the cost of participatory legitimacy.
d. **The Netherlands** proves that strong legal institutions and civil activism can turn CSR into binding environmental responsibility.
e. **The United States** highlights the role of markets and investor activism as alternative enforcement mechanisms.

For developing economies, the most promising way forward lies in blending these approaches: grounding CSR in clear legal requirements, supported by active civil society engagement and economic incentives for compliance. Strengthening judicial capacity, enforcing ESG disclosure, and integrating CSR into national sustainability agendas can transform it from a symbolic exercise into a meaningful instrument for environmental protection and inclusive growth.

6.6 Integrating CSR and the Energy Transition Emerging Trends and Strategic Innovations

The global shift from fossil fuels to renewable and low-carbon energy sources has profoundly redefined the aims and methods of Corporate Social Responsibility (CSR) within the energy sector. Once viewed primarily as agents of environmental harm, oil and gas companies are now recasting themselves as partners in the global energy transition. They do so by investing in cleaner technologies, building partnerships with local communities, and embedding sustainability into corporate governance frameworks (International Energy Agency [IEA], 2023).

6.6.1 CSR and Decarbonisation Strategies in the Energy Sector

Decarbonisation has become a defining test of corporate sustainability. Multinationals such as Shell, BP, and TotalEnergies have outlined energy transition plans consistent with the Paris Agreement's 1.5 °C target, highlighting investments in carbon capture and storage (CCS), renewable energy diversification, and methane abatement (TotalEnergies, 2024). However, implementation frequently trails behind ambition, raising persistent concerns about "greenwashing" and the credibility of voluntary disclosure systems (InfluenceMap, 2024).

For developing economies, the challenge is particularly complex. National oil companies such as Nigeria's NNPC Ltd. and Malaysia's Petronas operate in contexts where fossil fuels remain essential to fiscal stability. Achieving a balanced transition demands CSR models that stimulate economic diversification, expand clean energy access, and build local resilience (UNDP, 2023). In these settings, CSR is evolving from a philanthropic gesture into a platform for community-oriented climate adaptation supporting renewable microgrids, reforestation projects, and carbon offset initiatives that deliver tangible benefits to host populations (World Bank, 2024).

6.6.2 Integration of ESG and Sustainable Finance

The growing fusion of CSR with ESG finance has transformed sustainability into a measurable financial concern. Investors and lenders increasingly tie capital flows to environmental performance. The International Finance Corporation (IFC, 2023), for example, mandates compliance with its Performance Standards on Environmental and Social Sustainability for all energy investments.

In Nigeria, frameworks such as the Central Bank's Sustainable Banking Principles (2019) and the Nigerian Exchange (NGX) ESG Reporting Guidelines (2022) encourage firms to disclose data on carbon emissions, waste, and gender inclusion (NGX, 2022). This alignment of CSR with financing incentives has created a market logic for sustainability: companies with strong ESG profiles gain access to green bonds and sustainability-linked loans, while laggards face investor exclusion. In this new landscape, CSR is not just ethically desirable; it is financially prudent.

6.6.3 Community-Centric CSR and just Transition Principles

The notion of a "just transition" ensuring that energy transformation benefits workers and communities has become a cornerstone of contemporary CSR (ILO, 2023). In regions long dependent on fossil extraction, such as Nigeria's Niger Delta or South Africa's Mpumalanga coal belt, CSR is being reimagined as a tool for social reintegration. Firms are investing in retraining programmes, alternative livelihoods, and ecosystem rehabilitation to mitigate the social costs of decarbonisation.

Shell's *All On* initiative in Nigeria, for instance, supports off-grid renewable enterprises that expand energy access while empowering local entrepreneurs (Okeke et al., 2020). Likewise, Petrobras' social investment programmes in Brazil promote biofuel cooperatives and vocational training in green energy (Petrobras, 2024). These examples highlight a broader paradigm shift from CSR as compensation for damage to CSR as a driver of equitable, forward-looking transformation.

6.6.4 *Technology, Digitalisation, and Transparency Innovations*

Digital technologies are revolutionising the monitoring and verification of CSR commitments. Artificial intelligence, blockchain, and satellite imagery now make it possible to track emissions, spills, and compliance in real time. Platforms such as the Global Methane Tracker (IEA, 2024) and the Carbon Disclosure Project (CDP, 2024) provide open access to environmental data, empowering investors and the public to hold corporations accountable.

In developing countries, digital transparency tools are fostering civic oversight. Nigeria's **Extractive Industries Transparency Initiative** (NEITI) Open Data Dashboard (2023) allows citizens to follow extractive revenues and CSR projects, narrowing the information gap between corporations and communities. This trend signals a shift towards participatory accountability where technology strengthens environmental governance from the bottom up.

6.6.5 *Strategic Repositioning of CSR in the Energy Transition*

Across the global energy system, CSR is increasingly positioned as a strategic governance instrument linking innovation, climate responsibility, and inclusive development. Oil and gas majors are transforming into integrated energy companies with portfolios in solar, wind, and hydrogen. Their CSR agendas now centre on:

a. measurable emissions reductions and biodiversity restoration;
b. equitable renewable energy access for local communities;
c. inclusion of women and youth in clean energy employment; and
d. partnerships for sustainability education and infrastructure.

For developing economies, aligning CSR with national climate and development priorities presents an opportunity to achieve both equity and growth. Embedding CSR principles within national transition policies can mobilise corporate expertise towards the Sustainable Development Goals (SDGs) 7 (Affordable and Clean Energy), 13 (Climate Action), and 17 (Partnerships for the Goals).

Ultimately, the shift from "extractive responsibility" to "transformative sustainability" marks a conceptual breakthrough. CSR is no longer confined to damage mitigation; it has become a strategic pillar of the global energy transition, shaping how corporations, communities, and states collaborate towards a low-carbon future.

6.7 Conclusion

Corporate Social Responsibility (CSR) in the oil and gas sector has evolved from a voluntary act of philanthropy into a core component of corporate governance and environmental accountability. As the preceding analysis has shown, the environmental intensity and social complexity of this industry have compelled companies, governments, and global institutions to treat CSR not merely as reputation management, but as both a strategic necessity and a moral obligation. In developing economies such as Nigeria, Brazil, and China, where weak regulation and institutional fragility often undermine formal governance, CSR has become a practical instrument for pursuing environmental protection and community welfare.

The chapter began by situating CSR within its historical and theoretical evolution, noting how global demands for decarbonisation, human rights, and community inclusion have transformed the logic of corporate responsibility in the energy industry. It then explored the persistent obstacles to effective CSR implementation in developing contexts: fragmented legal systems, limited institutional capacity, poor stakeholder engagement, and deep socio-economic inequalities. These factors help explain why, despite decades of investment and numerous sustainability pledges, CSR has often failed to deliver meaningful environmental remediation or equitable social outcomes.

Even so, a new phase of CSR governance is emerging. Recent legal and policy reforms such as Nigeria's Petroleum Industry Act (2021), Brazil's strengthened ESG reporting standards, and China's national green development policies reflect a growing convergence between voluntary corporate initiatives and binding sustainability obligations. Landmark judicial decisions, including *Milieudefensie v. Shell* (2021) and *Okpabi v. Shell* (2021), have reinforced this transition by holding corporations accountable for environmental harm, expanding the boundaries of corporate liability across borders. Together, these developments point to the gradual consolidation of a "hard law" model of CSR, where environmental and human rights responsibilities are codified as conditions of corporate legitimacy and long-term financial performance.

Comparative lessons from the Netherlands and the United States reveal that CSR evolution is driven by multiple forces—judicial activism, civic participation, and market-based ESG integration among them. For developing countries, the challenge and opportunity lie in blending these approaches into hybrid governance models that combine legal enforcement, financial incentives, and participatory oversight. Such integration moves CSR beyond symbolic gestures, transforming it into a credible policy mechanism that supports national development objectives and aligns private enterprise with the Sustainable Development Goals (SDGs).

The chapter also underscored how the global energy transition is reshaping the meaning and scope of CSR. As attention shifts towards renewables, hydrogen, and sustainable mining, CSR is no longer limited to mitigating the damages of extraction; it now plays a central role in enabling equitable, low-carbon transformation. The emphasis on "just transition" principles ensures that workers, communities, and ecosystems are not left behind. Moreover, technological innovation through digital reporting, satellite monitoring, and open data platforms is enhancing transparency and empowering citizens to hold corporations accountable.

Ultimately, the evolution of CSR in the oil and gas industry mirrors a broader redefinition of corporate responsibility in the Anthropocene: from profit-driven growth to stewardship of the planet and its people. The critical question that follows, and the focus of the next chapter, is whether the renewable energy, electricity, and mining sectors can institutionalise CSR early enough to avoid repeating the environmental and social injustices of the fossil-fuel era.

Chapter Seven builds on this reflection by examining how CSR principles are being embedded in emerging energy systems, exploring whether these new industries can achieve sustainability by design rather than by correction.

References

Acheampong, T., & Wang, Y. (2021). Environmental regulation and oil governance in sub-Saharan Africa: Policy effectiveness and challenges. *Energy Policy, 156*, Article 112456. https://doi.org/10.1016/j.jpolmod.2021.03.011

Agbarakwe, U. H., & Bredino, S. M. (2024). Nigerian Petroleum Industry Act 2021 & host communities development: Issues & challenges. *Scholars Journal of Humanities and Social Sciences, 9*(2), 45–52. https://doi.org/10.36348/sjhss.2024.v09i02.002

Amnesty International. (2020). *Nigeria: No cleanup, no justice ten years after the UNEP report on Ogoniland* (AFR 44/1012/2020). Amnesty International. Nigeria: No Clean-Up, No Justice: An evaluation of the implementation of UNEP's environmental assessment of Ogoniland, nine years on—Amnesty International.

Bonini, S., & Swartz, S. (2014). *Profits with purpose: How organizing for sustainability can benefit the bottom line.* McKinsey & Company. https://www.mckinsey.com/~/media/McKinsey/Business%20Functions/Sustainability/Our%20Insights/Profits%20with%20purpose/Profits%20with%20Purpose.ashx

Carbon Disclosure Project (CDP). (2024). *CDP global climate disclosure report 2024.* CDP Worldwide. https://www.cdp.net

Carroll, A. B. (1999). Corporate social responsibility: Evolution of a definitional construct. *Business & Society, 38*(3), 268–295. https://doi.org/10.1177/000765039903800303

Doe v. Exxon Mobil Corp., 654 F.3d 11 (D.C. Cir. 2021).

Directive (EU) 2022/2464 of the European Parliament and of the Council of 14 December 2022 amending Regulation (EU) No 537/2014, Directive 2004/109/EC, Directive 2006/43/EC and Directive 2013/34/EU, as regards corporate sustainability reporting. (2022). *Official Journal of the European Union,* L 322/15. eur-lex.europa.eu

Ekhator, E. O., & Iyiola-Omisore, I. (2021). Corporate social responsibility in the oil and gas industry in Nigeria: The case for a legalised framework. In E. G. Pereira, R. Spencer, & J. W. Moses (Eds.), *Sovereign wealth funds, local content policies and CSR* (pp. 493–508). Springer. https://doi.org/10.1007/978-3-030-56092-8_25

Enabulele, O., & Ekhator, E. O. (2022). Improving environmental protection in Nigeria: A reassessment of the role of informal institutions. *The Journal of Sustainable Development, Law and Policy, 13*(1), 162–199. https://doi.org/10.4314/jsdlp.v13i1.7

Ervits, I. (2023). CSR reporting in China's private and state-owned enterprises: A mixed methods comparative analysis. *Asian Business & Management, 22*(1), 55–83. https://doi.org/10.1057/s41291-021-00147-1

Freudenburg, W. R., & Gramling, R. (2011). *Blowout in the Gulf: The BP oil spill disaster and the future of energy in America.* MIT Press. https://www.jstor.org/stable/j.ctt5hhggk

Friedman, M. (1970, September 13). The social responsibility of business is to increase its profits. *The New York Times Magazine*, 32–33, 122–126. https://www.nytimes.com/1970/09/13/archives/a-friedman-doctrine-the-social-responsibility-of-business-is-to.html

Frynas, J. G., & Yamahaki, C. (2016). Corporate social responsibility: Review and roadmap of theoretical perspectives. *Business Ethics: A European Review, 25*(3), 258–285. https://doi.org/10.1111/beer.12115

Global Reporting Initiative & Support the Goals. (2022). State of progress: *Business contributions to the SDGs.* https://www.globalreporting.org/media/ab5lun0h/stg-gri-report-final.pdf

Hilson, G. (2012). Corporate social responsibility in the extractive industries: Experiences from developing countries. *Resources Policy, 37*(2), 131–137. https://doi.org/10.1016/j.resourpol.2012.01.002

Hilson, G., & Maconachie, R. (2020). Artisanal and small-scale mining and the Sustainable Development Goals: Opportunities and new directions for sub-Saharan Africa. *Geoforum, 111*, 125–141. https://doi.org/10.1016/j.geoforum.2019.09.006

Hohnen, P. (2007). *Corporate social responsibility: An implementation guide for business.* International Institute for Sustainable Development.

Husted, B. W., & Allen, D. B. (2007). *Corporate social strategy in multinational enterprises: Antecedents and value creation.* Journal of Business Ethics, 74(4), 345–361.

InfluenceMap. (2024). *Energy transition and oil majors: Climate policy alignment analysis 2024.* InfluenceMap. https://influencemap.org

International Energy Agency (IEA). (2023). *World energy outlook 2023.* IEA. https://www.iea.org/reports/world-energy-outlook-2023

International Energy Agency (IEA). (2024). *Global methane tracker 2024.* IEA. https://www.iea.org/reports/global-methane-tracker-2024

International Finance Corporation (IFC). (2023). *Performance standards on environmental and social sustainability (updated edition).* World Bank Group. https://www.ifc.org

International Labour Organisation (ILO). (2023). *Just transition and climate action in the global energy sector.* ILO. https://www.ilo.org/topics-and-sectors/just-transition-towards-environmentally-sustainable-economies-and-societies

Isallah, H. (2023). The impact of the Petroleum Industry Act on corporate social responsibility and taxation in Nigeria's upstream oil and gas sector: A path towards sustainable development. *Sustainability, 15*(21), 15538. https://doi.org/10.3390/su152115538

Jamali, D., & Karam, C. (2018). Corporate social responsibility in developing countries as an emerging field of study. *International Journal of Management Reviews, 20*(1), 32–61. https://doi.org/10.1111/ijmr.12112

Jamali, D., Zadeh, M. H., & Samara, G. (2017). CSR implementation and institutional complexity: SMEs in developing countries. *Business & Society, 56*(3), 420–450. https://doi.org/10.1177/0007650315584303

Kolstad, I., & Wiig, A. (2009). Is transparency the key to reducing corruption in resource-rich countries? *World Development, 37*(3), 521–532. https://doi.org/10.1016/j.worlddev.2008.07.002

McKinsey & Company. (2023). *A more orderly transition: Navigating energy in 2023.* McKinsey & Company. https://www.mckinsey.com/~/media/mckinsey/industries/electric%20power%20and%20natural%20gas/our%20insights/a%20more%20orderly%20transition%20navigating%20energy%20in%202023/mck_energycompendium_v2.pdf

Milieudefensie et al. v. Royal Dutch Shell plc, Rechtbank Den Haag, ECLI:NL:RBDHA:2021:5339 (2021).

National Commission on the BP Deepwater Horizon Oil Spill and Offshore Drilling. (2011). *Deepwater: The Gulf oil disaster and the future of offshore drilling.* U.S. Government Printing Office. https://www.govinfo.gov

Nigeria Upstream Petroleum Regulatory Commission. (2022). *Nigeria upstream petroleum host communities development regulations, 2022.* https://www.nuprc.gov.ng/wp-content/uploads/2022/07/Nigeria-Upstream-Petroleum-Host-Communities-Development-Regulations-2022.pdf

Nigerian Exchange Group (NGX). (2022). *Sustainability disclosure guidelines for listed companies.* NGX. https://doclib.ngxgroup.com/regulation-site/IssuersRules/Sustainability%20Disclosure%20Guidelines.pdf

Okeke, M., Ifeanyi, T., Victoria, T., & Okechukwu, A. C. (2020). Multinational corporations and corporate social responsibility: An investigation of Shell and its relationship with their host communities in Nigeria. *Journal of Business and Management Studies, 4*(2), 127–135.

Organisation for Economic Co-operation and Development. (2023, June 8). *Updated guidelines lift ambition on responsible business conduct.* OECD. https://www.oecd.org/en/about/news/press-releases/2023/06/updated-guidelines-lift-ambition-on-responsible-business-conduct.html

Paiement, P. (2021). Transnational sustainability governance and the law. In P. Zumbansen (Ed.), *The Oxford handbook of transnational law.* Oxford University Press. https://doi.org/10.1093/oxfordhb/9780197547410.013.37

Petróleo Brasileiro S.A. (Petrobras). (2024). *Sustainability report 2024.* https://sustentabilidade.petrobras.com.br/documents/1449993/35174516/PETROBRAS_RA_SUST24_ENG_FINAL_2107_red.pdf/c169f58f-7b91-8095-2809-038dcae1b166?version=1.0&t=1753455407000&download=true

Pinto, L., & Allui, A. (2020). Critical drivers and barriers of corporate social responsibility in Saudi organisations. *Journal of Asian Finance, Economics and Business, 7*(9), 933–944.

Porter, M. E., & Kramer, M. R. (2011). Creating shared value. *Harvard Business Review, 89*(1/2), 62–77. https://hbr.org/2011/01/the-big-idea-creating-shared-value

Rechtbank Den Haag. (2021). *Milieudefensie et al. v. Royal Dutch Shell plc* (ECLI:NL:RBDHA:2021:5339). The Hague. https://uitspraken.rechtspraak.nl/#!/details?id=ECLI:NL:RBDHA:2021:5339

Sahara Reporters. (2025, September 5). *No escape for Shell: Amnesty insists oil giant must clean Niger Delta despite exit from Nigeria.* https://saharareporters.com/2025/09/05/no-escape-shell-amnesty-insists-oil-giant-must-clean-niger-delta-despite-exit-nigeria

Securities and Exchange Commission (Nigeria). (2021). *SEC guidelines on sustainable financial principles for the Nigerian capital market.* SEC. https://sec.gov.ng/documents/5/SEC-Guidelines-on-Sustainable-Financial-Principles-for-the-Capital-Market_Final.pd

Spence, D. B. (2011). Corporate social responsibility in the oil and gas industry: The importance of reputational risk. *Chicago-Kent Law Review, 86*(1), 59–85. https://scholarship.kentlaw.iit.edu/cklawreview/vol86/iss1/4

State Council of China. (2021). *Outline of the 14th Five-Year Plan for National Economic and Social Development (2021–2025).* Government of China. https://www.gov.cn/english/official/2021-03/13/content_5592681.htm

TotalEnergies. (2024). *Sustainability and climate 2024 progress report.* TotalEnergies SE. https://egyptoil-gas.com/news/totalenergies-unveils-sustainability-climate-2024-progress-report

Ubani, N. E. (2022). *A retrospective examination of Ogoniland environmental remediation in Nigeria's Niger Delta: Fundamental challenges and attendant benefits. Icheke Journal of the Faculty of Humanities, 20*(1), 1–15. https://ichekejournal.com/wp-content/uploads/2022/11/14.-A-Retrospective-Examination-of-Ogoniland-Environmental-Remediation-in-Nigerias-Niger-Delta.pdf

Ukhurebor, K. E., Athar, H., Adetunji, C. O., Aigbe, U. O., Onyancha, R. B., & Abifarin, O. (2021). Environmental implications of petroleum spillages in the Niger Delta region of Nigeria: A review. *Journal of Environmental Management, 293*, Article 112872. https://doi.org/10.1016/j.jenvman.2021.112872

United Nations. (2011). *Guiding principles on business and human rights: Implementing the United Nations Protect, Respect and Remedy framework.* https://www.ohchr.org/documents/publications/guidingprinciplesbusinesshr_en.pdf

United Nations Development Programme. (2023). *A just energy transformation beneficial for all.* UNDP. https://www.undp.org/energy/events/just-energy-transformation-beneficial-all

United Nations Environment Programme (UNEP). (2011, updated 2023). *Environmental assessment of Ogoniland.* UNEP. https://www.unep.org/ogoni

U.S. Environmental Protection Agency (EPA). (2021). *Deepwater Horizon oil spill: Response and restoration.* EPA. https://www.epa.gov/enforcement/deepwater-horizon-bp-gulf-mexico-oil-spill

U.S. Securities and Exchange Commission. (2024). *Proposed rule: The enhancement and standardisation of climate-related disclosures for investors.* SEC. https://www.sec.gov/files/rules/final/2024/33-11275.pdf

Visser, W. (2016). *The age of responsibility: CSR 2.0 and the new DNA of business.* Wiley.

Wilburn, K., & Wilburn, R. (2014). Social license to operate as a business strategy. *Organisational Cultures: An International Journal, 13*(4), 21–41. https://doi.org/10.18848/2327-8013/CGP/v13i03/50930

World Bank. (2024, February 12). *TDB and the World Bank to accelerate access to sustainable and clean energy in Africa.* World Bank Group. https://www.worldbank.org/en/news/press-release/2024/02/12/tdb-and-the-world-bank-to-accelerate-access-to-sustainable-and-clean-energy-in-afe-africa

Zhu, Q., & Zhang, Q. (2015). Evaluating practices and drivers of corporate social responsibility: The Chinese context. *Journal of Cleaner Production, 100*, 315–324. https://doi.org/10.1016/j.jclepro.2015.03.053

Chapter 7
Corporate Social Responsibility (CSR) in Other Energy Sectors: Renewables, Electricity, and Mining

7.1 Introduction

In recent years, the world has been moving quickly towards renewable and alternative energy sources, seen as essential for reducing carbon emissions and addressing climate change (International Energy Agency [IEA], 2024). However, behind this hopeful shift lies a growing awareness that problems such as environmental damage, displacement of local communities, and weak governance still occur across the broader energy industry (Cerchione et al., 2025; United Nations Environment Programme [UNEP], 2024). For instance, mining lithium for batteries or relocating communities to build hydropower and solar projects show that even *clean energy* can create new social and ecological challenges (Galvão Ferreira, 2020).

This chapter therefore expands the discussion of Corporate Social Responsibility (CSR) beyond oil and gas. It argues that CSR should serve as a shared foundation for promoting sustainability across *all* parts of the energy sector.

The main goal of this chapter is to explore how CSR is practiced and what challenges exist within renewable energy, electricity production and distribution, and the mining of critical minerals areas that are now key to global efforts to cut carbon emissions. By comparing company policies, legal rules, and community experiences, this chapter shows how CSR tools can help balance the fast growth of energy projects with the need to protect the environment over time (Paiement, 2021).

The discussion covers both industry and policy aspects, using examples from different regions such as the social impacts of wind farms in Kenya, CSR governance in Europe's electricity markets, and responsible mineral sourcing in Asia and Latin America. The chapter aims to present CSR as a broad sustainability tool that supports international regulations and climate goals.

In terms of method, it combines legal and policy analysis with real-world data and case studies to evaluate how companies can be held accountable. The chapter starts by redefining CSR beyond fossil fuels, then examines key issues in each sector, compares different CSR approaches, and finally highlights gaps in governance. These findings

J. A. Debski, *Corporate Social Responsibility in the Energy Sector*, CSR, Sustainability, Ethics & Governance, https://doi.org/10.1007/978-3-032-17748-3_7

connect directly to the experiences of host communities, which will be discussed in the following chapter.

7.2 CSR Beyond Fossil Fuels: Reframing the Debate

For a long time, discussions about environmental sustainability in the energy sector have focused mainly on oil and gas, treating these industries as the main sources of pollution and social conflict. While that focus once helped raise awareness about the damage caused by hydrocarbons, it now hides wider truth environmental problems exist across *all* types of energy production (Cerchione et al., 2025). As renewable technologies grow and demand for minerals rises, the conversation about sustainability needs to move beyond carbon emissions to include broader corporate responsibility. Corporate Social Responsibility (CSR), which used to be seen mainly as a way for oil and gas companies to offset their impact, has now become an important tool for ensuring that the push for clean energy does not repeat old injustices under a "green" label (UNEP, 2024).

7.2.1 The Persistence of Externalities Across Energy Forms

Every kind of energy fossil-based, renewable, or hybrid creates environmental and social side effects. Wind farms can disturb bird migration and take up large rural spaces (International Renewable Energy Agency [IRENA], 2024). Solar panels create waste after their lifespan ends, hydropower dams alter rivers and displace people, and mining for lithium, cobalt, and nickel pollutes soil and water (European Commission, 2023b). These examples show that the real problem is not the *type* of energy but how it is produced and managed.

7.2.2 CSR as a Cross-Sectoral Instrument

Given these widespread impacts, CSR needs to evolve from a tool used only in certain industries into a shared governance approach across all energy sectors. The International Energy Agency (2024) emphasises that as energy systems become more diverse, corporate accountability should cover environmental, social, and governance (ESG) issues throughout the entire supply chain from resource extraction to waste disposal. This shift involves three main changes in thinking.

First, CSR should take a *life-cycle approach*, looking at the full journey of energy products from how resources are sourced to how waste is managed after use. For example, the European Union's Battery Regulation (2023/1542) now requires companies to check their entire supply chain for responsible mineral sourcing, showing how CSR principles are being written into law (European Commission, 2023a).

Second, CSR should be *locally inclusive.* Many renewable and mining projects are based in developing countries where laws are weak and communities get few benefits (Paiement, 2021). True CSR means involving local people in project design and decision-making, ensuring they have a real voice in how resources are managed.

Third, CSR must *align with national and global sustainability goals.* Corporate actions should work together with public environmental policies, supporting the aims of the Paris Agreement and the United Nations Sustainable Development Goals (SDGs 7 and 12), rather than replacing government efforts.

7.2.3 Neglect in Academic and Policy Discourses

Even with the rapid growth of renewable energy and mineral extraction, most academic and policy discussions about CSR still focus heavily on fossil fuels. A UNEP (2024) review shows that between 2000 and 2022, more than 70% of CSR-energy research centred on oil and gas, while less than 10% examined renewable energy. This gap leaves little understanding of the ethical and governance issues facing new energy industries. It also feeds the illusion that clean energy is automatically sustainable, delaying the development of CSR standards for new technologies such as hydrogen, bioenergy, and energy storage.

The rising demand for critical minerals further exposes this gap. The International Energy Agency (2025) predicts that global demand for lithium and cobalt will increase five times by 2040, which will increase mining pressures in sensitive areas, especially in Latin America and Africa. Yet CSR reporting among mining companies that supply materials for renewable energy remains irregular and mostly voluntary. Without clear and enforceable transparency rules, the shift to green energy could create a new form of *resource colonialism.*

7.2.4 Empirical Indicators and Emerging Responses

Recent policies show that some progress is being made. The OECD's *Due Diligence Guidance for Responsible Supply Chains* of Minerals from Conflict-Affected and High-Risk Areas (2016) and the European Union's *Critical Raw Materials Act* (2024) include CSR-based requirements on human rights, labour conditions, and environmental protection. Big companies like Tesla, Siemens Gamesa, and Build Your Dreams Auto now publish detailed sustainability reports that include data on carbon emissions, community investments, and waste recycling (IEA, 2024). Still, smaller renewable-energy and mining firms often lack the capacity to apply CSR in a meaningful way.

Data from the IEA (2024) show that more than 80% of major oil companies produce sustainability reports following the Global Reporting Initiative (GRI) guidelines, while fewer than 35% of renewable-energy firms do the same. This difference highlights a major gap the practice and discussion of CSR have not yet caught up with the diversification of the global energy sector.

Looking at CSR beyond fossil fuels shows that sustainability problems are not limited to one industry, they are system-wide. Whether a company is drilling oil, mining lithium, or producing solar panels, it operates within the same environmental limits and social expectations. The success of the global energy transition therefore depends not only on new technologies but also on *ethical and responsible governance* built around CSR principles.

7.3 Renewable Energy and CSR: Hidden Costs of "Green Energy"

The global shift towards renewable energy is often seen as a clear moral and environmental victory, an essential step to reduce carbon emissions and slow climate change. However, as renewable projects like solar, wind, and hydropower grow, they also bring new ethical, social, and environmental challenges. These include land displacement, loss of biodiversity, and the growing problem of waste from energy technologies (IEA, 2024). In this context, Corporate Social Responsibility (CSR) is not just an optional practice but a key part of ensuring that the transition to green energy is fair, inclusive, and truly sustainable.

7.3.1 Solar Power: Clean Energy, Dirty Footprints

Solar energy represents the promise of clean and endless electricity, but its production and disposal tell a more complicated story. Making solar panels involves the use of toxic materials like cadmium telluride and silicon tetrachloride, while old or damaged panels generate massive amounts of non-biodegradable waste (European Environment Agency [EEA], 2024). The International Renewable Energy Agency (IRENA, 2024) predicts that by 2050, solar panel waste could reach over 78 million metric tons worldwide, posing serious recycling and waste management challenges.

In many parts of the world, recycling systems are weak, and informal waste handlers often work in unsafe conditions (UNEP, 2024). CSR policies must therefore focus on worker safety and encourage innovations in recycling and circular economy practices. Some large companies like First Solar and Trina Solar have started taking responsibility by collecting old panels for recycling and investing in safe dismantling technologies (IEA, 2024). However, smaller companies, especially in developing countries, often lack the means to do so. The European Union's Waste Electrical and Electronic Equipment (WEEE) Directive, which makes recycling and producer responsibility compulsory, is considered a leading CSR model in this area (European Commission, 2023b).

Large-scale solar farms also create social problems. In Rajasthan, India, for example, the Bhadla Solar Park the largest in Asia has been criticised for taking over grazing lands used by local herders, leading to the loss of livelihoods without proper consultation or compensation (Singh et al., 2024). Such cases show that the “green transition” must not sacrifice social justice for environmental gains. Genuine CSR means including affected communities in decision-making, ensuring fair compensation, and planning land use in ways that protect both livelihoods and the environment.

7.3.2 Wind Energy: Environmental Gains and Social Frictions

Wind power is often praised as one of the cleanest forms of energy, yet it also creates environmental and social tensions. Wind farms can disrupt ecosystems, produce noise, and change the visual character of rural and coastal areas (IRENA, 2024). Although each turbine may seem harmless, the cumulative impact of many can fragment habitats and affect wildlife.

A strong example is the Lake Turkana Wind Power Project in Kenya Africa’s largest wind farm. Despite being financed by global investors and promising economic growth, the project revealed several CSR shortcomings. Reports cited weak environmental assessments, inadequate consultation, and contested land acquisition (Simberg-Koulumies, 2024). Local communities in Turkana said they lost access to ancestral lands and received little benefit from the project’s profits. Although a community fund was later created, it came only after public criticism, showing that CSR was reactive rather than proactive.

To avoid such outcomes, CSR in the wind sector should focus on *anticipatory engagement* involving communities early and ensuring shared benefits. Mechanisms like community ownership, benefit-sharing agreements, and grievance systems can help transform CSR from charity into true partnership. Denmark and Germany have successfully used these approaches by allowing local residents to co-own wind farms, creating trust and shared prosperity (Cerchione et al., 2025).

Another growing concern involves wind-turbine blades, which are made of fibreglass and composites that are difficult to recycle. By 2030, over 200,000 tons of blade waste may pile up annually (IEA, 2024). The lack of recycling options shows that even renewable energy systems can produce new environmental problems precisely the kind that CSR is meant to prevent.

7.3.3 Hydropower: Clean Electricity, Displaced Communities

Hydropower generates more than 16% of global electricity, making it the largest source of renewable energy (IEA, 2024). Yet, its social and environmental consequences can be severe. The Belo Monte Dam in Brazil is a striking example. While built to provide sustainable power, it displaced over 20,000 people, mainly Indigenous groups living along the Xingu River (Pezzuti et al., 2024). It also damaged fisheries, changed river flows, and increased deforestation in surrounding rainforests. Investigations by the Inter-American Commission on Human Rights found violations of Indigenous consultation rights under the International Labour Organisation (ILO) Convention (Pezzuti et al., 2024).

CSR in hydropower should therefore move beyond compensation after displacement. It must be based on *rights and participation*, ensuring Free, Prior, and Informed Consent (FPIC) and continuous environmental monitoring. Companies such as Statkraft (Norway) and Sinohydro (China) have begun updating their CSR policies to include FPIC and ecosystem restoration (OECD, 2023), though their implementation varies greatly between countries.

Hydropower also reflects the tension between national development goals and local rights. Governments often promote dams as signs of progress, while local people see them as unfair sacrifices. CSR can help bridge this divide by ensuring transparency, fair compensation, and inclusive governance that respects both national and community interests.

7.3.4 The Policy and Governance Nexus

At the policy level, CSR is increasingly being built into renewable energy laws and financing programmes. The European Green Deal (2019) and the U.S. Inflation Reduction Act (2022), for example, require companies to disclose their environmental and social impacts as part of receiving state support (European Commission, 2023a). Similarly, the African Development Bank (2023) has introduced a Just Energy Transition Framework that requires developers to include CSR indicators such as community benefit plans, environmental risk control, and gender inclusion in their projects. These policies mark a shift from voluntary CSR to *regulated accountability* in sustainable finance systems (Paiement, 2021).

7.4 CSR in the Electricity Sector: Governance and Energy Justice

The electricity sector plays a key role in the global move towards cleaner energy. It connects the production of energy to its everyday use in homes, businesses, and industries. As many countries work to reduce carbon emissions through renewable energy, modern power grids, and electric vehicles, new sustainability issues have emerged. Corporate Social Responsibility (CSR) has therefore become an important framework for promoting responsible corporate behaviour, guiding government policy, and meeting public expectations in the electricity industry (International Energy Agency [IEA], 2024).

However, the practice of CSR in this sector is still inconsistent. Some companies adopt strong sustainability goals, while others ignore key social and governance issues such as fairness, access, and accountability.

7.4.1 Governance Challenges in Electricity CSR

The electricity sector is highly complex, covering generation, transmission, distribution, and retail. This structure creates unique challenges for CSR. Unlike the oil and gas industry, electricity is now often managed through a mix of public and private players private utilities, independent producers, and state-owned companies each operating under different laws and CSR expectations (D'Orazio & Vasishtha, 2024).

Traditionally, companies have focused on environmental issues like reducing emissions or improving energy efficiency. Yet, social aspects such as affordability, customer rights, and community involvement often receive less attention (Kourula et al., 2017). In many developing countries, the privatisation of electricity has led to higher tariffs, unreliable service, and the neglect of rural areas, which damages public trust (Estrin & Pelletier, 2018). For CSR to be meaningful, electricity companies must aim to serve the public interest, not just shareholder profit.

Governance problems are most visible in power transmission and distribution. Outdated systems and weak regulation often lead to huge energy losses and safety risks. In sub-Saharan Africa, for example, 15–20% of generated electricity is lost before reaching consumers, causing both financial and environmental harm (African Development Bank [AfDB], 2024). Despite this, many CSR reports ignore such issues. In contrast, electricity firms in Europe guided by the EU Corporate Sustainability Reporting Directive (2024) are required to report detailed environmental, social, and governance (ESG) data, including community and stakeholder impacts (European Commission, 2024).

7.4.2 *Regulatory and Policy Developments*

Across the world, the governance of CSR in electricity is changing due to stricter regulations and investor demands. In the European Union, electricity firms now report CSR data under the Sustainable Finance Disclosure Regulation (SFDR) and the Corporate Sustainability Due Diligence Directive (CSDDD). These require companies to disclose how they handle human rights, environmental risks, and supply-chain responsibilities (European Commission, 2024). This shift marks a move from voluntary CSR to legally enforced sustainability.

By contrast, many developing countries still depend on voluntary CSR or loose public–private partnerships. For instance, Nigeria's Electric Power Sector Reform Act (EPSRA) 2005 promotes CSR through community electrification programmes but does not make CSR a legal duty (Estrin & Pelletier, 2018). Similarly, India's Companies Act (2013) requires companies to spend a portion of profits on CSR but does not include clear indicators for electricity utilities (Upadhyay, 2017).

New frameworks, such as the African Union's Continental Power System Master Plan (2024) and the International Renewable Energy Agency's (IRENA) Just Energy Transition Framework (2024), are now linking electricity expansion with justice and fairness principles. Still, many of these plans struggle in practice because of weak institutions and poor coordination between corporate goals and national sustainability strategies.

7.5 CSR in the Mining of Critical Minerals

The shift towards clean energy has made minerals such as lithium, cobalt, nickel, and rare earth elements extremely important. These resources are vital for renewable technologies, electric vehicles, and battery storage systems (International Energy Agency [IEA], 2023). However, the rapid increase in their extraction has created new sustainability and governance problems many of which are just as serious as those in the oil and gas industry. As global demand rises, issues of ethical sourcing, environmental damage, and social fairness have become central to Corporate Social Responsibility (CSR) in the mining sector (Berthet et al., 2024; Li et al., 2025).

7.5.1 *The Paradox of Green Minerals*

Although critical minerals are often described as key to reducing carbon emissions, their extraction is far from environmentally friendly. For example, lithium mining in South America's "Lithium Triangle" (Chile, Argentina, and Bolivia) has led to water shortages, soil damage, and the displacement of local communities because of intensive water use in salt flat regions (Bainton & Holcombe, 2018). In the Democratic

Republic of Congo (DRC), which provides more than 70% of the world's cobalt, mining operations have been linked to child labour, unsafe working conditions, and pollution (Ulimwengu & Sanginga, 2025).

These examples show that while critical minerals are essential for clean energy, their production can create serious social and environmental harm. To truly support sustainability, CSR must go beyond carbon goals and include strong commitments to human rights, community well-being, and ecological balance.

7.5.2 CSR Frameworks and Regulatory Responses

In response to these challenges, several global frameworks have emerged to guide responsible mineral sourcing. The *OECD Due Diligence Guidance for Responsible Supply Chains of Minerals from Conflict-Affected and High-Risk Areas* (2016) gives companies a clear process to identify and reduce risks related to human rights and environmental impacts. Similarly, the European Union's *Battery Regulation (EU 2023/1542)* requires manufacturers and importers to prove that their materials are sourced responsibly, with transparency across the supply chain and proper recycling of batteries (European Commission, 2023b).

Other global initiatives, such as the Global Battery Alliance and the Extractive Industries Transparency Initiative (EITI), promote openness, traceability, and community participation in mineral supply chains (Galvão Ferreira, 2020). Together, these frameworks represent a major shift in CSR from voluntary donations or public-relations exercises to a more structured, rule-based approach integrated into trade and environmental policy.

However, putting these frameworks into action is still difficult. Many resource-rich countries such as the DRC, Indonesia, and Zambia lack strong national laws to ensure compliance (Hilson & Maconachie, 2020). This creates a *governance gap* between what multinational corporations claim to do and what local governments can actually enforce.

7.5.3 Environmental and Social Dimensions of Responsibility

CSR in mining is usually assessed in three connected areas: environmental care, social fairness, and transparent governance (Carroll & Brown, 2018). Environmentally responsible mining means proper water management, waste control, and protecting biodiversity. Yet, these goals often fail due to weak environmental reviews and poor law enforcement.

Social responsibility involves fair labour practices, meaningful dialogue with host communities, and a fair share of benefits. Unfortunately, many companies practice what researchers call "CSR minimalism", focusing on small, visible projects like donating school buildings or clinics while ignoring deeper issues such as land rights, gender inequality, or fair compensation (Cerchione et al., 2025; Jenkins et al., 2018).

Good governance also depends on transparent reporting and independent verification. Standards like the Global Reporting Initiative (GRI) and the Task Force on Climate-Related Financial Disclosures (TCFD) help companies report sustainability results in consistent ways. But without strong laws to enforce these reports, CSR often becomes more about ticking boxes than making real change (Berthet et al., 2024).

7.5.4 Comparative CSR Practices: Global North and South

CSR in the mining of critical minerals looks very different across regions. In the Global North especially the European Union companies must follow strict reporting requirements such as the *Corporate Sustainability Reporting Directive (CSRD)* (European Commission, 2023a). These rules force companies to disclose social and environmental impacts along their entire supply chains, indirectly pressuring suppliers in developing countries to do better.

In contrast, CSR in the Global South often mixes traditional community development with new sustainability goals. In countries like Nigeria, Zambia, and Indonesia, extractive companies often operate in places where government services are weak. As a result, CSR is used to provide basic infrastructure like water or roads instead of serving as a real accountability system (Hilson & Maconachie, 2020).

This imbalance between North and South shows why a more inclusive approach to CSR is needed. Stronger cooperation among governments, corporations, and civil society can help ensure that the green mineral boom benefits local communities instead of deepening inequality.

7.5.5 Towards Ethical and Sustainable Mining Transitions

The demand for critical minerals is expected to grow sixfold by 2040 if current net-zero policies continue (IEA, 2023). For this expansion to be sustainable, CSR must become a central part of mining operations not just a public relations tool. Companies that truly integrate environmental, social, and governance (ESG) principles into their business models can help build a fairer and more sustainable global energy system.

Transparency, traceability, and community involvement will be key to maintaining public trust. In the long run, CSR in the mining of critical minerals reflects a deeper ethical challenge: how to achieve clean energy without repeating the injustices of past extractive industries. The goal is not only technological progress but also moral responsibility ensuring that the transition to green energy respects both the planet and the people who depend on it.

7.6 Comparative CSR Models Across Energy Sectors

Corporate Social Responsibility (CSR) has become a central governance instrument across the global energy landscape, though its meaning and application differ markedly between sectors. These differences arise from the unique industrial structures, policy frameworks, and socio-political contexts that shape each energy domain (Carroll & Brown, 2018; Cerchione et al., 2025). While the fossil-fuel industry provided the earliest and most studied examples of CSR, the rapid diversification of the world's energy systems driven by decarbonisation and technological innovation has produced distinct CSR approaches in renewable energy, electricity, and mining. Building on the preceding discussion of sectoral CSR challenges, this section examines these variations comparatively, identifying both shared trends and sector-specific patterns in corporate responsibility and governance.

7.6.1 CSR Archetypes Across Energy Sectors

In the oil and gas sector, CSR has historically followed a reactive and compensatory model. Many companies adopted CSR primarily as a form of reputational management responding to environmental degradation, community unrest, and mounting global scrutiny (Jenkins et al., 2018). Common initiatives include community development projects, environmental remediation, and philanthropic donations, often undertaken independently of core business activities (Hilson & Maconachie, 2020). This legacy form of CSR reflects an extractivist logic rooted more in damage control than in long-term transformation.

The renewable energy industry, by contrast, tends to promote a more proactive and integrated CSR model. Because renewables are closely linked with sustainability and climate goals, companies in this sector often emphasise ethical governance, transparent supply chains, and enduring partnerships with host communities (UNEP, 2024). However, the image of renewables as inherently sustainable can obscure difficult trade-offs, such as land acquisition for wind or solar farms and population displacement caused by hydroelectric projects (Berthet et al., 2024). CSR in renewables therefore embodies a complex balance between genuine sustainability and the need to manage the unintended consequences of "green" development.

The electricity sector presents a hybrid model centred on governance, service delivery, and what has come to be known as "energy justice". Whether publicly or privately owned, electricity utilities operate within heavily regulated systems where CSR focuses on the accessibility, affordability, and reliability of power (IEA, 2024). In this context, CSR becomes a tool to promote fairness in energy distribution and to address inequalities that hinder inclusive development (McCauley, 2018). For example, following Nigeria's power sector privatisation, CSR programmes have concentrated on rural electrification and subsidised tariffs for low-income consumers. In the European Union, the Clean Energy Package mandates consumer protection and encourages community involvement in energy governance (European Commission, 2023b).

Mining for critical minerals essential to renewable technologies such as batteries and wind turbines follows a supply chain–oriented CSR approach. Firms in this sector rely on global frameworks such as the OECD Due Diligence Guidance and the Extractive Industries Transparency Initiative (EITI) to ensure responsible sourcing, ethical labour practices, and traceable supply chains (Galvão Ferreira, 2020). Unlike community-based CSR in fossil fuels or utilities, this model operates across borders, linking local mining practices to international standards, investor expectations, and sustainability reporting. CSR in mining thus represents a transnational form of responsibility embedded in the architecture of sustainable finance and environmental, social, and governance (ESG) regimes.

7.6.2 Convergence and Divergence

Despite sectoral differences, several unifying trends are visible. CSR has shifted from being an entirely voluntary practice to a more formalised component of governance through soft-law instruments and hybrid regulatory frameworks (Paul & Parra, 2021). Global standards such as the Global Reporting Initiative (GRI), the Task Force on Climate-Related Financial Disclosures (TCFD), and ISO 26000 have encouraged companies to adopt comparable sustainability reporting and accountability mechanisms. At the same time, the stakeholder governance model where businesses are expected to balance profit with broader social and environmental responsibilities has gained widespread acceptance (Carroll & Brown, 2018).

Nevertheless, meaningful divergences remain. CSR in fossil fuels continues to revolve around environmental mitigation and compensation, while renewables prioritise climate alignment and ethical branding. Electricity-sector CSR centres on equity and public trust, and mining-sector CSR emphasises due diligence and supply chain integrity (Cerchione et al., 2025; Jenkins et al., 2018). These differences are influenced by each sector's risk exposure, regulatory context, and visibility of impact. For instance, mining faces upstream risks such as labour exploitation and environmental harm, whereas the electricity sector's challenges lie downstream in ensuring fair pricing, consumer protection, and reliable service.

7.6.3 Regional Contrasts and Governance Capacities

CSR implementation also varies across regions, reflecting differing levels of institutional maturity and civic participation. In the European Union, CSR has become semi-mandatory through instruments such as the Corporate Sustainability Reporting Directive (CSRD), which integrates non-financial reporting into corporate disclosure obligations (European Commission, 2023a). In the United States, CSR has evolved under the influence of ESG investing, with stock exchanges and institutional investors increasingly demanding evidence-based sustainability performance (Camilleri, 2017).

In contrast, CSR in Sub-Saharan Africa and South Asia often serves developmental functions, compensating for weak state capacity and limited infrastructure. In these regions, extractive and electricity firms frequently step in to provide basic services such as schools, hospitals, and electrification projects that governments cannot deliver effectively (Hilson & Maconachie, 2020). While such initiatives yield short-term social benefits, they risk fostering dependency and reinforcing corporate dominance if not implemented through transparent, participatory governance structures.

7.7 Challenges and Gaps

Although Corporate Social Responsibility (CSR) is now widely practiced across the global energy industry, major challenges remain in turning these commitments into real environmental and social results. Many of these challenges are connected to weak laws, limited community involvement, and poor coordination between sectors. This section highlights the main gaps that still limit the impact of CSR in renewable energy, electricity, and mining industries, focusing on governance, data, participation, and policy alignment.

7.7.1 Regulatory Fragmentation and Weak Enforcement

A major problem facing CSR in the energy sector is the lack of common and enforceable standards. In many countries, CSR is still voluntary, which leads to uneven implementation and reporting (Paul & Parra, 2021). While regions such as the European Union (EU) have introduced mandatory sustainability rules through the Corporate Sustainability Reporting Directive (CSRD) and green taxonomy policies, several developing nations such as Nigeria, Indonesia, and the Democratic Republic of Congo still lack effective monitoring systems (European Commission, 2023a; Hilson & Maconachie, 2020).

This creates what some scholars call *CSR arbitrage*, where companies adjust their level of commitment based on how strict local laws are (Jenkins et al., 2018). Multinational corporations often follow high standards in Europe or North America but take minimal action in countries where regulations are weak. This situation turns CSR into more of a reputation tool than a real instrument of accountability, reinforcing existing inequalities in global energy governance (Berthet et al., 2024).

7.7.2 Data Transparency and Accountability Deficits

Another major weakness is the lack of reliable and comparable data for assessing CSR outcomes. Even though global frameworks like the Global Reporting Initiative (GRI) and the Task Force on Climate-related Financial Disclosures (TCFD) encourage standard reporting, most disclosures remain self-assessed and rarely verified by independent auditors (Cerchione et al., 2025).

In renewable energy, companies often report expected benefits rather than real results using projections of carbon savings or unverified social benefits (UNEP, 2024). In the mining of critical minerals, many firms still struggle with tracing supply chains and monitoring subcontractors (Hilson & Maconachie, 2020). This lack of credible, third-party data reduces public trust and limits governments and investors from holding firms accountable for their CSR claims.

7.7.3 Limited Host Community Participation

CSR projects frequently fail to include meaningful participation from host communities, especially in the Global South where local governance is weak (Bainton & Holcombe, 2018; Hilson & Maconachie, 2020). Community consultations are often symbolic, giving people little influence over decisions or benefit-sharing.

Large renewable projects, such as solar or wind farms, have sometimes displaced communities without fair compensation or long-term engagement (Berthet et al., 2024). In mining areas, women and other marginalised groups are often excluded from CSR planning and decision-making (UNDP, 2023). This lack of participation weakens trust, reduces the legitimacy of CSR projects, and contradicts the core idea of *procedural justice* that guides fair energy transitions (McCauley, 2018).

7.7.4 Policy Incoherence and Cross-Sectoral Disconnect

Many CSR efforts fail because energy, environmental, and social policies are not properly coordinated. In several countries, different government agencies work in isolation, creating overlaps or contradictions (IEA, 2024). For example, renewable energy policies might promote large-scale solar projects but ignore their local ecological impacts, while mining policies focused on foreign investment can reduce environmental safeguards (Li et al., 2025).

This lack of policy alignment allows companies to operate in grey areas where CSR obligations are unclear. Without proper coordination between CSR laws, environmental rules, and energy strategies, CSR becomes fragmented and less capable of driving real sustainability (Paul & Parra, 2021).

7.7.5 Greenwashing and Symbolic CSR

As CSR spreads into renewable and "green" sectors, new risks of *greenwashing* have emerged where companies use sustainability rhetoric to appear responsible without changing harmful practices (Carroll & Brown, 2018; Cerchione et al., 2025). For instance, firms may highlight their clean energy investments while ignoring water use in lithium mining or pollution from manufacturing solar panels (Berthet et al., 2024).

This type of symbolic CSR weakens the concept's transformative value, shifting focus from real performance to image management. Since ESG (Environmental, Social, and Governance) metrics are now tied to investor confidence, some firms also manipulate data or use selective reporting to improve rankings (Li et al., 2025). The real task is ensuring CSR reports reflect measurable and context-sensitive progress, not just marketing narratives.

7.7.6 Capacity and Resource Constraints in Developing Economies

Developing countries face additional barriers due to limited institutional capacity. Many regulators lack the funds, expertise, or independence to monitor CSR effectively (Hilson & Maconachie, 2020). In such cases, corporations often step in to fill the gap building schools, hospitals, or roads but these actions are usually short-term and not aligned with national development goals.

This dependence creates a cycle where communities rely on corporate generosity instead of enforceable rights. Nigeria's experience shows that despite heavy CSR spending by oil and electricity firms, poverty and environmental damage persist because projects are poorly coordinated with government plans (UNDP, 2023). Similar trends appear in Zambia's mining regions and India's coal-dependent states.

7.7.7 Lack of Integration Between CSR and Energy Transition Frameworks

Finally, CSR policies often fail to connect directly with global energy transition goals. Although many companies reference the Paris Agreement or Sustainable Development Goals (SDGs), these are rarely translated into concrete targets or operational plans (IEA, 2024). Most CSR programmes remain short-term, focused on isolated projects rather than broader systems change (Berthet et al., 2024).

To make CSR truly effective, it needs to be embedded in national energy transition strategies integrating decarbonisation, ethical supply chains, and social inclusion as core business commitments. Only then can CSR evolve from a voluntary gesture into a central tool for achieving sustainable and fair energy systems.

7.8 Conclusion

This chapter has explored how Corporate Social Responsibility (CSR) has developed and operated across different parts of the global energy industry, focusing on its links to governance, sustainability, and energy justice. From the extractive and mining sectors to renewable and electricity industries, CSR has become an important but often debated tool for promoting responsible corporate behaviour. Originally introduced as a voluntary and philanthropic concept, CSR has gradually taken on a more structured and regulatory role, promoting environmental care, social inclusion, and ethical business conduct (Carroll & Brown, 2018; Paul & Parra, 2021).

The comparison across sectors revealed that while CSR principles share common goals, their application differs. In mining and other extractive industries, CSR programmes are usually aimed at managing conflicts, repairing environmental damage, and maintaining companies' social licences to operate. However, these initiatives often remain reactive and controlled by corporations, showing persistent power imbalances and weak oversight in host countries (Hilson & Maconachie, 2020). In contrast, the renewable energy sector presents CSR as a forward-thinking and climate-centred approach that supports innovation, decarbonisation, and inclusive growth (Cerchione et al., 2025). Still, this sector also faces contradictions, such as disputes over land, environmental disturbances, and unfair decision-making processes that often disadvantage local communities (Berthet et al., 2024).

In the electricity sector, CSR serves as a link between corporate governance and the goal of improving energy access and affordability. The effort to combine CSR with energy justice especially fairness in distribution and participation reflects growing awareness that sustainability must also involve equality and community voice (McCauley, 2018). However, ongoing policy and institutional fragmentation continue to limit CSR's ability to produce deep, long-term change.

The section on challenges and gaps highlighted several major problems: uneven regulations, weak enforcement, limited data transparency, shallow community engagement, and misleading sustainability claims. These issues show the ongoing struggle between CSR's voluntary origins and the rising global expectation for corporations to take real accountability for their social and environmental impacts. In developing countries, particularly across Africa and parts of Asia, poor institutional capacity and policy misalignment make it even harder for CSR to achieve its development goals (UNDP, 2023).

Despite these limits, CSR continues to serve as a valuable space for innovation, learning, and dialogue among stakeholders. Its flexibility allows it to adapt to different national and cultural settings, while its global recognition makes it a useful framework for aligning corporate practices with global sustainability goals like the Paris

Agreement and the Sustainable Development Goals (SDGs) (European Commission, 2023a; IEA, 2024). The central question is therefore not whether CSR should continue, but how it can evolve moving from a voluntary and image-based model to one that is law-driven, participatory, and focused on justice.

A truly transformative CSR model in the energy sector would make transparency, fairness, and accountability key pillars of governance. This means aligning laws across different countries, ensuring that communities actively participate in decision-making, promoting cooperation across sectors, and requiring independent verification of sustainability claims. As CSR shifts from being an act of charity to a policy instrument, its success will depend on measurable social progress and the ability of local communities to become partners in governance rather than passive recipients of benefits.

In the end, CSR in the energy sector reflects a powerful paradox it is both a product of global corporate growth and a possible solution to its negative consequences. Its credibility in the future will depend on how well it balances profit with public good, turning CSR from a statement of responsibility into a practice rooted in justice and shared sustainability.

This naturally leads to Chapter 8, which looks more closely at how CSR actually affects host communities and the environment. While this chapter focused on governance and institutional issues, the next one explores real-world experiences examining whether CSR activities in oil, gas, electricity, and renewable energy truly promote environmental recovery, social welfare, and sustainable community development.

References

African Development Bank. (2023). *Just energy transition framework.* Abidjan: AfDB. https://www.afdb.org/sites/default/files/documents/publications/just_transition_-_18-09-2023.pdf

Amnesty International. (2022). *Powering change: Principles for businesses and governments in the battery value chain.* London: Amnesty International. https://www.amnesty.org/en/documents/ACT30/3544/2021/en/#:~:text=This%20paper%20lays%20out%20the%20principles%20that%20businesses,and%20other%20human%20rights-consistent%20solutions%20to%20climate%20change

Bainton, N., & Holcombe, S. (2018). A critical review of the social aspects of mine closure. *Resources Policy, 59*, 468–478. https://doi.org/10.1016/j.resourpol.2018.08.020

Berthet, E., Lavalley, J., Anquetil-Deck, C., Ballesteros, F., Stadler, K., Soytas, U., Hauschild, M., & Laurent, A. (2024). Assessing the social and environmental impacts of critical mineral supply chains for the energy transition in Europe. *Global Environmental Change, 86*, Article 102841. https://doi.org/10.1016/j.gloenvcha.2024.102841

Camilleri, M. A. (2017). Corporate social responsibility policy in the United States of America. In M. A. Camilleri (Ed.), *Corporate sustainability, social responsibility and environmental management: An introduction to theory and practice with case studies* (pp. 129–143). Springer. https://doi.org/10.1007/978-3-319-52839-7_7

Cerchione, R., Morelli, M., Passaro, R., & Quinto, I. (2025). Balancing sustainability and circular justice: The challenge of the energy transition. *Journal of Cleaner Production, 494*, Article 144942. https://doi.org/10.1016/j.jclepro.2025.144942

Carroll, A. B., & Brown, J. A. (2018). Corporate social responsibility: A review of current concepts, research, and issues. In J. Weber & D. Wasieleski (Eds.), *Corporate social responsibility* (pp. 39–68). Emerald Group Publishing. https://doi.org/10.1108/S2514-175920180000002002

D'Orazio, P., & Vasishtha, G. (2024). Critical minerals and the low-carbon transition: Economic implications for emerging markets and developing economies. *Energy Proceedings, 45, Part VIII*. https://doi.org/10.46855/energy-proceedings-11093

Estrin, S., & Pelletier, A. (2018). Privatisation in developing countries: What are the lessons of recent experience? *The World Bank Research Observer, 33*(1), 65–102. https://doi.org/10.1093/wbro/lkx007

European Commission. (2023a). *Corporate Sustainability Reporting Directive (CSRD), Directive (EU) 2022/2464*. Official Journal of the European Union. https://eur-lex.europa.eu/legal-content/EN/TXT/?uri=CELEX%3A32022L2464

European Commission. (2023b). *Regulation (EU) 2023/1542 on batteries and waste batteries*. Official Journal of the European Union. https://eur-lex.europa.eu/eli/reg/2023/1542/oj

European Commission. (2024). *Critical Raw Materials Act*. Single Market and Economy. https://single-market-economy.ec.europa.eu/sectors/raw-materials/areas-specific-interest/critical-raw-materials/critical-raw-materials-act_en

European Environment Agency. (2024). *Accelerating the circular economy in Europe: State and outlook 2024* (EEA Report No. 13/2023). Publications Office of the European Union. https://doi.org/10.2800/055236

Galvão Ferreira, P. (2020). The Extractive Industries Transparency Initiative (EITI): Using global hybrid regulation to promote domestic governance reform. In *Global hybrid and private governance: Standard-setting, market regulation, and institutional design* (Oxford University Press, forthcoming). Available at SSRN: https://ssrn.com/abstract=3559659

Hilson, G., & Maconachie, R. (2020). Artisanal and small-scale mining and the sustainable development goals: Opportunities and new directions for sub-Saharan Africa. *Geoforum, 111*, 125–141. https://doi.org/10.1016/j.geoforum.2019.09.006

International Energy Agency. (2024). *World energy outlook 2024*. Paris: IEA. https://www.iea.org/reports/world-energy-outlook-2024

International Energy Agency. (2025). *Global critical minerals outlook 2025*. https://www.iea.org/reports/global-critical-minerals-outlook-2025

International Renewable Energy Agency. (2024). *Just and inclusive energy transition*. IRENA. https://www.irena.org/How-we-work/Collaborative-frameworks/Just-and-Inclusive-Energy-Transition

International Renewable Energy Agency. (2024, July). *Renewable energy statistics 2024*. IRENA. https://www.irena.org/Publications/2024/Jul/Renewable-energy-statistics-2024

Jenkins, K., Sovacool, B. K., & McCauley, D. (2018). Humanizing sociotechnical transitions through energy justice: An ethical framework for global transformative change. *Energy Policy, 117*, 66–74. https://doi.org/10.1016/j.enpol.2018.02.036

Kourula, A., Pisani, N., & Kolk, A. (2017). Corporate sustainability and inclusive development: Highlights from international business and management research. *Current Opinion in Environmental Sustainability, 24*, 14–18. https://doi.org/10.1016/j.cosust.2017.01.003

Li, Y., Umair, M., Guliyeva, S., & Shakaraliyeva, Z. (2025). The extractive industries transparency initiative. Achieving disclosure, but falling short on corruption reduction. *The Extractive Industries and Society, 22*, Article 101602. https://doi.org/10.1016/j.exis.2024.101602

McCauley, D. (2018). *Energy justice: Re-balancing the trilemma of security, poverty and climate change*. Palgrave Macmillan. https://doi.org/10.1007/978-3-319-62494-5

OECD (2016). *OECD due diligence guidance for responsible supply chains of minerals from conflict-affected and high-risk areas: Third Edition*, OECD Publishing, Paris. https://doi.org/10.1787/9789264252479-en.

Organisation for Economic Co-operation and Development. (2023, June 8). *Updated guidelines lift ambition on responsible business conduct*. OECD. https://www.oecd.org/en/about/news/press-releases/2023/06/updated-guidelines-lift-ambition-on-responsible-business-conduct.html

Paiement, P. (2021). Transnational sustainability governance and the law. In P. Zumbansen (Ed.), *The Oxford handbook of transnational law*. Oxford University Press. https://doi.org/10.1093/oxfordhb/9780197547410.013.37

Paul, K., & Parra, C. M. (2021). Corporate social responsibility in international business literature: Results from text data mining of the *Journal of International Business Studies*. *International Journal of Corporate Social Responsibility, 6*(1), 12. https://doi.org/10.1186/s40991-021-00066-6

Pezzuti, J. C. B., Zuanon, J., Lopes, P. F. M., Carneiro, C., Sawakuchi, A. O., Montovanelli, T. R., Akama, A., Ribas, C. C., Juruna, D., & Fearnside, P. M. (2024). Brazil's Belo Monte license renewal and the need to recognize the immense impacts of dams in Amazonia. *Perspectives in Ecology and Conservation, 22*(2), 112–117. https://doi.org/10.1016/j.pecon.2024.05.001

Singh, S., Kumar, P., & Versha. (2024). Impact of Bhadla solar power plant on the rainfall: A study of western Rajasthan, India. *International Journal of Geography, Geology and Environment, 6*(2), 242–245. https://www.geojournal.net/uploads/archives/7-1-1-987.pdf

Simberg-Koulumies, N. (2024). Just sustainabilities: Lessons from the Lake Turkana wind power project in Kenya. *Local Environment, 29*(1), 40–56. https://doi.org/10.1080/13549839.2023.2249497

Ulimwengu, J. M., & Sanginga, B. (2025). The complex economics of a complete ban on child labor in the cobalt supply chain: The case of the DR Congo. *The Extractive Industries and Society, 23*, Article 101687. https://doi.org/10.1016/j.exis.2025.101687

United Nations Development Programme. (2023). *Human development report 2023/24: Breaking the gridlock—Reimagining cooperation in a polarized world*. New York: UNDP. https://hdr.undp.org/content/human-development-report-2023-24

United Nations Environment Programme. (2024, February 19). *What are energy transition minerals and how can they unlock the clean energy age?* https://www.unep.org/news-and-stories/story/what-are-energy-transition-minerals-and-how-can-they-unlock-clean-energy-age

United Nations Environment Programme. (2025, February). *We are all in this together: Annual Report 2024*. https://wedocs.unep.org/20.500.11822/47082

United Nations Environment Programme. (2024). *Emissions Gap Report 2024: No more hot air … please!* https://wedocs.unep.org/bitstream/handle/20.500.11822/46404/EGR2024.pdf?sequence=3&isAllowed=y

United Nations Environment Programme & International Resource Panel. (2024). *Global resources outlook 2024: Bend the trend—Pathways to a liveable planet as resource use spikes* (PDF). https://wedocs.unep.org/bitstream/handle/20.500.11822/44901/Global-Resource-Outlook_2024.pdf?sequence=3&isAllowed=y

Upadhyay, C. S. M. K. (2017). The Indian Company's Act 2013—A boon or bane to sustainable development. *IOSR Journal of Business and Management (IOSR-JBM), 19*(7, Ver. V), 08–16.

Chapter 8
Host Communities and Environmental Sustainability Impacts in the Energy Sector

8.1 Introduction

Communities that host energy-sector projects whether involving oil and gas extraction, hydropower dams, wind farms, solar installations, or the mining of critical minerals are increasingly recognised as pivotal actors in achieving a sustainable global energy transition. Historically, academic and policy attention has centred largely on host communities in the oil and gas sector (Ediagbonya, 2023). However, this chapter broadens the analytical lens to encompass the full energy landscape, including renewable energy systems, electricity infrastructure, and extractive operations. The overarching aim is to explore how host-community relationships both influence and are influenced by environmental sustainability across diverse energy value chains.

Specifically, this chapter examines four key themes:

1. How host communities are defined and engaged across different segments of the energy sector;
2. The environmental sustainability challenges these communities face such as land-use change, displacement, pollution, and the equitable sharing of benefits (Kaze et al., 2025; Lennon, 2019);
3. The evolving governance and legal frameworks that shape the interaction between energy projects and local communities (Adeshina et al., 2024); and
4. Case studies from developing-country contexts, with a particular focus on Nigeria, that illustrate both effective and problematic practices.

This inquiry is timely and significant. Global energy systems are undergoing profound transformation, marked by the transition from fossil fuels to renewable sources, the expansion of decentralised electricity systems, and the intensifying demand for minerals critical to green technologies. Amid these shifts, host-community dynamics remain central to securing a social licence to operate, ensuring

J. A. Debski, *Corporate Social Responsibility in the Energy Sector*, CSR, Sustainability, Ethics & Governance, https://doi.org/10.1007/978-3-032-17748-3_8

fair benefit distribution, and achieving genuinely sustainable outcomes. In particular, community-based renewable energy initiatives depend on local participation, shared decision-making, and inclusive governance to generate both environmental and social value (Kaze et al., 2025).

The discussion in this chapter unfolds in five main parts. It begins with a conceptual clarification of the term "host communities" within the energy context, followed by an examination of key environmental and social sustainability impacts across energy sub-sectors. The next section analyses governance mechanisms, engagement practices, and legal frameworks that mediate community–industry relations. This is followed by case studies, primarily from Nigeria and comparable jurisdictions, which demonstrate the diversity of experiences and lessons learned. The chapter concludes with critical reflections and a forward linkage to Chapter 9, which focuses on multi-stakeholder governance strategies for advancing sustainability in the energy sector. Together, these discussions lay the groundwork for understanding how governments, corporations, and communities can collaborate to promote environmental sustainability within energy-sector host-community contexts.

8.2 Concept and Definition of "Host Communities" in the Energy Sector

The idea of a "host community" is not fixed; it shifts depending on the context, sector, and jurisdiction. Traditionally, the term was most closely linked to petroleum development, referring to communities situated around oil fields, gas installations, or related infrastructure. Yet, as the global energy transition accelerates, a broader and more flexible understanding has become necessary one that includes the entire energy ecosystem. This encompasses not only oil and gas but also electricity infrastructure, large-scale renewable energy projects such as wind, solar, and hydropower, as well as mining operations that supply the critical minerals required for low-carbon technologies. Consequently, the way host communities are defined varies across legal systems, industry practices, and specific policy objectives whether for determining entitlement to benefits, conducting environmental assessments, or structuring stakeholder engagement (Ipieca, 2022; Spaces for Change, 2013).

Two main approaches to defining host communities are widely recognised in both research and practice. The first is a legal or jurisdictional approach, where statutes and regulations identify which communities are entitled to particular rights or benefits. For instance, Nigeria's *Petroleum Industry Act* (PIA) of 2021, especially Chapter 3, establishes a framework for Host Communities Development Trusts to ensure that local populations benefit from petroleum operations (Petroleum Industry Act, 2021; Nigerian Upstream Petroleum Regulatory Commission [NUPRC], 2022).

The second is an impact-based or operational approach, reflected in international industry standards such as those developed by Ipieca (2022). Here, host communities are not defined strictly by geography or political boundaries but by the scope of a project's influence, its physical footprint, and its potential, social, or environmental effects. Under this broader view, host communities include those that directly host energy infrastructure, those who experience secondary effects such as pollution or restricted access to resources, and those whose livelihoods or cultural heritage are indirectly affected.

International human rights frameworks further shape how host communities should be identified and engaged. The *United Nations Declaration on the Rights of Indigenous Peoples* (UNDRIP) and the *International Labour Organisation (ILO) Convention No. 169* both affirm the rights of Indigenous and tribal peoples to consultation, cultural protection, and, where appropriate, free, prior, and informed consent (FPIC) before any development project proceeds (ILO, 1989; United Nations, 2007). While these instruments do not prescribe a single global definition of "host community", they reinforce a universal principle: affected populations must be meaningfully involved in decisions that impact their lands, resources, and livelihoods.

In practice, the boundaries of a host community in the energy sector often overlap and evolve. They typically encompass three interrelated categories:

1. **Direct host communities** those on whose land or territory the energy infrastructure is located;
2. **Neighbouring or adjacent communities** those exposed to operational effects such as noise, pollution, or reduced access to land; and
3. **Resource-dependent communities** those whose livelihoods or cultural practices rely on natural resources affected by the project, such as fishers, farmers, or pastoralists (Spaces for Change, 2013; NUPRC, 2022).

Increasingly, researchers highlight that the impacts of energy projects extend beyond their immediate sites. For example, Sonter et al. (2020) show that the global shift towards renewable energy has intensified mining for critical minerals, often in biodiverse regions, thereby extending environmental and social impacts far beyond local project boundaries.

For the purpose of this chapter and to enable meaningful cross-sector comparison, host communities are defined as:

> *Communities and social groups that (i) host energy infrastructure or extractive operations within their territory; (ii) are situated within the broader environmental or socio-economic zone of influence of such operations, including both direct and indirect effects; or (iii) depend materially or culturally on natural resources or ecosystem services significantly affected by energy activities.*

This working definition is intentionally broader than most sector-specific legal formulations. A wider framing is essential to capture the complex and evolving forms of community–industry interaction emerging in today's energy landscape from land disputes linked to solar and wind projects to displacement caused by hydropower development and biodiversity loss associated with critical-mineral mining.

Recent policy developments illustrate how definitions of host communities have tangible governance implications. In Nigeria, for instance, the *Energy Transition Plan* and the *Electricity* Act (2023) signal a growing recognition of community engagement in renewable energy and electrification programmes (Federal Government of

Nigeria, 2022; Electricity Act, 2023). Meanwhile, petroleum-specific frameworks such as the Petroleum Industry Act (2021) and its implementing guidelines (NUPRC, 2022) continue to influence eligibility for benefits, governance arrangements, and oversight mechanisms factors that directly affect inclusion, accountability, and the prevention of elite capture.

Promoting environmental sustainability across the energy sector therefore requires an inclusive, impact-sensitive understanding of host communities one informed by law but not confined by it. Such an approach makes it possible to draw coherent comparisons across oil, gas, electricity, renewables, and mining, and provides a strong foundation for equitable and integrated policy development in support of a just energy transition. The next section builds on this conceptual grounding to examine the main environmental and social sustainability challenges confronting host communities across different energy sub-sectors.

8.3 Host Communities and Environmental Sustainability Challenges Across the Energy Sector

Host communities across the global energy landscape whether in oil and gas regions, renewable energy zones, electricity infrastructure corridors, or mining districts face a complex mix of environmental and social sustainability challenges. These challenges differ in scale and character across sectors and geographies, yet they share a common thread: the unequal distribution of environmental risks and economic benefits that accompanies energy production (Bainton & Holcombe, 2018; World Bank, 2019). Historically, large energy and extractive projects have been located in areas marked by poverty, weak governance, and limited institutional oversight. This combination has made host communities especially vulnerable to ecological degradation, social displacement, and economic marginalisation (Hilson, 2020).

8.3.1 Pollution and Ecological Degradation

Pollution remains one of the most visible and persistent threats to environmental sustainability in host communities. In the oil and gas sector, spills, gas flaring, and hydrocarbon leaks contaminate water and soil, destroying farmland, fisheries, and biodiversity while causing long-term health problems for local populations (United Nations Environment Programme [UNEP], 2011). The Niger Delta stands as a tragic emblem of these challenges decades of oil production have left the region heavily polluted, with clean-up and remediation processes progressing slowly and compensation often inadequate (Bamidele & Erameh, 2023).

Mining activities linked to the energy transition present a new generation of environmental risks. The extraction of critical minerals such as cobalt, lithium, and rare earth elements vital for renewable technologies has been associated with deforestation, toxic waste discharge, and habitat destruction (Ulimwengu & Sanginga, 2025).

Even renewable energy projects, often regarded as inherently "green", can generate unintended ecological consequences. Large solar and wind installations require vast tracts of land, sometimes located in fragile ecosystems or productive agricultural zones. The result can be habitat fragmentation, soil degradation, and localised conflicts over land use (Rehbein et al., 2020). Similarly, hydropower dams while producing low-carbon electricity can radically alter river systems, disrupt sediment flow, and undermine downstream fisheries and livelihoods (Ansar et al., 2014). These examples illustrate that environmental sustainability cannot be assumed simply because a project contributes to decarbonisation.

8.3.2 Land Use, Displacement, and Livelihood Disruption

Energy projects, by their nature, demand substantial land acquisition, which often leads to displacement and loss of livelihoods. In many African and Asian contexts, insecure land tenure systems leave local people without formal titles, making them vulnerable to expropriation and inadequate compensation (Hilson & Maconachie, 2020).

Cases from northern Kenya and India reveal tensions where solar and wind developers have restricted pastoralists' access to grazing land, undermining traditional livelihoods and cultural practices (Liu et al., 2020). Hydropower projects across Southeast Asia and sub-Saharan Africa have also displaced thousands, fracturing social networks and eroding community cohesion (World Commission on Dams, 2000).

In Nigeria, similar challenges are beginning to surface in the renewable energy sector. Projects under the Rural Electrification Agency's mini-grid and solar park programmes sometimes intersect with communal farmlands, leading to disputes over ownership, compensation, and benefit distribution (Adeshina et al., 2024). Without clear consultation processes and fair resettlement frameworks, the renewable transition risks repeating the social injustices historically associated with fossil fuel development.

8.3.3 Inequality in Benefit-Sharing

A recurring issue across the energy sector is the inequitable sharing of benefits. While companies and governments often emphasise local development promises, host communities frequently receive only a fraction of the economic gains relative to the profits extracted from their lands (Hilson, 2012).

This imbalance is evident in regions such as Nigeria's Niger Delta and Canada's Alberta province, where resource wealth has coincided with poverty, unemployment, and periodic unrest a dynamic widely referred to as the "resource curse" (Watts, 2004).

Even in the renewable energy sector, benefit-sharing remains uneven. Many large-scale wind and solar projects are financed and operated by external investors, creating limited local employment or ownership opportunities (Brummer, 2018). By contrast, community-owned and cooperative renewable models where residents share in governance and profits have demonstrated greater social acceptance and longer-term sustainability outcomes (Bauwens et al., 2022). These experiences reinforce the idea that fair participation and transparent benefit distribution are central to sustainable energy transitions.

8.3.4 Climate Change and Cumulative Impacts

Host communities are not only affected by local environmental changes but also by broader climate-related pressures. Rising sea levels, prolonged droughts, and extreme weather events compound existing vulnerabilities in areas hosting energy infrastructure. Coastal regions such as the Niger Delta and East Africa's Lamu Basin are particularly at risk, where flooding and erosion exacerbate pollution, economic fragility, and social displacement (Intergovernmental Panel on Climate Change [IPCC], 2022).

The cumulative impacts of ongoing fossil extraction combined with expanding renewable and mining operations create complex, interlinked stresses. As Li and Guliyeva (2025) observe, these overlapping pressures can accelerate land degradation, social tension, and migration particularly in contexts where environmental governance remains weak.

8.3.5 Governance Deficits and Institutional Weakness

At the heart of many sustainability challenges lies a deeper governance problem. Weak regulatory enforcement, corruption, and fragmented institutional responsibilities often allow unsustainable practices to persist unchecked. In developing countries, overlapping mandates and opaque licencing processes undermine accountability and environmental justice for affected communities (Enabulele & Ekhator, 2022; Hilson, 2020).

Even in more developed jurisdictions, procedural compliance does not always translate into genuine participation. In Canada, for instance, Indigenous consultation requirements are often treated as formalities rather than opportunities for shared decision-making (Biezenbos, 2023).

Addressing these issues requires a re-orientation of energy governance one that places host-community rights, voices, and livelihoods at the centre of policy and project design. The next section examines how the relationship between corporations and host communities has evolved, focusing on emerging principles of engagement, accountability, and shared responsibility for environmental sustainability.

8.4 Understanding Between Energy Corporations and Host Communities

The relationship between energy corporations and host communities has changed profoundly over the past three decades. What was once a largely transactional exchange focused on compensation, compliance, and damage control has gradually evolved into a more relational and legitimacy-based partnership built on trust, accountability, and shared benefit (Moffat & Zhang, 2014; Prno & Slocombe, 2012). This evolution reflects wider global shifts in sustainability norms, public expectations, and governance standards. As the energy landscape diversifies spanning oil and gas, electricity networks, renewables, and the mining of critical transition minerals the understanding of what constitutes meaningful corporate–community relations must also broaden to reflect this new complexity.

8.4.1 The Evolution of Corporate–Community Relations

In the traditional oil and gas context, corporate engagement with communities was typically framed through the lens of corporate social responsibility. Under this model, companies sought to offset harm through philanthropic gestures or compensatory schemes. However, as several scholars have noted, these initiatives often reinforced paternalistic dynamics providing short-term relief while leaving deeper structural inequalities untouched (Idemudia, 2009).

The emergence of the Social Licence to Operate (SLO) concept marked a significant turning point. It highlighted the fact that regulatory compliance alone was no longer enough to sustain corporate legitimacy or operational stability. Instead, firms were expected to earn community trust by demonstrating fairness, responsiveness, and long-term commitment to mutual benefit (Moffat & Zhang, 2014).

Today, this legitimacy imperative extends well beyond the fossil fuel sector. Renewable energy and mining projects face similar social and ethical expectations. Where developers ignore local consent or fail to deliver tangible benefits, they encounter community resistance and reputational damage. For instance, in Canada, several energy and mining projects have faced litigation and protest for proceeding without meaningful engagement or the free, prior, and informed consent of Indigenous peoples (Biezenbos, 2023; Lennon, 2019). These experiences reinforce the reality that sustainability is as much a social process as it is a technical or environmental one.

8.4.2 Trust, Transparency, and Social Legitimacy

Trust is the foundation upon which all durable corporate–community relationships rest. Research consistently shows that when communities perceive openness, fairness, and accountability, cooperation tends to flourish and partnerships endure (Edelman, 2021; Moffat et al., 2016). Conversely, when decisions are made behind closed doors or promises go unfulfilled, distrust grows, often leading to protests, litigation, or outright project failure (Enabulele & Ekhator, 2022).

Transparency, therefore, must go beyond simply publishing reports or disclosing payments. It involves clear communication about environmental risks, project impacts, and mitigation measures ideally in formats communities can understand and use. Initiatives such as the Extractive Industries Transparency Initiative (EITI) and the Global Reporting Initiative (GRI) have expanded disclosure standards on community investments and environmental performance (Li et al., 2025). Still, transparency has little meaning without empowerment. Communities must have the knowledge, capacity, and opportunity to interpret information and use it to influence outcomes. Genuine trust emerges when disclosure is paired with dialogue and when accountability mechanisms are not merely symbolic but practical and participatory.

8.4.3 Towards Shared Value and Co-Creation

In recent years, corporate–community relations have increasingly shifted towards shared value creation, a concept that encourages collaboration in identifying opportunities that serve both business objectives and community priorities (Porter & Kramer, 2011; Van Tulder, 2018).

This approach moves beyond philanthropy by embedding community development within the core of business strategy. For instance, investments in local skills training, entrepreneurship, or renewable mini-grid systems can enhance both community resilience and operational stability (IRENA & AfDB, 2022). In the renewable energy sector, community energy models where residents co-own or co-finance renewable assets illustrate how shared ownership can foster trust, reduce project risks, and generate sustainable income streams (Bauwens et al., 2022).

Mining firms have also begun to institutionalise relationships through Community Development Agreements (CDAs) and Impact and Benefit Agreements (IBAs), which clarify mutual responsibilities and benefits (O'Faircheallaigh, 2015). When designed collaboratively and monitored transparently, these agreements can transform corporate–community dynamics from adversarial to cooperative, tying the well-being of communities directly to the success of the project.

8.4.4 *Persistent Tensions and Emerging Lessons*

Despite progress, deep structural imbalances persist particularly in developing economies where communities often lack the legal, financial, or technical capacity to negotiate on equal terms. In some cases, CSR and shared-value programmes are still used to manage dissent rather than to promote genuine inclusion, framing participation within corporate priorities rather than community needs (Idemudia, 2018).

Experiences from across the energy spectrum (both fossil and renewable), suggest that sustainable engagement depends on four essential elements:

1. **Early and continuous dialogue**, initiated at the design stage rather than after key decisions are made.
2. **Recognition of community agency** and respect for traditional governance and cultural structures.
3. **Benefit-sharing mechanisms** that deliver long-term outcomes rather than one-off compensation.
4. **Independent oversight and facilitation**, ensuring accountability, transparency, and equitable monitoring (Organisation for Economic Co-operation and Development [OECD], 2019).

Where these principles are ignored, even well-intentioned "green" projects can generate conflict. This is evident in the resistance to large-scale wind farms in Kenya's Turkana region and to hydropower developments across Southeast Asia, both of which highlight that the energy transition must be socially just as well as environmentally sound (Ansar et al., 2014; Liu et al., 2020).

8.5 Stakeholder Engagement Strategies Across Energy Sub-Sectors

Effective stakeholder engagement has become central to achieving sustainable energy governance. As global energy systems expand and diversify from fossil-fuel operations to renewable infrastructure and the extraction of transition minerals the number and diversity of stakeholders have increased dramatically. Host communities, once peripheral to project design and policy formulation, are now recognised as indispensable partners in ensuring both environmental sustainability and social stability (Organisation for Economic Co-operation and Development [OECD], 2019; World Bank, 2019).

This section examines how stakeholder engagement strategies have evolved across energy sub-sectors, identifies emerging best practices, and highlights persistent barriers that continue to limit inclusion, accountability, and long-term legitimacy.

8.5.1 Models of Stakeholder Engagement

Stakeholder engagement can be understood as a continuous, two-way process through which governments, corporations, and communities exchange information, negotiate expectations, and co-create solutions to shared challenges (Reed, 2008). Across the energy landscape, three broad models have shaped this process:

a. The Inform–Consult–Involve Model (Linear Model)

This traditional approach, rooted in early Environmental Impact Assessment (EIA) frameworks, emphasises disclosure and consultation as key mechanisms of accountability. It remains common in fossil-fuel and large-scale hydropower projects, where engagement is often reactive and compliance-oriented (Hilson, 2020). While this model increases transparency, it often treats communities as passive recipients rather than active decision-makers, thereby limiting the potential for genuine co-creation.

b. The Collaborative Governance Model

Renewable-energy projects and electricity-grid reforms have increasingly adopted a collaborative approach in which governments, civil-society organisations (CSOs), and host communities jointly define project objectives and monitor outcomes - a collaborative process (Ansell & Gash, 2008). In Kenya and Nigeria, for example, participatory rural electrification and solar mini-grid programmes have integrated gender considerations, livelihood support, and environmental safeguards into project design (Adeshina et al., 2024). This model recognises the interdependence between technical feasibility and social legitimacy, bridging institutional and community perspectives.

c. The Empowerment and Co-Ownership Model

The most progressive model is the empowerment and co-ownership approach, visible in community-energy initiatives across Europe and parts of Africa. Here, communities hold equity stakes in renewable facilities, linking ownership directly to environmental stewardship (Bauwens et al., 2022). This model enhances legitimacy and ensures long-term sustainability by aligning community welfare with project success. However, it relies on supportive policy frameworks such as feed-in tariffs, microfinance access, and decentralised regulation to become viable.

8.5.2 Direct Engagement: Corporations and Host Communities

Corporate–community engagement has evolved from one-off consultations to structured, ongoing dialogue supported by formalised mechanisms. Many corporations now use stakeholder mapping to identify diverse social groups women, youth, and

Indigenous peoples who may be affected differently by energy projects (International Finance Corporation [IFC], 2007).

Two engagement mechanisms have gained prominence:

a. Community Development Agreements (CDAs): These legally binding frameworks, widely used in oil, gas, and mining projects, establish mutual obligations between companies and host communities (O'Faircheallaigh, 2015). Nigeria's Petroleum Industry Act (2021) institutionalises this approach through Host Communities Development Trusts (HCDTs), which allocate a fixed percentage of operational expenditure to local development initiatives.
b. Impact and Benefit Agreements (IBAs): Originating in Canada and Australia, IBAs require companies to commit to employment targets, revenue sharing, and environmental management plans with Indigenous or local communities (Biezenbos, 2023).

In the renewable-energy sector, engagement processes are increasingly guided by the principle of Free, Prior and Informed Consent (FPIC), which ensures that communities understand potential impacts and give voluntary consent before project implementation (International Labour Organisation [ILO], 1989; United Nations, 2007). This marks a crucial step towards respecting community autonomy and embedding human rights within corporate practice.

Indirect Engagement: The Role of Government, Civil Society, and Multilateral Actors

Beyond direct corporate–community interactions, governments and civil-society organisations play a vital facilitative role in ensuring fair, transparent, and inclusive engagement. Governments provide the regulatory scaffolding for consultation, compensation, and benefit-sharing, while CSOs often act as intermediaries building community capacity, monitoring compliance, and advocating for justice (Enabulele & Ekhator, 2022).

Multilateral institutions such as the World Bank, African Development Bank (AfDB), and United Nations Development Programme (UNDP) have integrated stakeholder-engagement standards into their funding and operational frameworks. For instance, the World Bank's Environmental and Social Framework (ESF) mandates early stakeholder mapping and continuous consultation throughout a project's life cycle (World Bank, 2019). Similarly, the AfDB's Integrated Safeguards System requires borrower countries to involve host communities in designing environmental and social mitigation plans (African Development Bank [AfDB], 2021).

Nonetheless, several challenges persist. Engagement is too often initiated late in the project cycle or excludes marginalised groups such as women, pastoralists, and youth. Political interference and elite capture can further distort benefit allocation and erode public trust (Hilson, 2020). Successful engagement therefore requires multi-level dialogue platforms local, regional, and national to promote representation, coherence, and sustained accountability.

8.5.3 Participatory Monitoring and Accountability Mechanisms

True engagement extends beyond consultation to participatory monitoring, where communities directly contribute to assessing environmental and social performance. Mechanisms such as grievance-redress systems, community scorecards, and joint monitoring committees have been effective in both extractive and renewable-energy projects (Ipieca, 2022; OECD, 2019).

Technological innovations ranging from mobile data tools to satellite-based environmental tracking now enable real-time reporting and greater transparency. In Nigeria, for instance, partnerships between CSOs and the Nigeria Extractive Industries Transparency Initiative (NEITI) have improved oversight and accountability in host-community fund management (NEITI, 2023). These participatory systems not only enhance governance but also empower communities to shape outcomes that affect their environment and livelihoods.

8.5.4 Key Principles for Effective Stakeholder Engagement

Drawing lessons from across energy sub-sectors, several principles consistently underpin effective engagement:

1. Inclusivity: Ensure participation of vulnerable and under-represented groups, including women, youth, and Indigenous peoples.
2. Transparency: Communicate project information in accessible formats and languages.
3. Continuity: Maintain dialogue throughout the project's full life cycle, not just during consultation phases.
4. Mutual Benefit: Align community welfare with corporate and environmental sustainability goals.
5. Legal Backing: Embed engagement and benefit-sharing processes within contractual or statutory frameworks.

When these principles are applied holistically, stakeholder engagement becomes far more than a procedural requirement, it becomes a governance instrument that links environmental justice, social inclusion, and corporate accountability.

Stakeholder engagement in the energy sector has evolved from a peripheral activity to a strategic necessity. Whether in oil, gas, renewables, or mining, the ability of corporations and governments to engage stakeholders meaningfully determines not only a project's social acceptance but also its environmental and economic viability.

The next section turns to the legal and policy frameworks that govern host-community relations across jurisdictions, examining how legislative and regulatory instruments can institutionalise participatory practices and embed sustainability within corporate governance structures.

8.6 Legal and Policy Frameworks Governing Host-Community Relations in the Energy Sector

Legal and policy frameworks form the foundation for how host communities interact with corporations, governments, and other stakeholders in the energy sector. These frameworks determine the distribution of rights, responsibilities, and benefits while setting the parameters for environmental protection, consultation, and social justice. As the global energy transition accelerates, regulatory regimes are expanding beyond fossil-fuel governance to encompass renewable energy, electricity networks, and the extraction of critical minerals essential for clean-energy technologies.

This section explores how host-community relations are shaped and regulated across three levels: national frameworks (focusing on Nigeria and selected African contexts), comparative international models (with examples from Canada and the European Union), and global soft-law instruments that establish broader sustainability norms.

8.6.1 National Legal Frameworks: Nigeria and the Expanding Energy Mandate

Nigeria offers one of the most comprehensive examples of evolving host-community regulation within a dynamic energy sector. The Petroleum Industry Act (PIA) of 2021 represents a major reform in the governance of oil and gas. Part III of the Act establishes the Host Communities Development Trust (HCDT), which requires oil companies to contribute 3% of their annual operating expenditure to a community-managed trust fund. The aim is to foster inclusion, reduce conflict, and ensure that communities benefit tangibly from petroleum operations (Petroleum Industry Act, 2021).

Despite its significance, the PIA has been critiqued for its limited scope focusing narrowly on petroleum resources and excluding other energy activities such as renewables and electricity infrastructure (Enabulele & Ekhator, 2022). Recognising this gap, the Electricity Act (2023) introduces broader provisions for community engagement within renewable and decentralised energy systems. It promotes local content, equitable access, and participatory governance across generation, transmission, and distribution projects (Electricity Act, 2023).

These developments are reinforced by the Nigeria Energy Transition Plan (2022), which explicitly integrates host-community concerns into the national decarbonisation agenda. The Plan underscores the need for a *just and inclusive transition* protecting livelihoods in oil-dependent regions while creating green jobs in emerging energy industries (Federal Government of Nigeria, 2022). Collectively, these instruments mark a shift from sector-specific corporate responsibility towards a coordinated, multisectoral sustainability regime.

8.6.2 Regional Developments in Africa

Across Africa, legislative reforms are increasingly recognising the social dimensions of energy governance. Ghana's Local Content and Local Participation Regulations (2013) and Tanzania's Extractive Industries (Transparency and Accountability) Act (2015) both incorporate provisions for benefit-sharing and community development. In Kenya, the Energy Act (2019) and accompanying Renewable Energy Regulations mandate public consultation and participatory decision-making at county level particularly during the siting of renewable-energy projects (Lamhamedi & de Vries, 2024).

These developments indicate a continental trend towards inclusive energy governance, although implementation remains uneven. Persistent challenges such as limited institutional capacity, weak monitoring systems, and the capture of community benefits by local elites continue to hinder effective realisation of these reforms. Nevertheless, the growing alignment between national policies and sustainability principles signals important progress in embedding host-community rights across African energy systems.

8.6.3 Comparative International Perspectives: Canada and the European Union

Comparative experiences from Canada and the European Union illustrate distinct yet complementary approaches to integrating community participation within energy governance.

In Canada, host-community relations are closely linked to Indigenous self-determination and constitutional rights. The Impact Assessment Act (2019) requires project proponents to engage Indigenous and local communities early in the planning process and to incorporate traditional ecological knowledge into environmental assessments (Government of Canada, 2019). Indigenous communities have also leveraged Impact and Benefit Agreements (IBAs) to secure employment, revenue sharing, and environmental monitoring commitments in both extractive and renewable-energy projects (Biezenbos, 2023). This model has been instrumental in formalising equitable partnerships and embedding local oversight within project governance.

In the European Union (EU), while extractive industries play a smaller role, participatory principles are deeply integrated into energy and corporate legislation. The Renewable Energy Directive (RED II, 2018) promotes community ownership and citizen participation in renewable-energy production, while the Corporate Sustainability Due Diligence Directive (CSDDD, 2024) obliges companies to identify and mitigate human rights and environmental risks throughout their global supply chains (European Commission, 2024). Together, these instruments advance a governance framework that aligns due diligence with social justice and just-transition principles.

8.6.4 Global and Soft-Law Frameworks

At the global level, a series of soft-law instruments though not legally binding have significantly shaped the norms guiding host-community relations in the energy sector. These include:

a. The United Nations Declaration on the Rights of Indigenous Peoples (UNDRIP), which enshrines the principle of Free, Prior, and Informed Consent (FPIC) for projects affecting Indigenous lands (United Nations, 2007).
b. ILO Convention No. 169, which reinforces communities' procedural rights to consultation, cultural preservation, and participation in resource governance (International Labour Organisation [ILO], 1989).
c. The OECD Guidelines for Multinational Enterprises (2011) and the Guiding Principles for Durable Extractive Contracts (2019), which promote transparency, equitable benefit-sharing, and environmental accountability (OECD, 2019).
d. The Paris Agreement (**2015**) and subsequent COP27 and COP28 decisions, which emphasise the need for a *just transition* that protects vulnerable communities while accelerating decarbonisation (United Nations Framework Convention on Climate Change [UNFCCC], 2023).

Though voluntary, these instruments exert substantial normative influence on corporate and governmental behaviour, shaping expectations around fairness, inclusion, and sustainability (Macchi, 2022). They also empower communities to make stronger claims for compensation, participation, and environmental protection under international law and public scrutiny.

8.6.5 Emerging Trends and Policy Innovations

Globally, host-community governance is evolving through several interrelated trends:

a. **Integration into Renewable-Energy Law:** Recognition that clean-energy projects can generate social and environmental conflicts similar to fossil-fuel operations (Liu et al., 2020).
b. **Just Transition Legislation:** Linking decarbonisation with social justice, exemplified by South Africa's *Just Energy Transition Investment Plan (JET-IP)* and the EU's *Just Transition Mechanism* (European Commission, 2024).
c. **Digital Transparency Platforms:** Initiatives such as the *Extractive Industries Transparency Initiative (EITI) Open Data Standard* enhance visibility and accountability in benefit-sharing and revenue transfers.
d. **Multi-Stakeholder Governance:** Expanding collaboration between governments, corporations, and civil society to co-design energy policies and monitor sustainability outcomes.
e. **Regional Harmonisation:** Efforts within frameworks like the **African Continental Free Trade Area (AfCFTA)** are promoting continent-wide convergence on environmental and social standards (African Union, 2023).

These trends suggest a gradual convergence between national laws and international soft-law norms, contributing to a more coherent and rights-based global framework for host-community governance.

While domestic legislation remains the primary legal foundation for host-community engagement, the influence of international and soft-law norms has grown steadily across energy sub-sectors. This convergence is redefining how corporations, governments, and communities share responsibility for sustainable development.

In essence, host communities are no longer peripheral beneficiaries of energy projects but central actors in shaping a just and inclusive energy transition. The next section presents case studies from Nigeria, Canada, and selected developing contexts, examining how these legal frameworks operate in practice and the challenges involved in turning policy commitments into equitable, community-centred outcomes.

8.7 Case Studies: Host Communities and Environmental Sustainability in Practice

Examining real-world experiences reveals how legal, policy, and corporate frameworks shape outcomes for host communities. This section presents case studies from Nigeria, Canada, and Kenya, covering oil and gas, renewable energy, and electricity infrastructure. Together, they highlight tensions and opportunities in balancing community welfare, corporate accountability, and environmental sustainability within the global energy transition.

8.7.1 Nigeria: From Oil Dependence to Renewable Transition

Nigeria's experience embodies both the legacy of extractive-sector conflict and the promise of inclusive energy governance. The Niger Delta remains emblematic of environmental injustice decades of oil exploitation have left behind degraded ecosystems, entrenched poverty, and recurrent unrest (UNEP, 2011; Watts, 2004). Although the Petroleum Industry Act (PIA) 2021 sought to reform this dynamic through the Host Communities Development Trust (HCDT) allocating 3% of operating expenditure to community projects implementation has faced challenges, including elite capture, opacity, and limited inclusion of women and youth (Enabulele & Ekhator, 2022).

Recent renewable-energy initiatives are testing new engagement models. Under the Nigeria Electrification Project, co-funded by the World Bank and the Rural Electrification Agency, off-grid solar mini-grids have expanded rural access using participatory design involving local leaders, cooperatives, and civil-society organisations (Adeshina et al., 2024). For instance, the Rubitec Solar Mini-Grid in Ogun State employs local labour and reinvests profits in community infrastructure illustrating how inclusivity fosters social acceptance and operational efficiency.

Nonetheless, land-tenure conflicts, weak regulation, and limited technical capacity threaten sustainability. Integrating the Nigeria Energy Transition Plan (2022) with community-driven mechanisms remains crucial to ensuring that the renewable shift does not replicate extractive-era inequities.

8.7.2 Canada: Indigenous Peoples, Impact Agreements, and Renewable Projects

Canada represents a mature model of host-community governance grounded in Indigenous rights and environmental accountability. The Impact Assessment Act (2019) mandates early and continuous consultation with Indigenous peoples, recognising traditional knowledge in project evaluation (Government of Canada, 2019). Indigenous nations have leveraged Impact and Benefit Agreements (IBAs) to secure employment, environmental stewardship roles, and revenue sharing rights across extractive and renewable projects (Biezenbos, 2023).

A leading case is the Henvey Inlet Wind Project in Ontario, a 300 MW joint venture between Pattern Energy and the Henvey Inlet First Nation. The co-management arrangement ensures Indigenous leadership in biodiversity protection and reinvestment of revenues into education and social programmes (Natural Resources Canada, 2022). This model transforms host communities into co-owners of energy transitions rather than passive recipients.

Still, concerns persist that consultation processes can prioritise procedure over substance. Some Indigenous groups report projects proceeding despite unresolved land claims or cumulative ecological impacts (Papillon & Rodon, 2020). Hence, while Canada institutionalises best practices, it also underscores that consultation must evolve into consent.

8.7.3 Kenya: Renewable-Energy Expansion and Community Participation

Kenya's rapid growth in renewable energy particularly wind, geothermal, and solar positions it as a continental leader in low-carbon development. Yet, social sustainability challenges persist. The Lake Turkana Wind Power (LTWP) project, Africa's largest wind farm, significantly expanded power generation but drew criticism over insufficient consultation and loss of grazing lands, resulting in litigation and local tension (Liu et al., 2020).

Conversely, smaller-scale projects such as the Ngong Hills Wind Farm and Olkaria Geothermal Development have progressively enhanced community engagement. The Geothermal Development Company (GDC) established community liaison offices, benefit-sharing frameworks, and gender-responsive initiatives to strengthen local trust (World Bank, 2019). These experiences highlight that early consultation, fair compensation, and transparency are central to achieving socially sustainable renewables.

The Energy Act (2019) now mandates county-level consultation and participatory environmental assessments (Lamhamedi & de Vries, 2024), reflecting Kenya's recognition that social legitimacy is integral to project success.

8.8 Challenges and Criteria for Host-Community Acceptance in the Energy Sector

Host-community acceptance is one of the most decisive factors influencing the success and sustainability of energy projects. Whether in traditional fossil fuel operations or in the fast-growing renewable energy sector, community approval or its absence can determine project timelines, cost efficiency, and overall legitimacy. This section explores the main challenges that hinder host-community acceptance and outlines the essential criteria for building enduring and equitable partnerships in the changing global energy landscape.

8.8.1 Structural and Historical Inequalities

In many resource-rich developing countries, relationships between energy companies and host communities are shaped by long histories of environmental neglect, economic marginalisation, and weak governance. The Niger Delta remains a striking example: decades of pollution and underdevelopment have deepened mistrust and community resistance to new energy initiatives (Bamidele & Erameh, 2023; Watts, 2004). These structural inequalities often result in the exclusion of local voices from key decisions, elite capture of community development funds, and the neglect of gender and youth perspectives (Enabulele & Ekhator, 2022).

Even within renewable energy projects, similar patterns are emerging. Large-scale solar and wind developments have displaced pastoralists and smallholder farmers, sometimes without adequate consultation or compensation (Liu et al., 2020). This reproduces what some scholars describe as the "extractive logic" of fossil capitalism under a new green label, fuelling scepticism towards clean energy transitions (Macchi, 2022).

8.8.2 Deficits in Transparency and Information Flow

A major obstacle to community acceptance lies in poor transparency and weak communication channels between companies, governments, and affected populations. Too often, environmental and social impact assessments (ESIAs) are disclosed only after key project decisions have been made, making consultations seem tokenistic (Hilson, 2020). Moreover, technical reports are frequently presented in formats or languages inaccessible to local communities.

Although global initiatives like the Extractive Industries Transparency Initiative (EITI) have improved fiscal disclosure, information on community-level expenditure, compensation, and environmental performance remains inconsistent (Li & Guliyeva, 2025). When communities lack timely, clear, and reliable information, they cannot participate meaningfully or hold institutions accountable conditions that perpetuate distrust and conflict.

8.8.3 Inadequate Legal and Institutional Protections

Legal and institutional frameworks across many developing economies remain fragmented, focusing heavily on extractive industries while neglecting the broader energy ecosystem. For example, Nigeria's Petroleum Industry Act (2021) offers specific community benefits for oil operations, yet renewable and electricity projects still operate with limited social safeguards (Electricity Act, 2023). Weak enforcement, overlapping institutional responsibilities, and corruption further erode the effectiveness of community protection measures (Enabulele & Ekhator, 2022; OECD, 2019).

By contrast, countries such as Canada and Australia have established robust instruments like Impact and Benefit Agreements (IBAs), which formalise consultation, monitoring, and benefit-sharing between companies and Indigenous or local communities (Biezenbos, 2023; O'Faircheallaigh, 2015). These models could guide legal reforms in developing countries seeking to embed social responsibility within renewable and power sector policies.

8.8.4 Economic and Benefit-Sharing Imbalances

Community resistance frequently stems from perceptions of unfair benefit distribution. In extractive regions, community development funds are often mismanaged or diverted, providing little visible improvement to local livelihoods (Hilson, 2012). Renewable energy projects sometimes replicate this pattern when employment promises are unmet, as many rely on imported technologies and foreign contractors, limiting local participation (Brummer, 2018).

A balanced benefit-sharing system should therefore include:

a. Revenue participation: Allocating a fair portion of profits or royalties to local development trusts.
b. Employment and skills development: Prioritising local labour and technical capacity-building.
c. Infrastructure co-benefits: Linking projects to tangible improvements in electrification, water access, and education.
d. Sustainability funds: Establishing long-term financing mechanisms to ensure benefits persist beyond the project's lifespan (World Bank, 2019).

When these frameworks are clearly defined, transparent, and legally enforced, they enhance social legitimacy and reduce conflict.

8.8.5 Environmental and Climate Vulnerabilities

Climate change adds a new layer of complexity to community–energy relations. Rising temperatures, flooding, and drought are increasingly affecting host regions, compounding pre-existing vulnerabilities (IPCC, 2022). In the Niger Delta, for instance, coastal communities face both sea-level rise and oil contamination, while highland regions hosting hydropower dams struggle with shifting rainfall patterns that undermine agriculture (Adeshina et al., 2024).

Energy projects especially renewable ones must integrate climate resilience into their design. This includes adaptive land-use planning, ecosystem restoration, and water management strategies that protect community livelihoods. By doing so, project developers can reinforce local confidence in the sustainability and fairness of energy transitions.

8.8.6 *Criteria for Genuine Host-Community Acceptance*

Sustainable acceptance does not occur automatically; it must be cultivated through fair processes and enduring trust. Based on the challenges discussed, several core criteria emerge as prerequisites for meaningful and lasting community approval:

a. Legitimacy of Process: Early, continuous, and inclusive consultations that recognise local governance structures and cultural values (Reed, 2008).
b. Equity and Fairness: Transparent benefit-sharing mechanisms that prevent elite capture and ensure gender inclusion.
c. Accountability: Clear systems for monitoring, grievance redress, and enforceable obligations within project agreements.
d. Capacity Building: Support for legal literacy, education, and technical skills to empower communities as informed participants.
e. Environmental Integrity: Demonstrated compliance with environmental standards and proactive mitigation of cumulative impacts.
f. Long-Term Partnership: A shift from seeing communities as beneficiaries to recognising them as partners and co-owners in energy development.

When these criteria are institutionalised, host communities are more likely to see energy projects as aligned with their long-term interests. Conversely, their absence can turn even well-intentioned initiatives into flashpoints of tension and distrust.

Host-community acceptance is not a one-time achievement but a continuous, negotiated process grounded in trust, equity, and mutual accountability. As the global energy system transitions towards renewables, these human and social dimensions must be embedded in the legal, policy, and operational frameworks guiding energy development. The next section will synthesise these findings and build a conceptual bridge to Chapter 9, which explores how multi-stakeholder strategies can foster just, inclusive, and sustainable energy governance.

8.9 Conclusion

Host communities occupy an increasingly vital position in the governance of environmental sustainability within the global energy sector. As demonstrated throughout this chapter, their experiences highlight the profound connection between social justice, environmental management, and the legitimacy of energy transitions. From the oilfields of the Niger Delta to the Indigenous territories of Canada and the renewable-energy landscapes of Kenya, community participation and acceptance consistently determine whether energy projects succeed or falter.

The analysis in this chapter has shown that expanding the lens of energy governance beyond the traditional focus on oil and gas to include renewables, electricity infrastructure, and mining reveals recurring challenges of inequality, environmental degradation, and governance fragmentation. Yet, this broader view also exposes new possibilities for reform and collaboration. Emerging legal and policy frameworks, such as Nigeria's *Electricity* Act (2023), Canada's *Impact Assessment Act* (2019), and the European Union's *Corporate Sustainability Due Diligence Directive* (2024), signal growing international recognition that host-community welfare must be integral to sustainable energy planning.

Across diverse contexts, several consistent themes stand out:

1. Trust and legitimacy: Communities that are genuinely consulted and fairly compensated tend to show stronger collaboration and long-term acceptance.
2. Transparency and accountability: Open access to information and participatory monitoring systems help build confidence and reduce disputes.
3. Shared value and co-ownership: Projects that enable local equity participation or livelihood benefits cultivate durable partnerships.
4. Institutional coherence: Legal and policy frameworks must align across energy sub-sectors to prevent silos that marginalise communities involved in renewable and electricity projects.
5. Environmental integrity: Sustainability efforts must extend beyond carbon reduction to include biodiversity conservation, as well as land and water protection.

Despite these encouraging developments, persistent challenges remain. Weak enforcement capacity, fragmented legislation, and entrenched mistrust continue to undermine meaningful progress in many developing contexts. Moreover, as renewable energy expands, new conflicts around land rights, benefit distribution, and cultural preservation are emerging underscoring that the transition to clean energy is not inherently a just one (Liu et al., 2020; Macchi, 2022). Achieving justice in this transition requires community-centred governance models and adaptive policy frameworks that recognise host communities not as passive beneficiaries but as co-architects of a sustainable energy future.

The lessons drawn from this discussion naturally lead to Chapter **9**, which explores how multi-stakeholder collaboration among governments, corporations, host communities, and civil society can translate these principles into practical governance mechanisms. Building upon the foundations of trust, fairness, and transparency outlined here, the next chapter examines institutional models and partnership frameworks capable of fostering genuine co-governance in the energy sector. The central question that follows, therefore, is how diverse stakeholders can jointly manage the energy transition in ways that ensure environmental integrity, social inclusion, and long-term resilience for host communities.

References

Adeshina, M. A., et al. (2024). From potential to power: Advancing Nigeria's energy policies and sustainable energy development. *Sustainability, 16*(20), 8803. https://doi.org/10.3390/su16208803

African Development Bank (AfDB). (2021). *Integrated safeguards system: Policy statement and operational safeguards*. African Development Bank.

African Union. (2023). *Continental power system master plan (AfCFTA Energy Integration Framework)*. Addis Ababa: African Union Commission.

Ansell, C., & Gash, A. (2008). Collaborative governance in theory and practice. *Journal of Public Administration Research and Theory, 18*(4), 543–571. https://doi.org/10.1093/jopart/mum032

Ansar, A., Flyvbjerg, B., Budzier, A., & Lunn, D. (2014). Should we build more large dams? *Energy Policy, 69*, 43–56. https://doi.org/10.1016/j.enpol.2013.10.069

Bainton, N., & Holcombe, S. (2018). *The social aspects of mine closure: A global literature review*. Centre for Social Responsibility in Mining, University of Queensland.

Bamidele, S., & Erameh, N. I. (2023). Environmental degradation and sustainable peace dialogue in the Niger Delta region of Nigeria. *Resources Policy, 80*, Article 103274. https://doi.org/10.1016/j.resourpol.2022.103274

Bauwens, T., Schraven, D., Drewing, E., Radtke, J., Holstenkamp, L., Gotchev, B., & Yildiz, Ö. (2022). Conceptualizing community in energy systems: A systematic review of 183 definitions. *Renewable and Sustainable Energy Reviews, 156*, Article 111999. https://doi.org/10.1016/j.rser.2021.111999

Biezenbos, K. (2023). When social license and sovereignty collide on First Nations land in Canada. In G. Wood, J. Górski, & G. Mete (Eds.), *Palgrave handbook of social license to operate and energy transitions* (pp. 321–341). Palgrave Macmillan. https://doi.org/10.1007/978-3-030-74725-1_6-1

Brummer, V. (2018). Community energy – Benefits and barriers: A comparative literature review of community energy in the UK, Germany and the USA, the benefits it provides for society and the barriers it faces. *Renewable and Sustainable Energy Reviews, 94*, 187–196. https://doi.org/10.1016/j.rser.2018.06.013

Edelman. (2021). *Edelman trust barometer 2021*. Edelman Research Group.

Ediagbonya, V. (2023). Towards sustainable prosperity for host communities: The role of community development in Nigeria's oil and gas sector. In S. Ojo (Ed.), *Sustainability and development in African energy systems* (pp. 55–78). Routledge.

Enabulele, O., & Ekhator, E. O. (2022). Improving environmental protection in Nigeria: A reassessment of the role of informal institutions. *The Journal of Sustainable Development, Law and Policy, 13*(1), 162–199. https://doi.org/10.4314/jsdlp.v13i1.7

Electricity Act. (2023). Federal Republic of Nigeria.

Commission, E. (2024). *Corporate Sustainability Due Diligence Directive (CSDDD)*. European Union.

Federal Government of Nigeria. (2022). *Nigeria energy transition plan*. Abuja: Office of the Vice President.

Government of Canada. (2019). *Impact Assessment Act (S.C. 2019, c. 28)*. Ottawa: Department of Justice.

Hilson, G. (2012). Corporate social responsibility in the extractive industries: Experiences from developing countries. *Resources Policy, 37*(2), 131–137. https://doi.org/10.1016/j.resourpol.2012.01.002

Hilson, G. (2020). 'Formalisation Bubbles': A Blueprint for Sustainable Artisanal and Small-Scale Mining (ASM) in Sub-Saharan Africa. *The Extractive Industries and Society, 7*, 1624–1638. https://doi.org/10.1016/j.exis.2020.11.001

Hilson, G., & Maconachie, R. (2020). Artisanal and small-scale mining and the sustainable development goals: Opportunities and new directions for sub-Saharan Africa. *Geoforum, 111*, 125–141. https://doi.org/10.1016/j.geoforum.2019.09.006

Idemudia, U. (2009). Rethinking the role of corporate social responsibility in the Nigerian oil conflict. *Journal of International Development, 22*(7), 833–845. https://doi.org/10.1002/jid.1644

Idemudia, U. (2018). Shell–NGO partnership and peace in Nigeria: Critical insights and implications. *Organisation & Environment, 31*(4), 384–405. https://doi.org/10.1177/1086026617718428

International Finance Corporation. (2007). *Stakeholder engagement: A good practice handbook for companies doing business in emerging markets.* World Bank Group. https://www.ifc.org/content/dam/ifc/doc/mgrt/ifc-stakeholderengagement.pdf

International Labour Organisation (ILO). (1989). *Indigenous and Tribal Peoples Convention (No. 169).* Geneva: ILO.

International Renewable Energy Agency. (2022, January 16). *IRENA-AfDB report: Energy transition central to Africa's economic future.* DevelopmentAid. https://www.developmentaid.org/news-stream/post/136150/irena-afdb-africa-energy

Intergovernmental Panel on Climate Change (IPCC). (2022). *Climate change 2022: Impacts.* Cambridge University Press. https://doi.org/10.1017/9781009325844

IpiECA. (2022). *Working with local communities.* IPIECA.

Kaze, K., Balta-Ozkan, N., & Shrimpton, E. (2025). Connecting power to people: Integrating community renewable energy and multi-level governance towards a low-carbon energy transition in Nigeria. *Energy Research & Social Science, 121*, Article 103938. https://doi.org/10.1016/j.erss.2025.103938

Lamhamedi, B. E. H., & de Vries, W. T. (2024). Comparative analysis of rural communities' trade-offs in large-scale and small-scale renewable energy projects in Kenya. *Discover Sustainability, 5*, Article 392. https://doi.org/10.1007/s43621-024-00637-0

Lennon, B. (2019). Community acceptability and the energy transition: A citizens' perspective. *Energy Sustainability & Society, 9*(1), 21. https://doi.org/10.1186/s13705-019-0218-z

Li, Y., & Guliyeva, S. (2025). The extractive industries transparency initiative: Achieving disclosure but falling short on corruption reduction. *The Extractive Industries and Society, 22*, Article 101602. https://doi.org/10.1016/j.exis.2024.101602

Liu, L., Bouman, T., Perlaviciute, G., & Steg, L. (2020). Public participation in decision making, perceived procedural fairness and public acceptability of renewable energy projects. *Energy and Climate Change, 1*, Article 100013. https://doi.org/10.1016/j.egycc.2020.100013

Macchi, C. (2022). Towards a business and human rights binding treaty: Opportunities and challenges. In *Business, human rights and the environment: The evolving agenda.* T.M.C. Asser Press, The Hague. https://doi.org/10.1007/978-94-6265-479-2_7

Moffat, K., & Zhang, A. (2014). The paths to social licence to operate: An integrative model explaining community acceptance of mining. *Resources Policy, 39*, 61–70. https://doi.org/10.1016/j.resourpol.2013.11.003

Moffat, K., Lacey, J., Zhang, A., & Leipold, S. (2016). The social licence to operate: A critical review. *Forestry, 89*(5), 477–488. https://doi.org/10.1093/forestry/cpv044

Natural Resources Canada. (2022). *Indigenous partnerships in Canada's renewable energy transition.* NRCan.

Nigeria Extractive Industries Transparency Initiative (NEITI). (2023). NEITI audits and industry reporting: Solid Minerals and extractive sector performance. Retrieved [date you accessed it], from https://neiti.gov.ng/audits

Nigerian Upstream Petroleum Regulatory Commission (NUPRC). (2022). *Host Communities' Development Trust Implementation Template.* Abuja: NUPRC.

O'Faircheallaigh, C. (2015). Social equity and large mining projects: Voluntary industry initiatives, public regulation and community development agreements. *Journal of Business Ethics, 132*(1), 91–103. https://doi.org/10.1007/s10551-014-2308-3

Organisation for Economic Co-operation and Development (OECD). (2019). *Guiding principles for durable extractive contracts.* OECD Publishing. https://doi.org/10.1787/55c19888-en

Papillon, M., & Rodon, T. (2020). The transformative potential of indigenous-driven approaches to implementing free, prior and informed consent: Lessons from two Canadian cases. *International Journal on Minority and Group Rights, 27*(2), 314–335. https://doi.org/10.1163/15718115-02702009

Petroleum Industry Act. (2021). Federal Republic of Nigeria.

Porter, M. E., & Kramer, M. R. (2011). Creating shared value. *Harvard Business Review, 89*(1–2), 62–77.

Prno, J., & Slocombe, D. S. (2012). Exploring the origins of social licence to operate in the mining sector. *Resources Policy, 37*(3), 346–357. https://doi.org/10.1016/j.resourpol.2012.04.002

Reed, M. S. (2008). Stakeholder participation for environmental management: A literature review. *Biological Conservation, 141*(10), 2417–2431. https://doi.org/10.1016/j.biocon.2008.07.014

Rehbein, J. A., Watson, J. E. M., Lane, J. L., Sonter, L. J., Venter, O., & Possingham, H. P. (2020). Renewable energy development threatens many globally important biodiversity areas. *Global Change Biology, 26*(6), 3040–3051. https://doi.org/10.1111/gcb.15067

Sonter, L. J., Dade, M. C., Watson, J. E. M., & Valenta, R. K. (2020). Renewable energy production will exacerbate mining threats to biodiversity. *Nature Communications, 11*, 4174. https://doi.org/10.1038/s41467-020-17928-5

Spaces for Change. (2013). *What is a host community? A framework for Nigeria's oil region.* Lagos: Spaces for Change.

United Nations. (2007). *United Nations Declaration on the Rights of Indigenous Peoples (UNDRIP).* UN General Assembly.

United Nations Environment Programme (UNEP). (2011). *Environmental Assessment of Ogoniland.* Nairobi: UNEP.

United Nations Framework Convention on Climate Change (UNFCCC). (2023). *Sharm El-Sheikh Implementation Plan: COP27 Outcome.* Bonn: UNFCCC Secretariat.

Ulimwengu, J. M., & Sanginga, B. (2025). The complex economics of a complete ban on child labour in the cobalt supply chain: The case of the DR Congo. *The Extractive Industries and Society, 23*, Article 101687. https://doi.org/10.1016/j.exis.2025.101687

van Tulder, R. (2018). *Business & The sustainable development goals: A framework for effective corporate involvement.* RSM positive change series. http://hdl.handle.net/1765/110689

Van Tulder, R., Crane, A., & Husted, B. (2022). *Business and the sustainable development goals: A research handbook.* Edward Elgar Publishing. https://doi.org/10.4337/9781800375611

Watts, M. (2004). Resource curse? Governmentality, oil and power in the Niger Delta. *Geopolitics, 9*(1), 50–80. https://doi.org/10.1080/14650040412331307812

World Bank. (2019, December 15). *Good practice note for energy sector adaptation.* Washington, DC: World Bank.

World Commission on Dams. (2000). *Dams and development: A new framework for decision-making.* Earthscan.

Chapter 9
Effective Multi-Stakeholder Strategies: Roles of Government, Corporations, and Host Communities Across the Energy Sector

9.1 Introduction

The relationship between host communities, governments, and corporations plays a central role in determining whether activities in the energy sector lead to sustainable environmental results. The 2030 Agenda for Sustainable Development views sustainability as a shared responsibility that depends on collaboration among different stakeholders (United Nations, 2015). Research on corporate responsibility also shows that businesses today are expected to embed social and environmental goals within their main operations, rather than treating them as side charitable efforts (McElhaney, 2009). Similarly, stakeholder theory explains that every organisation operates within a web of interest groups whose power, legitimacy, and urgency shape corporate decisions. Understanding and ranking these groups is therefore crucial for building effective partnerships (Freeman, 1984; Mitchell et al., 1997).

This chapter explores strategies for multi-stakeholder collaboration in the energy industry, including oil and gas, power, renewables, and mining. It aims to: (1) explain the different but complementary roles of governments, companies, and host communities in promoting environmental sustainability; (2) assess both mandatory and voluntary policy tools that support responsible and long-term partnerships; and (3) suggest governance structures such as a dedicated coordinating body and corporate sustainability offices that can align incentives and promote transparency. The discussion looks beyond single-sector practices to highlight approaches that can be applied across the energy value chain, from large-scale extractive projects to smaller renewable initiatives.

This chapter is especially relevant because weak regulation, poor enforcement, and inconsistent corporate behaviour often create gaps that prevent sustainability goals from being achieved (see, for example, the reforms in the Petroleum Industry Act, 2021). The analysis combines legal and policy review with institutional and stakeholder analysis to explore how binding rules (like statutory obligations and reporting requirements) and voluntary measures (such as company sustainability

J. A. Debski, *Corporate Social Responsibility in the Energy Sector*, CSR, Sustainability, Ethics & Governance, https://doi.org/10.1007/978-3-032-17748-3_9

units, community agreements, and industry standards) can work together or sometimes conflict. The chapter is organised as follows: Sect. 9.2 identifies the main stakeholders and criteria for determining their importance; Sect. 9.3 compares compulsory and voluntary instruments; Sect. 9.4 presents ideas for institutional design, including a proposed Sustainability Commission and corporate CSR departments; Sect. 9.5 looks at strategic CSR and Institutional Reform: Embedding Sustainability through the CSR Commission Framework; Sect. 9.6 looks at community participation and trust-building mechanisms; and the Conclusion summarises key lessons.

9.2 Stakeholder Mapping and Salience: Roles for Government, Corporations, and Host Communities

Building a sustainable energy sector starts with understanding who the key players are and what responsibilities they hold. Stakeholder theory offers a useful foundation for this understanding. Freeman (1984) described stakeholders as any individuals or groups that can influence or are influenced by an organisation's goals. Later, Mitchell et al. (1997) identified three main factors power, legitimacy, and urgency that determine how important a stakeholder is. Using this framework, the energy sector can be seen as relying on three essential groups: governments, corporations, and host communities.

(a) *Government: Regulator, Enabler, and Partner*

Governments act both as regulators setting and enforcing environmental rules and as partners that encourage collaboration among companies and communities. In the energy sector, public institutions create the policies that shape environmental and social performance. For instance, Nigeria's Petroleum Industry Act (PIA) 2021 led to the establishment of the Nigerian Upstream Petroleum Regulatory Commission (NUPRC) and the Host Communities Development Trust (HCDT), both aimed at formalising relations between companies and host communities. Likewise, the European Union's Corporate Sustainability Due Diligence Directive (CSDDD) 2024 and China's 14th Five-Year Energy Plan (2021–2025) require businesses to embed environmental and social protections in their operations.

Beyond law-making, effective government action also involves coordinating policies and designing incentives. Measures such as renewable energy subsidies, emissions trading schemes, and tax benefits for green innovation show how regulation and partnership can work together (International Energy Agency [IEA], 2024). Governments also improve transparency through mandatory reporting systems for example, Nigeria's Extractive Industries Transparency Initiative (NEITI) and the EU's Corporate Sustainability Reporting Directive (European Commission, 2022) which reduce information gaps between companies and the public.

(b) *Corporations: Implementers and Innovators*

Corporations are at the heart of putting sustainability goals into practice. Their role goes beyond simply meeting legal requirements they must also integrate environmental and social priorities into their business models (Aguinis & Glavas, 2012). Frameworks such as the United Nations Global Compact (UNGC, 2024) help guide companies in aligning their strategies with the Sustainable Development Goals (SDGs) and in disclosing their sustainability performance.

In this process, companies often take the lead in innovation developing cleaner technologies, improving energy efficiency, and adopting responsible resource management practices. Firms such as Seplat Energy in Nigeria and Ørsted in Denmark show that it is possible to combine profitability with decarbonisation and community engagement (Ørsted, 2023; Seplat Energy, 2024). To make these efforts lasting, many companies now appoint Chief Sustainability Officers (CSOs) and establish CSR committees, ensuring that sustainability oversight becomes a permanent part of their governance structure (Velte & Stawinoga, 2017).

(c) *Host Communities: Custodians and Beneficiaries*

Host communities hold a special place in the sustainability equation they are both the main beneficiaries of energy projects and the protectors of the environments those projects affect. Their involvement is essential to ensure that sustainability initiatives respond to local needs rather than being top-down gestures. The PIA 2021 requires host communities to participate in managing the Host Community Development Trusts (HCDTs), though concerns remain about whether they have enough voice in executive decisions (NUPRC, 2022). Effective partnerships depend on open consultation, transparent benefit-sharing, and a shared sense of environmental responsibility to maintain peace and secure the "social licence to operate" (Górski, 2022).

When communities are included in environmental monitoring, impact assessment, and project evaluation, sustainability becomes something that is co-created rather than imposed. This approach reflects the principles of environmental democracy found in global frameworks such as the Aarhus Convention 1998, which upholds access to information, public participation, and justice in environmental decision-making.

(d) *Integrative Approach*

The connections between governments, corporations, and host communities make collaboration essential. Governments provide the legal and policy foundation; corporations turn these goals into real outcomes through technology, finance, and management; and communities ensure accountability, trust, and local relevance. Each depends on the others to achieve long-term sustainability.

Overall, multi-stakeholder engagement in the energy sector should not be viewed as an administrative burden but as a strategic necessity. When the responsibilities of these actors are unclear or ignored, the result is often poor environmental outcomes, social tensions, and weak governance (Table 9.1).

Table 9.1 Core Stakeholders in Energy-Sector Sustainability

Stakeholder	Primary roles	Key instruments/Frameworks	Examples
Government	Regulator, enabler, and policy coordinator	Petroleum Industry Act PIA 2021, EU CSDDD 2024; China's 14th Five-Year Energy Plan	NUPRC, NESREA, NEITI; Renewable subsidies and carbon-pricing schemes
Corporations	Implementers, innovators, and sustainability leaders	UN Global Compact (2024), GRI Standards 2023, TCFD 2017	Seplat Energy, Ørsted, TotalEnergies
Host Communities	Custodians and beneficiaries; ensure legitimacy and local ownership	Host Communities Development Trusts (HCDTs); Aarhus Convention (1998)	Niger Delta host communities; Ghana's Community Mining Programme 2022

9.3 Mandatory and Voluntary Frameworks for Multi-Stakeholder CSR

The question of whether corporate social responsibility (CSR) should be a legal duty or a voluntary commitment remains a key issue in the energy sector's sustainability debate. Around the world, regulations increasingly combine legal reporting requirements with voluntary performance incentives. The most effective approach is not to choose one side but to blend both using mandatory rules to ensure accountability and voluntary measures to encourage innovation, flexibility, and trust.

(a) *The Case for Mandatory CSR*

Making CSR compulsory helps guarantee minimum standards, consistency, and transparency. It limits the risk of "greenwashing" by requiring companies to provide verifiable information and by establishing clear penalties for non-compliance. Several countries have taken this route. For example, India's Companies Act 2013 requires eligible firms to spend at least 2% of their average profits on CSR activities, while Indonesia's Law No. 40/2007 makes CSR a legal obligation for natural resource companies. In China, the 14th Five-Year Energy Plan (2021–2025) includes mandatory environmental reporting and carbon reduction targets for the energy sector (Stern & Xie, 2022).

In Nigeria, the Petroleum Industry Act (PIA) 2021 formalised corporate duties towards host communities through the Host Communities Development Trusts (HCDTs), which allocate 3% of a company's previous year's operating expenses to community development. However, this arrangement mainly covers the oil and gas sector. To promote consistency across all energy industries, an updated Energy Sustainability Act could expand similar provisions to include renewables, electricity, and mining.

Mandatory reporting initiatives such as the EU's Corporate Sustainability Reporting Directive (European Commission, 2022) and the Task Force on Climate-related Financial Disclosures (TCFD, 2017) show that legal disclosure requirements can reshape corporate governance culture. These frameworks are most effective when they:

1. Set clear performance indicators for CSR and ESG;
2. Appoint a dedicated government body to monitor compliance; and
3. Provide transparent sanctions and incentives.

For Nigeria, this chapter recommends establishing a dedicated CSR or Sustainability Commission to coordinate the overlapping duties currently handled by NUPRC, National Environmental Standards and Regulations Enforcement Agency (NESREA), NOSDRA, and NEITI. Such a Commission could harmonise sustainability data, assess corporate CSR reports, and encourage knowledge sharing across oil, gas, renewable, and power sectors (Table 9.2).

(b) *The Value of Voluntary CSR*

While legal rules create a foundation, voluntary CSR builds initiative, creativity, and long-term commitment. It allows companies to go beyond compliance and form genuine partnerships with local communities. Globally, voluntary frameworks such as the UN Global Compact (2024), OECD Guidelines for Multinational Enterprises (OECD, 2023), and GRI Standards (2023) help companies embed sustainability within their culture and align with international best practices.

Research shows that voluntary CSR can improve both corporate reputation and financial performance. Companies that use GRI-based sustainability reporting, for instance, often show stronger environmental outcomes and stakeholder engagement (Velte & Stawinoga, 2017). In Nigeria, firms such as Seplat Energy, TotalEnergies,

Table 9.2 Comparison of mandatory and voluntary CSR frameworks

Approach	Main characteristics	Advantages	Limitations	Examples
Mandatory CSR	Legally enforced through statutes or directives	Ensures compliance, consistency, and accountability	May limit innovation; risk of box-ticking	India's Companies Act 2013, Indonesia's Law No. 40/2007; Nigeria's PIA 2021; European Commission (2022)
Voluntary CSR	Firm-driven; based on moral and reputational incentives	Encourages innovation, flexibility, and trust-building	Risk of greenwashing; weak monitoring	UN Global Compact; OECD Guidelines (2023); GRI Reporting Standards
Hybrid Model	Combines legal mandates with voluntary innovation	Balances accountability with flexibility; enables co-regulation	Requires strong coordination capacity	Philippines CSR Act 2020; China's dual reporting model; Nigeria's proposed CSR Commission

and Dangote Industries have voluntarily adopted global ESG disclosure standards. These efforts complement legal obligations by fostering public trust and reinforcing companies' social licence to operate (Górski, 2022).

However, voluntary CSR can fall short when it lacks transparency or meaningful community involvement. When used mainly as a public-relations exercise, CSR projects often fail to produce lasting results. To avoid this, voluntary initiatives should be supported by co-regulatory tools such as public databases of CSR projects, community scorecards, and joint evaluation systems that include civil society and host communities.

(c) *A Hybrid Model for Nigeria and Other Developing Economies*

Developing countries like Nigeria face unique governance challenges: weak enforcement, fragmented institutions, and corruption (Adegbite, 2015). In such contexts, neither purely mandatory nor entirely voluntary approaches are enough. A balanced or "hybrid" CSR framework can combine the strengths of both by:

i. Requiring minimum CSR reporting and environmental standards;
ii. Encouraging voluntary innovation through tax reliefs, awards, and licencing incentives; and
iii. Extending community co-management models (like the HCDT structure) to all energy sectors.

This hybrid approach aligns with the concept of "smart regulation", which promotes cooperation, adaptability, and continuous learning in sustainability governance (Baldwin et al., 2012). It envisions governments as facilitators, corporations as innovators, and host communities as active partners in achieving shared sustainability goals.

(d) *Comparative Insights*

i. Philippines: The Corporate Social Responsibility Act (2020) promotes voluntary CSR but supports it with tax incentives and public recognition for outstanding projects (Cervantes, 2020).
ii. European Union: The CSRD (European Commission, 2022) enforces mandatory sustainability disclosures, complemented by voluntary initiatives under the European Green Deal Industrial Plan (2023).
iii. China: Combines compulsory environmental reporting with CSR-related financial incentives, particularly for renewable energy firms (Stern & Xie, 2022).

Drawing from these examples, Nigeria's proposed CSR or Sustainability Commission could design a regulatory ecosystem that merges accountability with innovation, embedding sustainability across the entire energy landscape.

9.4 Institutional Design for Effective Multi-Stakeholder Partnership

The way institutions are designed often determines whether sustainability goals are transformed into tangible outcomes or remain aspirational policy declarations. In the energy sector, institutional design is particularly crucial because of the sector's long value chains, interdependent systems, and overlapping mandates among regulators, corporations, and host communities. Fragmented governance structures, inconsistent policy enforcement, and weak inter-agency coordination have historically undermined sustainability efforts. Effective multi-stakeholder governance therefore requires a coordinated institutional framework that connects the actions of government agencies, private-sector entities, and local communities under a common vision of sustainable development. Such coordination depends on clear mandates, defined responsibilities, mutual accountability, and transparent communication channels that ensure every actor contributes constructively to shared sustainability goals.

In Nigeria, energy governance has traditionally operated through separate institutional silos, where environmental agencies, petroleum regulators, and corporate bodies work largely in isolation. This fragmentation often leads to policy duplication, uneven enforcement, and limited community participation. Achieving sustainability thus demands not only new policies but also a fundamental redesign of how institutions interact. The principle of institutional coherence—that is, aligning mandates and actions across sectors—becomes essential to transform sustainability objectives into measurable progress.

(a) ***Establishing a National CSR and Sustainability Commission***

Nigeria currently maintains several agencies tasked with regulating environmental and corporate practices, including the Nigerian Upstream Petroleum Regulatory Commission (NUPRC)**, the** National Environmental Standards and Regulations Enforcement Agency (NESREA)**, and the** Nigeria Extractive Industries Transparency Initiative (NEITI)**.** Although these bodies perform important roles, their mandates often overlap, resulting in inefficiency, inconsistent data reporting, and policy gaps (Chijoke-Mgbame & Mgbame, 2018). To overcome these challenges, Nigeria should establish a National CSR and Sustainability Commission (NCSC) through an enabling Act of the National Assembly.

The proposed Commission would act as the country's coordinating hub for sustainability and CSR, bringing together the functions currently dispersed across multiple agencies. The NCSC would:

(a) Develop and coordinate national CSR policies across the oil, gas, power, mining, and renewable-energy sectors;
(b) Monitor and review sustainability reports using harmonised templates aligned with the Global Reporting Initiative (GRI) and the Sustainability Accounting Standards Board (SASB);
(c) Recommend fiscal incentives for companies that adopt clean technologies and low-carbon innovations;

(d) Serve as a platform for conflict resolution and dialogue between corporations and host communities; and
(e) Forge strategic partnerships with regional and international organisations such as the African Development Bank (AfDB), the International Energy Agency (IEA), and the UN Global Compact to ensure Nigeria's CSR practices remain consistent with global sustainability standards.

The NCSC could adopt a hybrid governance model similar to the Philippines' Department of Trade and Industry CSR Board (Cervantes, 2020) and South Africa's National Business Initiative, both of which combine public oversight with private-sector leadership and stakeholder participation. In the Nigerian setting, such an approach would institutionalise what Baldwin et al. (2012) describe as a "partnership state", a system that moves beyond traditional command-and-control regulation towards a cooperative, transparent, and incentive-based regime. Through this arrangement, the Commission would not only coordinate agencies but also act as a policy laboratory, promoting continuous learning and adaptation in sustainability governance.

Beyond coordination, the NCSC would cultivate a culture of compliance that is supportive rather than punitive. By introducing transparent performance benchmarks and public recognition for exemplary firms, it could encourage voluntary excellence alongside regulatory enforcement. Over time, the Commission would serve as both a standard-setter and a trust-builder, bridging the historical divide between corporations and host communities.

(b) ***Integrating Corporate Sustainability Departments and Chief Sustainability Officers***

Institutional design for effective multi-stakeholder partnership must also extend into the corporate architecture of energy companies. National institutions cannot deliver sustainability goals in isolation if firms themselves lack internal structures to implement them. Therefore, each major energy company should establish formal CSR or sustainability departments responsible for developing strategy, preparing sustainability reports, and managing stakeholder engagement. In addition, the appointment of Chief Sustainability Officers (CSOs) at the executive level would ensure that environmental, social, and governance (ESG) issues are considered in every major business decision.

Empirical research has demonstrated that corporations with dedicated CSOs and board-level CSR committees perform significantly better on environmental and social indicators. They are also more likely to maintain transparent disclosures and to respond quickly to sustainability risks (Hussain et al., 2018; Peters et al., 2019). The UK Corporate Governance Code (United Kingdom Financial Reporting Council, 2018) further reinforces this principle by urging boards to incorporate stakeholder perspectives directly into sustainability strategy and reporting.

In Nigeria, however, sustainability functions often exist informally within public relations or community-affairs units, with little influence on corporate strategy. Making the CSO role a permanent structural feature of every major energy company would enhance internal accountability and create consistent performance benchmarks across firms. Moreover, collaboration with professional training institutions such as the GRI Academy (GRI, 2024) would help develop indigenous expertise in sustainability reporting and ESG management. Such partnerships could build a new cadre of Nigerian sustainability professionals capable of meeting international disclosure and assurance standards.

Integrating sustainability departments within firms also promotes vertical alignment between national and corporate institutions. While the NCSC coordinates national policy, corporate CSOs would implement these frameworks internally, ensuring consistency of practice from headquarters to field operations. This alignment can produce a virtuous cycle: stronger companies inform better policy, while coherent policy encourages more responsible corporate behaviour.

(c) ***Coordination Platforms for Stakeholder Engagement***

For institutional design to yield real transformation, stakeholder engagement must be systematic, continuous, and inclusive. Ad-hoc consultations are insufficient; there must be permanent platforms for dialogue, joint planning, and progress evaluation. Three interconnected mechanisms are therefore proposed:

(a) National Energy Sustainability Forum (NESF): A flagship public–private platform led by the NCSC that convenes annually to assess progress towards energy-related Sustainable Development Goals (SDGs). The Forum would bring together ministries, corporations, civil-society organisations, and universities to review performance indicators, share innovations, and issue annual communiqués on sustainability priorities.
(b) Regional Host-Community Liaison Councils: Decentralised structures under the NCSC to oversee the work of Host Community Development Trusts (HCDTs) in strategic regions such as the Niger Delta, North-Central mining corridors, and renewable-energy hubs in the North-East. These councils would foster two-way communication, ensure fair benefit-sharing, and prevent local grievances from escalating into conflicts.
(c) Integrated Reporting and Data Portal: A digital platform managed by the NCSC to collect, verify, and publish sustainability data from all licenced energy companies. Modelled on the European Union's central sustainability-reporting hub, this portal would increase transparency, reduce duplication of reports, and provide open access to verified information for investors, researchers, and the public.

All these mechanisms encourage both vertical coordination linking federal, state, and community levels and horizontal alignment across industries. Over time, they would cultivate trust among stakeholders, reduce policy contradictions, and create an evidence base for adaptive policymaking.

9.5 Strategic CSR and Institutional Reform: Embedding Sustainability Through the CSR Commission Framework

The idea of Corporate Social Responsibility (CSR) in Nigeria's energy industry has evolved far beyond its earlier conception as a charitable or philanthropic undertaking. What used to consist mainly of ad hoc donations, community handouts, or occasional infrastructure projects has gradually transformed into a broader societal expectation for companies to demonstrate measurable commitment to sustainability, ethical governance, and long-term community well-being. This shift reflects a deeper recognition that businesses, particularly those operating in sensitive sectors such as oil, gas, and energy, are not isolated economic actors but integral components of the social and ecological systems within which they operate.

Over the past two decades, Nigeria's energy landscape has faced a complex interplay of challenges, including environmental degradation, local unrest, climate vulnerability, and social inequality. Against this backdrop, CSR can no longer be an occasional act of goodwill or a public relations strategy; it must be strategic, embedded, and institutionalised. As Debski and Ezeani (2022) emphasise, modern CSR should be viewed as a comprehensive management approach that weaves social and environmental awareness into the fabric of corporate governance and everyday operations, rather than being treated as an optional publicity exercise. This perspective resonates strongly with Nigeria's current realities, where sustainability has become a prerequisite for long-term viability, community trust, and global competitiveness.

Strategic CSR in the Nigerian context therefore requires a structural transformation in how energy companies define and pursue corporate success. It calls for a re-orientation from short-term profit maximisation to long-term value creation that integrates economic, social, and environmental dimensions. For energy firms whose operations often intersect directly with local livelihoods, ecosystems, and national policy, CSR cannot be peripheral; it must be a core element of strategy, governance, and risk management.

(a) *Strategic CSR as a Corporate Imperative*

Strategic CSR treats social, environmental, and governance objectives as interdependent with corporate growth and profitability. Instead of perceiving CSR as a regulatory burden or external obligation, forward-looking companies view it as a strategic investment that enhances innovation, reduces operational risks, and builds social capital. In the energy sector, where the cost of environmental failure or community distrust can be immense, integrating sustainability into the core of business operations has become a defining feature of modern corporate success.

For example, companies such as Ørsted, TotalEnergies, and Seplat Energy have demonstrated that aligning CSR with overall business strategy produces dual outcomes: better environmental performance and stronger financial results (Ørsted, 2023; Seplat Energy, 2024). These firms have internalised sustainability metrics into their performance evaluations, tied executive compensation to environmental targets, and embedded community development into their supply chain and innovation agendas. This model shows that CSR, when strategically embedded, is not an additional cost but a catalyst for innovation, efficiency, and resilience.

In the Nigerian context, the implication is clear: companies must move beyond token gestures of social responsibility towards institutionalising CSR within decision-making systems. Strategic CSR compels corporations to assess the broader social and ecological impact of their activities at every stage of planning and execution. It also ensures that investments in technology, production, and human resources are aligned with environmental preservation and social development goals. As Debski and Ezeani (2022) argue, CSR should create a shared responsibility in which business success reinforces social progress, and social stability in turn supports business sustainability.

This alignment becomes even more critical as Nigeria positions itself within global sustainability frameworks and energy transition agendas. The integration of CSR into national development policy can facilitate economic diversification, attract sustainable investment, and strengthen Nigeria's credibility in the global energy market. Making CSR a core part of national energy policy rather than leaving it as a voluntary corporate practice would help ensure that the sector contributes systematically to inclusive growth, energy equity, and environmental stewardship.

(b) *The CSR Commission as the Institutional Core of Strategic Sustainability*

Institutionalisation is essential to sustain CSR beyond corporate goodwill. The proposed National CSR and Sustainability Commission (NCSC) offers a structured mechanism for embedding CSR into Nigeria's governance architecture. Presently, Nigeria's main formal CSR mechanism, the Host Communities Development Fund (HCDF), established under the Petroleum Industry Act (PIA) of 2021, is designed primarily to address the aftermath of environmental and social damage. The Fund is managed under the supervision of the Nigerian Upstream Petroleum Regulatory Commission (NUPRC) and focuses largely on compensation, remediation, and community infrastructure following harmful incidents (NUPRC, 2023).

While this framework represents progress, its orientation remains reactive. It seeks to repair harm after it occurs rather than preventing it. Such a remedial approach may provide temporary relief but does not address the systemic issues that lead to conflict, degradation, and mistrust. A forward-looking institutional framework, therefore, must shift from post-impact intervention to pre-impact prevention, integrating sustainability principles into policy and business conduct from the outset.

The NCSC would be designed as a central coordination and oversight body with a proactive and cross-sectoral mandate that cuts across oil, gas, renewable energy, electricity, and mining. Its key responsibilities would include:

(a) Promoting preventive environmental practices by setting unified Environmental, Social, and Governance (ESG) standards, enforcing continuous monitoring mechanisms, and aligning these with global sustainability reporting frameworks.

(b) Integrating multiple agencies such as NUPRC, the National Environmental Standards and Regulations Enforcement Agency (NESREA), and the Nigeria Extractive Industries Transparency Initiative (NEITI) under a coherent sustainability strategy.
(c) Advising policymakers by providing research, technical guidance, and recommendations to the Ministry of Energy and related institutions on matters of incentives, transparency, capacity building, and regulatory harmonisation.
(d) Empowering host communities through participatory governance structures, fair benefit distribution, and strengthened local accountability mechanisms under reformed Host Community frameworks.

Positioning the NCSC within the Energy Directorate but granting it operational independence would enable it to balance policy alignment with impartial oversight. It would function as a bridge between government regulators, corporate actors, and host communities, ensuring that sustainability is pursued collectively rather than in isolation. Through such a coordinated approach, Nigeria can build an energy governance model that is transparent, inclusive, and future-oriented.

(c) *From Remediation to Strategic Prevention*

Although the Host Communities Development Fund remains valuable for remediation and compensation, Nigeria's ecological and social realities demand a preventive, strategic orientation. The energy sector operates in a context of environmental fragility: oil spills, gas flaring, deforestation, and biodiversity loss continue to threaten livelihoods. Communities in the Niger Delta and other resource-rich regions have experienced decades of neglect and pollution, leaving behind deep distrust between corporations and citizens. In such a context, a reactive CSR approach is insufficient.

The CSR Commission would therefore aim to institutionalise strategic prevention, encouraging companies to internalise environmental responsibility and community engagement as integral components of project design and operational planning. Rather than waiting for disasters to trigger compensation, companies would be incentivised to adopt technologies, practices, and governance systems that minimise harm from the beginning.

This preventive approach mirrors global trends in strategic CSR, where firms increasingly recognise that proactive environmental and social investment enhances competitiveness and protects long-term shareholder value. As McElhaney (2009) noted, strategic CSR is not about philanthropy but about integrating social and environmental considerations into the core business model, thereby achieving mutual benefit for companies and society.

In practical terms, preventive CSR would encourage companies to invest in environmental protection technologies, renewable energy diversification, and sustainable livelihood programmes. It would require them to engage host communities in participatory planning, conduct thorough environmental and social impact assessments, and ensure continuous monitoring and reporting. In doing so, CSR becomes an instrument of long-term stability, reducing the likelihood of community conflict, regulatory penalties, and reputational crises.

(d) *Embedding CSR within National Sustainability Goals*

For CSR to truly drive national transformation, it must align with Nigeria's broader sustainable development and energy transition objectives. Strategic CSR should not exist in isolation from public policy; rather, it should complement and reinforce government efforts to achieve sustainable growth. The proposed CSR Commission can serve as the institutional platform for integrating CSR into the implementation of national frameworks such as the Petroleum Industry Act, the National Renewable Energy and Energy Efficiency Policy, and Nigeria's Climate Change Act.

Embedding CSR into these frameworks would ensure that corporate sustainability initiatives contribute directly to national priorities: reducing carbon emissions, improving energy access, and fostering inclusive economic growth. It would also help standardise CSR reporting and accountability, allowing for consistent evaluation of companies' social and environmental performance. This level of alignment between business and government objectives would further enhance investor confidence and position Nigeria as a regional leader in responsible energy governance (Figs. 9.1 and 9.2).

(e) *Towards an Integrated and Accountable CSR System*

Finally, achieving such an ambitious transformation requires robust accountability mechanisms. The CSR Commission must have the authority to monitor compliance, enforce penalties for violations, and reward companies that demonstrate exceptional sustainability performance. Transparent reporting standards, independent audits, and public disclosure of CSR activities will foster trust among stakeholders and discourage tokenism.

Equally important is community participation. Host communities should be involved not merely as beneficiaries but as partners in governance, planning, and evaluation. Their inclusion in decision-making processes will ensure that CSR initiatives

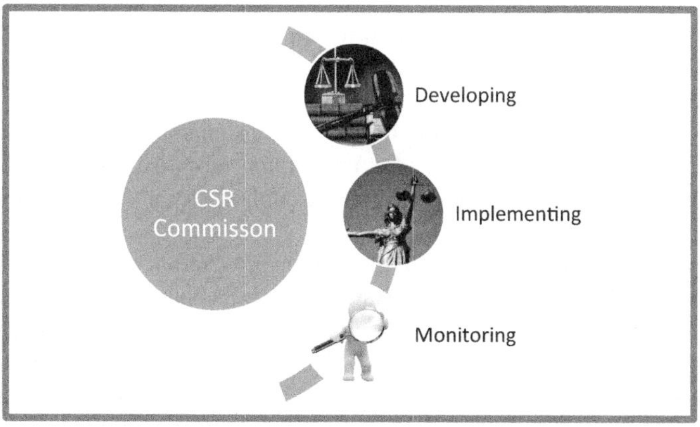

Fig. 9.1 CSR Bill framework (Debski, 2023)

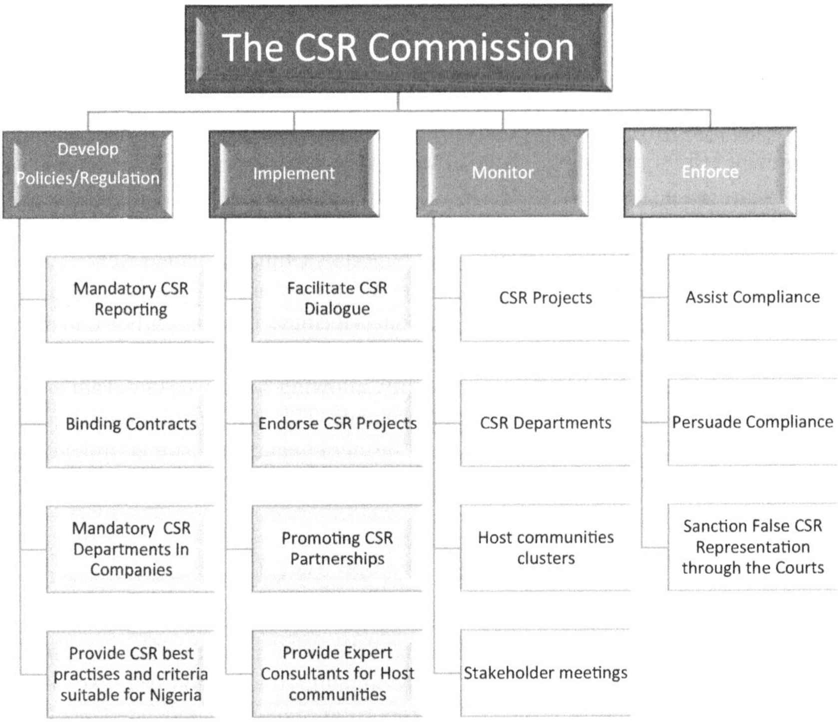

Fig. 9.2 An organogram for the proposed CSR commission (Debski, 2023)

address genuine local needs and yield measurable outcomes. Strengthening institutional capacity through training, funding, and technical support will further enable communities to engage effectively with corporate and government actors.

The institutional reform of CSR in Nigeria's energy industry represents a shift from fragmented, reactive practices towards an integrated, preventive, and strategic system. Strategic CSR, as envisioned by Debski and Ezeani (2022), demands that companies view sustainability not as a cost but as a cornerstone of long-term competitiveness. The creation of a National CSR and Sustainability Commission would provide the institutional backbone for embedding sustainability into the energy governance framework, ensuring coherence, accountability, and collaboration across sectors.

By transitioning from remediation to strategic prevention, and by linking CSR to national sustainability goals, Nigeria can transform its energy sector into a catalyst for inclusive growth, environmental protection, and social stability. Such a model would align corporate objectives with community well-being and national progress, marking a new chapter in the evolution of CSR—one that integrates strategy, accountability, and shared prosperity at the very heart of corporate governance (Debski & Ezeani, 2022; McElhaney, 2009; NUPRC, 2022; Ørsted, 2023; Seplat Energy, 2024).

9.6 Host-Community Participation and Environmental Stewardship

Host communities play a central role in ensuring environmental sustainability in the energy sector. They live closest to areas of extraction, generation, and transmission, and therefore experience both the benefits and the negative effects of energy projects firsthand. Despite this proximity, their involvement in decisions that affect them has often been minimal. This exclusion has contributed to mistrust, social tension, and even project failures. A more effective multi-stakeholder approach should therefore recognise host communities not as passive beneficiaries of company goodwill, but as active partners and co-creators of sustainable outcomes.

(a) *From Beneficiaries to Partners*

Global experience shows that when communities are meaningfully involved, both social harmony and environmental performance improve. The Aarhus Convention 1998 and the Escazú Agreement 2018 formally established the principles of environmental democracy ensuring communities have the right to information, participation, and access to justice on environmental matters. Applying these principles in Nigeria and other energy-producing regions means involving local people at every stage from project design to environmental assessment and ongoing monitoring.

The Petroleum Industry Act (PIA) 2021 made progress in this area by introducing Host Communities Development Trusts (HCDTs), designed to give communities a role in managing development benefits. However, gaps remain. The current structure gives corporations (referred to as "settlors") substantial control over fund administration, while community voices are underrepresented in decision-making (NUPRC, 2022). This imbalance can weaken transparency and reduce local trust.

To address these issues, subsidiary regulations and clear guidance should be developed to define how trustees and management committees of HCDTs are chosen. Criteria should emphasise representation from local residents or indigenous members, gender balance, and technical qualifications. This would bring the process closer to the African Union's *Guidelines for Public Participation in Environmental Governance* (African Union, 2023), which promote fairness and inclusivity in environmental decision-making.

(b) *Integrating Communities Across All Energy Industries*

Although the PIA applies specifically to the petroleum sector, similar participatory models are needed in other energy industries, such as renewables, electricity, and mining. The Nigeria Renewable Energy Master Plan (REMP, 2023 update) and the Energy Transition Plan (ETP) 2022 both prioritise decentralised energy systems and job creation, but they provide little guidance on community ownership or benefit-sharing. Introducing Community Energy Trusts (CETs) built on the same principles as HCDTs across renewable and mining projects would ensure fair revenue distribution and encourage local responsibility for environmental protection.

Mining communities face similar challenges, including land degradation and pollution. Integrating Extractive Industries Transparency Initiative (EITI) standards into mining and renewable energy projects could help standardise how benefits are shared. Under the proposed National CSR and Sustainability Commission (NCSC), these various frameworks could be harmonised to avoid duplication and guarantee consistent community participation across the energy value chain.

(c) *Environmental Monitoring and the Social Licence to Operate*

Community involvement in environmental monitoring is essential for building trust and improving compliance. When communities are trained and equipped to monitor aspects such as water quality, waste management, and biodiversity, they become partners in maintaining environmental standards. For example, Ghana's Community Mining Programme of 2022 allows local committees to report environmental breaches directly to authorities, while South Africa's Renewable Energy Independent Power Producer Programme (REIPPPP) ensures communities hold ownership stakes of 2–5% in renewable projects, enhancing social acceptance (World Bank, 2023).

In Nigeria, similar practices could be formalised through *Community Environmental Observatories* supported by the NCSC and funded through CSR contributions. Such a system would put into practice the concept of the Social Licence to Operate (SLO), that is, the informal but vital approval that communities give to companies that demonstrate responsible conduct (Górski, 2022). Without this community trust, even legally approved projects can face resistance and delays.

(d) *Financing and Capacity-Building Mechanisms*

Empowering communities also depends on access to sustainable funding and technical skills. While the HCDT's 3% operating expenditure provision offers a financial base, it may not cover broader sustainability goals such as renewable energy access, biodiversity protection, and climate adaptation. Additional funding sources could include:

(a) Partnerships with development finance institutions like the African Development Bank's Sustainable Energy Fund for Africa;
(b) Green bonds and community investment trusts managed transparently through the NCSC portal; and
(c) Skills training for youth and local workers in line with the workforce needs identified in Nigeria's National Energy Transition Plan (Federal Government of Nigeria, 2022).

Training should focus on environmental management, financial accountability, and technical knowledge so that communities can effectively take part in sustainability governance.

(e) *Towards Co-Governance and Long-Term Legitimacy*

Lasting environmental stewardship depends on shared authority and responsibility among host communities, corporations, and government agencies. The proposed NCSC could help formalise this shared governance by:

Table 9.3 Mechanisms for host-community Participation

Mechanism	Purpose	Implementation example	Challenges / notes
Host Communities Development Trusts (HCDTs)	Ensure direct benefit-sharing from oil and gas projects	Nigeria PIA 2021	Limited representation in governance NUPRC (2022)
Community Energy Trusts (CETs)	Extend benefit-sharing to renewables and mining	Proposed under NCSC framework	Requires enabling legislation
Community Environmental Observatories	Facilitate local environmental monitoring and reporting	Ghana's Community Mining Programme 2022	Needs sustained funding and training
Regional Liaison Councils	Coordinate host-community dialogues across regions	Proposed under NCSC	Risk of bureaucratic overlap if poorly defined

i. Creating joint panels to review Environmental and Social Impact Assessments (ESIAs);
ii. Making CSR and environmental data easily accessible to the public;
iii. Offering mediation services to help prevent conflicts; and
iv. Including community contributions to sustainability in national Sustainable Development Goal (SDG) reports (Table 9.3).

By recognising communities as co-decision-makers rather than peripheral actors, Nigeria can build stronger and more sustainable partnerships in its energy transition. Extending this inclusive model to renewable and mining projects will also prevent the repetition of exclusionary practices that once characterised the oil industry.

9.7 Conclusion

This chapter has explored how effective multi-stakeholder strategies can reshape environmental sustainability governance across the energy sector. It has shown that although governments, corporations, and host communities pursue different goals, their interdependence forms the foundation of sustainable energy development. In Nigeria, fragmented institutional mandates and limited community participation have historically constrained the impact of corporate social responsibility (CSR) initiatives. Addressing these gaps requires a more coherent, collaborative, and accountable governance system—one that combines legal mandates, voluntary innovation, and inclusive participation.

The discussion reaffirms the relevance of stakeholder theory in understanding how legitimacy, power, and urgency influence sustainability outcomes. Governments function as both regulators and facilitators; corporations act as implementers and innovators; and host communities serve as custodians of local ecosystems and direct beneficiaries of energy projects. Effective sustainability governance depends on establishing a mutually reinforcing partnership among these actors, underpinned by clearly defined roles, transparency, and shared accountability.

To operationalise this vision, the chapter proposes the creation of a *National CSR and Sustainability Commission (NCSC)* to unify the currently dispersed functions of agencies such as NUPRC, NESREA, and NEITI. The Commission would provide the institutional backbone for Nigeria's sustainability governance by harmonising CSR reporting standards, coordinating cross-sector policy, and institutionalising community participation across oil, gas, renewables, electricity, and mining. Complementary corporate reforms, especially the establishment of sustainability departments and the appointment of Chief Sustainability Officers (CSOs), would embed environmental and social responsibility at the highest level of decision-making.

Equally important is the transformation of host communities from passive beneficiaries into active co-governors. Their engagement in project planning, monitoring, and evaluation is critical for legitimacy and long-term stability. Mechanisms such as the *Host Communities Development Trusts (HCDTs)* under the Petroleum Industry Act (PIA) 2021, and proposed *Community Energy Trusts (CETs)* for renewables and mining, offer promising models for participatory governance. Strengthening these through clearer regulations, transparent funding frameworks, and sustained capacity-building will enhance both accountability and public trust.

In conclusion, the chapter argues that the path to sustainable energy governance lies in integrated, multi-level collaboration—a framework that blends state leadership, corporate accountability, and community empowerment. Genuine sustainability is not achieved through isolated regulations but through an ecosystem of shared responsibility, mutual learning, and trust.

References

Adegbite, E. (2015). Good corporate governance in Nigeria: Antecedents, propositions and peculiarities. *International Business Review, 24*(2), 319–330. https://doi.org/10.1016/j.ibusrev.2014.08.004

African Union. (2023, March 29). *The environmental, social, and governance: An African private sector study*. https://au.int/en/announcements/20230329/environmental-social-and-governance-african-private-sector-study

Aguinis, H., & Glavas, A. (2012). What we know and don't know about corporate social responsibility: A review and research agenda. *Journal of Management, 38*(4), 932–968. https://doi.org/10.1177/0149206311436079

Baldwin, R., Cave, M., & Lodge, K. (2012). *Understanding regulation: Theory, strategy, and practice* (2nd ed.). Oxford University Press.

Cervantes, F. M. (2020, May 20). Corporate social responsibility bill gets final house nod. *Philippine News Agency*. https://www.pna.gov.ph/articles/1103485

Chijoke-Mgbame, A., & Mgbame, C. (2018). Discretionary environmental disclosures of corporations in Nigeria. *International Journal of Disclosure and Governance, 15*(4), 252–261.

Debski, J. A., & Ezeani, E. C. (2022). Corporate social responsibility under the petroleum industry act 2021: Achieving environmental sustainability through multi-stakeholder partnership. *African Journal of Engineering and Environment Research, 3*(1), 1–24. https://ajoeer.org.ng/otn/ajoeer/2022/qtr-1/01.pdf

Debski, J. A. (2023). *An effective multi-stakeholder strategy for environmental sustainability in oil and gas-producing areas* (PhD thesis). Robert Gordon University, Aberdeen, UK. https://doi.org/10.48526/rgu-wt-2071585

European Commission. (2022, December 14). *Directive (EU) 2022/2464 on corporate sustainability reporting (Corporate Sustainability Reporting Directive, CSRD).* Official Journal of the European Union, L 322, 15–80. https://eur-lex.europa.eu/eli/dir/2022/2464/oj

European Union. (2024, June 13). *Directive (EU) 2024/1760 of the European Parliament and of the Council on corporate sustainability due diligence and amending Directive (EU) 2019/1937 and Regulation (EU) 2023/2859* (OJ L 2024/1760). https://eur-lex.europa.eu/eli/dir/2024/1760/oj

Federal Government of Nigeria. (2022, March). *Investing in Nigeria's energy transition* [Report]. https://www.energytransition.gov.ng/wp-content/uploads/2022/05/Investing-in-Nigeria-Energy-Transition.pdf

Freeman, R. E. (1984). *Strategic management: A stakeholder approach.* Pitman–Ballinger.

Global Reporting Initiative. (2024). *Professional certification program.* https://www.globalreporting.org/reporting-support/gri-academy/professional-certification-program/

Górski, J. (2022). Social licence to operate (SLO) in the extractive and energy sectors Introduction. *Oil, Gas & Energy Law Journal,* 1. https://www.ogel.org/article.asp?key=3856

Hussain, N., Rigoni, U., & Orij, R. (2018). Corporate governance and sustainability performance: Analysis of triple bottom line performance. *Journal of Business Ethics, 149*(2), 411–432. https://doi.org/10.1007/s10551-016-3099-5

International Energy Agency. (2024). *World energy investment 2024.* https://www.iea.org/reports/world-energy-investment-2024

McElhaney, K. (2009). *Just good business: The strategic guide to aligning corporate responsibility and brand.* Berrett-Koehler Publishers.

Mitchell, R. K., Agle, B. R., & Wood, D. J. (1997). Toward a theory of stakeholder identification and salience: Defining the principle of who and what really counts. *Academy of Management Review, 22*(4), 853–886. https://doi.org/10.2307/259247

Nigerian Upstream Petroleum Regulatory Commission. (2022). *Nigeria upstream petroleum host communities development regulations, 2022* [Regulation]. https://www.nuprc.gov.ng/wp-content/uploads/2022/07/Nigeria-Upstream-Petroleum-Host-Communities-Development-Regulations-2022.pdf

OECD. (2023). *OECD guidelines for multinational enterprises on responsible business conduct.* OECD. https://doi.org/10.1787/81f92357-en

Organisation for Economic Co-operation and Development. (2023). *OECD guidelines for multinational enterprises on responsible business conduct.* https://mneguidelines.oecd.org

Ørsted. (2023). *Sustainability report 2023.* Ørsted A/S. https://orsted.com/en/sustainability/sustainability-reportsPetroleum Industry Act, 2021 (Nigeria).

Peters, G. F., Romi, A. M., & Sánchez, J. M. (2019). The influence of corporate sustainability officers on performance. *Journal of Business Ethics, 159*(4), 1065–1087. https://doi.org/10.1007/s10551-018-3818-1

Seplat Energy. (2024). *Annual report and financial statements 2024.* https://seplatenergy.com

Stern, N., & Xie, C. (2022). China's new growth story: Linking the 14th five-year plan with the 2060 carbon neutrality pledge. *Journal of Chinese Economic and Business Studies, 21*(1), 5–25. https://doi.org/10.1080/14765284.2022.2073172

United Kingdom Financial Reporting Council. (2018). *The UK Corporate Governance Code 2018.* Financial Reporting Council. https://www.frc.org.uk/getattachment/88bd8c45-50ea-4841-95b0-d2f4f48069a2/2018-UK-Corporate-Governance-Code-FINAL.pdf

United Nations. (2015). *Transforming our world: The 2030 agenda for sustainable development.* https://sdgs.un.org/2030agenda

United Nations Global Compact. (2024). *Communication on progress: Business leadership for the SDGs.* https://unglobalcompact.org

Velte, P., & Stawinoga, M. (2017). Integrated reporting: The current state of empirical research, limitations and future research implications. *Journal of Management Control, 28*(3), 275–320. https://doi.org/10.1007/s00187-016-0235-4

World Bank. (2023, January 24). *South Africa: Renewable Energy Independent Power Producer Procurement Programme (REIPPPP) Lessons for emerging markets.* World Bank. https://documents.worldbank.org/curated/en/357291468302453849/pdf/913030BR0SecM2000SA0renewale0energy.pdf

Index

J. A. Debski, *Corporate Social Responsibility in the Energy Sector*, CSR, Sustainability, Ethics & Governance, https://doi.org/10.1007/978-3-032-17748-3

The manufacturer's authorised representative in the EU is Springer Nature Customer Service Centre GmbH, Europaplatz 3, 69115 Heidelberg, Germany. If you have any concerns regarding our products, please contact ProductSafety@springernature.com

Printed and bound by CPI Group (UK) Ltd, Croydon, CR0 4YY
05/10/2026
02228023-0003